European Romanticism

A Brief History with Documents

D0980006

Related Titles in
THE BEDFORD SERIES IN HISTORY AND CULTURE
Advisory Editors: Lynn Hunt, *University of California, Los Angeles*
David W. Blight, *Yale University*
Bonnie G. Smith, *Rutgers University*
Natalie Zemon Davis, *Princeton University*
Ernest R. May, *Harvard University*

THE BEDFORD SERIES IN HISTORY AND CULTURE

European Romanticism
A Brief History with Documents

Warren Breckman

University of Pennsylvania

BEDFORD/ST. MARTIN'S   Boston ♦ New York

For Bedford/St. Martin's

Publisher for History: Mary V. Dougherty
Director of Development for History: Jane Knetzger
Editorial Assistant: Laurel Damashek
Senior Production Supervisor: Dennis J. Conroy
Production Associate: Sarah Ulicny
Executive Marketing Manager: Jenna Bookin Barry
Project Management: Books By Design, Inc.
Index: Books By Design, Inc.
Cover Design: Liz Tardiff
Cover Art: Angel of the Revelation (Book of Revelation, chapter 10), by William Blake, ca. 1803–1805. The Metropolitan Museum of Art, Rogers Fund, 1914. (14.81.1). Photograph © 1980 The Metropolitan Museum of Art.
Composition: Stratford/TexTech
Printing and Binding: RR Donnelley & Sons Company

President: Joan E. Feinberg
Editorial Director: Denise B. Wydra
Director of Marketing: Karen Melton Soeltz
Director of Editing, Design, and Production: Marcia Cohen
Manager, Publishing Services: Emily Berleth

Library of Congress Control Number: 2007920787

Copyright © 2008 by Bedford/St. Martin's

Manufactured in the United States of America.

2 1 0 9 8 7
f e d c b a

For information, write: Bedford/St. Martin's, 75 Arlington Street, Boston, MA 02116 (617-399-4000)

ISBN-10: 0-312-45023-0
ISBN-13: 978-0-312-45023-6

Acknowledgments

Acknowledgments and copyrights are continued at the back of the book on page 205, which constitutes an extension of the copyright page.

Foreword

The Bedford Series in History and Culture is designed so that readers can study the past as historians do.

The historian's first task is finding the evidence. Documents, letters, memoirs, interviews, pictures, movies, novels, or poems can provide facts and clues. Then the historian questions and compares the sources. There is more to do than in a courtroom, for hearsay evidence is welcome, and the historian is usually looking for answers beyond act and motive. Different views of an event may be as important as a single verdict. How a story is told may yield as much information as what it says.

Along the way the historian seeks help from other historians and perhaps from specialists in other disciplines. Finally, it is time to write, to decide on an interpretation and how to arrange the evidence for readers.

Each book in this series contains an important historical document or group of documents, each document a witness from the past and open to interpretation in different ways. The documents are combined with some element of historical narrative—an introduction or a biographical essay, for example—that provides students with an analysis of the primary source material and important background information about the world in which it was produced.

Each book in the series focuses on a specific topic within a specific historical period. Each provides a basis for lively thought and discussion about several aspects of the topic and the historian's role. Each is short enough (and inexpensive enough) to be a reasonable one-week assignment in a college course. Whether as classroom or personal reading, each book in the series provides firsthand experience of the challenge— and fun—of discovering, recreating, and interpreting the past.

Lynn Hunt
David W. Blight
Bonnie G. Smith
Natalie Zemon Davis
Ernest R. May

Preface

The intellectual and artistic spirit of Romanticism was inextricably bound to the great age of European revolutions from 1789 to 1848. Yet even though the Romantic period may be given a beginning and an end, its impact persists to our day. From stylistic innovations in the arts to new perceptions of the human self, from deep engagement with the vexing religious questions inherited from the Enlightenment to new political ideas about community, history, and the nation, Romanticism permanently transformed the intellectual and cultural landscape of Europe and the Americas. Romanticism is thus not only necessary to an understanding of the nineteenth century, but more generally of the culture and politics that continue to shape us.

This volume presents Romantic thought in its rich diversity, including writings on religion, politics, aesthetics, nature, and human identity. The introduction explores the history of Romanticism, setting major themes within the political, social, and intellectual context of the early nineteenth century. It balances attention to the specific national contexts of Romanticism with awareness of the shared experience that made Romanticism a Europe-wide phenomenon. Designed to give the reader a comprehensive overview of the history and characteristic concerns of Romanticism, the introduction is augmented by headnotes accompanying each selected reading, explanatory notes, a chronology, questions for discussion, and suggestions for further reading.

The primary readings are drawn from the "core" cultures of European Romanticism, England, Germany, and France. Many are canonical classics of Romantic writing. Others are less well known but have been chosen because they express Romantic concerns with exemplary power; some appear here for the first time in English. Many important Romantic themes run through these selections: the distinction between the "classic" and the "romantic"; humanity's relationship to nature; art and religion; creativity and imagination; the forms of authentic religious sensibility; the relationship between reason and passion, "Enlightenment" and "Romanticism," nature and history; the place of the nation in the search for self-realization.

Recognition of the border-crossing nature of Romantic thought has guided the decision to organize the readings chronologically, rather than thematically. As no thematic heading could exhaust the meaning of texts that liberally mix aesthetics, religion, and politics, to place such writings under one or another rubric would already decide issues that should instead provide intriguing and productive topics of discussion. Chronological order helps to reveal patterns of change, accumulation, and dissemination, while leaving more substantive questions of presentation and meaning to the individual reader. This last remark—indeed this hope—is offered in the spirit of Romanticism itself. After all, it was a German Romantic poet, Joseph von Eichendorff, who once claimed, "those are the right readers, who compose with and over the book."

ACKNOWLEDGMENTS

I would like to thank Lynn Hunt for suggesting the idea of a Romantic anthology and entrusting me with it. Numerous scholars have shared their expertise with me, including Joseph Luzzi, Marion Kant, Samuel Moyn, and the participants of the Columbia Faculty Seminar on Romanticism. For information on Romantic painting in Switzerland, I am grateful to Professor Sharon Hirsh of Dickinson College; for information on Scandinavian art, I am thankful to Professor Michelle Facos of Indiana University. An honors seminar on European Romanticism at the University of Pennsylvania in autumn 2002 allowed me to "test" many of these texts with a lively and engaged group of students. An Alexander von Humboldt Fellowship in 2004–2005 allowed me time to complete the manuscript in Berlin, Germany. I would also like to acknowledge the helpful comments of the scholars who reviewed the manuscript in an earlier form: Susan Crane of the University of Arizona, Stuart Hilwig of Adams State College, Gerald Izenberg of Washington University in St. Louis, Richard Kortum of East Tennessee State University, Helena Rosenblatt of Hunter College, Andrzej Warminski of the University of California, Irvine, and George Williamson of the University of Alabama. I would also like to acknowledge the supportive efforts of the editors at Bedford/St. Martin's, especially Laurel Damashek and Jane Knetzger. Finally, I am delighted to record my deepest debt to my wife, Cordula Grewe, a historian of German Romantic art, who was always willing to share her knowledge and was unfailingly generous in her love and support.

Warren Breckman

Contents

APPENDIXES

Illustrations

European Romanticism

A Brief History with Documents

PART ONE

Introduction:
A Revolution in Culture

Romanticism emerged in the tumult of the 1790s as the reverberations of the French Revolution swept through Europe. The new sensibility that came to be called Romantic first emerged simultaneously in Britain and Germany in the 1790s. Expressions of the same mood appeared in France around 1800, but the flowering of French Romanticism did not come until the 1820s. The 1820s and 1830s saw the spread of Romantic ideas into all parts of Europe, even though by then the initial power of British and German Romanticism had waned. In many parts of Europe, Romanticism persisted as a powerful cultural force up to the failed revolutions of 1848. The Romantic period thus spanned some fifty years, but its effects have been permanent. Indeed, measured by its impact, Romanticism was itself a "cultural revolution," a decisive turn in Western culture and thought. For Romanticism irrevocably altered the arts, music, and literature; our idea of the artist and of creativity; our views of nature; our political and social ideas; and our convictions about personal identity.

At first glance, the claim that Romanticism amounts to a cultural revolution may be surprising. Consider that the name "Romantic" stemmed in large part from the enthusiasm of some young German writers for the medieval literary genre of the "romance." This would seem to be an extraordinarily narrow base from which to trace a revolution, not to mention a paradoxical base, suggesting as it does a return to the past instead of the plunge into the future that we normally associate with revolutions. Yet what attracted these writers' imaginations were not only tales of knightly derring-do and courtly love but also the expressive powers of a genre that seemed to burst out of the confines of artistic rules and conventions, freely mixing narrative with lyrical flights, the real with the visionary, the religious with the mythical, the human with the divine, and the temporal with the eternal. The Romantic appreciation for old literary forms did not imply a slavish reverence for the past; it was, instead, a declaration of freedom for artists who had come to believe that the paramount task of art lies in the struggle to create external forms that adequately express the artist's inner vision. It suggested a new critical distance from the dominant tastes and artistic conventions of the eighteenth century, which had judged the literature of Christian Europe—from medieval romances like *Le Roman de la Rose* (*Romance of the Rose*) and *La Chanson de Roland* (*The Song of Roland*) to *The Inferno*, Dante's Christian epic, to the plays of Shakespeare and the poetry of Milton—to be vastly inferior to the classical models offered by ancient Greece and Rome.

The precise nature of these ideas has perplexed many generations of scholars. Romanticism spanned several generations and unfolded against a historical drama that encompassed the French Revolution, Napoleon, the rise of nationalism, the acceleration of European imperial conquest, the industrial revolution, and the beginnings of socialism. Romanticism was no more monolithic and unchanging than the history of which it was a part. Nor was it ever the only artistic style or manner of thought during its time. We call the period Romantic because in retrospect we recognize certain dominant themes that stamp the age; but a full picture would require us to acknowledge other artistic and intellectual currents that coexisted and competed with Romanticism. Romanticism itself is marked by an extreme pluralism that seems to defy all efforts to identify a specific set of essential Romantic elements. In Romantic art, we find an array of literary, painting, and musical styles that do not, on the surface, seem to have much in common. Gathered under the rubric of Romanticism, we can find sophisticated urbanites and admirers of rural simplicity. In politics, we can find Romantic conservatives, liberals, and even socialists.* Any

---

*Throughout this volume, "liberal" is used in the continental European sense of a political commitment to individual rights, constitutionalism, and representative government. This is not to be confused with the specific meaning that "liberal" has acquired in recent American politics.

definition of Romantic nationalism would have to include the conservative Adam Müller and the democrats Giuseppe Mazzini and Jules Michelet. In questions of religion, we encounter devout Romantics calling for a revival of medieval Christendom; Romantics who transferred religious feeling to their response to nature; lapsed Christians like the English poet Lord Byron, who spoke knowingly of "The innate torture of that deep despair, / Which is remorse without the fear of hell";[1] optimistic atheists like the English poet Percy Bysshe Shelley who foresaw a godless future with glittering eyes; aesthetes like the German essayist Wilhelm Heinrich Wackenroder who elevated art itself to a quasi-religion (see Document 1); and those like the young philosopher F. W. J. Schelling, who dreamed of inventing new religions and mythologies that would better serve the needs of modernity.

Scholarly attempts to reach a neat and tidy definition of Romanticism have shattered on its contradictory diversity. Yet, far from hindering our attempts at definition, contradiction itself should be recognized as a defining feature of Romanticism. Indeed, when the literary critic Frank Paul Bowman speaks of the "exacerbated polarities" of French Romanticism, he in fact provides us with a useful general rubric for the specific quality of innovation and creative energy typifying the Romantic period as a whole.[2] Exacerbated polarities in the culture of the period give us perhaps the truest index of how the arts and intellectual life belonged to, contributed to, and reflected an age of revolutionary upheaval and change.

Important as it is always to bear in mind the complex and divergent tendencies in the period, the contradictory impulses of Romanticism were not simply random. We can speak of *the* Romantic age and identify it as a new phase in European intellectual and cultural history because, despite all the pluralism of styles and convictions, we can identify core issues, recurrent concerns, and shared challenges. For our purposes, we may identify three fundamental and closely interrelated features of Romanticism: a commitment to self-expression, a desire to unite the liberated individual with a greater whole, and a dynamic style of thought.

The commitment to individual self-expression pitted Romantic artists against the constraints of aesthetic rules, hierarchies, and ideals of formal perfection, and it launched them into an endless search for new and adequate forms. This emphasis on self-expression tapped directly into the new sense of individual liberation born of the revolutionary age. At the same time, however, in the wake of a century of skeptical attacks on religion and the events of a political revolution that seemed to have snapped the thread of historical time, Romantics were acutely aware of the inadequacy of a naked individuality shorn of roots, connections, and belonging. The tension in Romanticism's basic view of the human person fueled a search for a principle that would combine a liberating ideal of individuality with the fullest possible identification of the individual with a greater whole. In political terms, we might say that Romanticism desired the individual freedom promised by modernity with none of its centrifugal, alienating, and divisive effects. Stated more broadly, this desire drove a Romantic quest for the most radical emancipation of the creative person, *and*, with equal fervor, it fed a yearning for connection with something larger and grander than the self, whether with nature and God or with community and nation. The goal of this Romantic dream was not the obliteration of the individual but a harmonious and endlessly enriching exchange between the individual and the totality. This was, strictly speaking, impossible. This underlying impossibility helps to explain why in Romanticism, despite the Romantics' dream of harmonious unity, emphasis could swing between the self and the totality, the individual and the collective, and the assertion of autonomous selfhood and the submission to a higher power. These vacillations were a source of frustration and instability for the Romantics, but they were also the source of much of Romanticism's expressive power and philosophical insight. This search for mediation between individual and world thus presents the third basic element: the tendency of Romanticism toward a dynamic style of thought based on paradox, contradiction, ideas of organic growth, and the dialectical reconciliation of opposites.

ROMANTICISM AND THE EIGHTEENTH-CENTURY LEGACY

Scholarly understanding of the Romantic era was itself long subject to an exacerbated polarity, namely the idea that Romanticism marked a radical rupture with the eighteenth-century Enlightenment. Undoubtedly, Romanticism did break with significant elements of the Enlightenment. It challenged the dominant aesthetic ideals and artistic practices of the eighteenth-century, and, on a whole range of philosophical issues, Romantic thinking opened new perspectives that contrast with those of the Enlightenment. In place of a rationalist, skeptical approach to religion, Romanticism recognized the historical importance of religion, the apparent necessity or inevitability of faith, and the intuitive sense of the transcendent and mysterious. Romanticism challenged the very style of thinking that had, by the end of the eighteenth century, become identified as the Enlightenment. The dominant impulse of eighteenth-century thought was to search for system, order, and classification. Natural law, politics, social interactions, the mind, and the body were all understood in static, nonhistorical, and universalistic terms. The "machine" provided a dominant metaphor for the operation of nature, society, and man; the relationship of cause and effect furnished the main explanatory framework for all phenomena. Romantic thought contains a notable dynamism in contrast to these typical features of Enlightenment rationalism. Romanticism uses paradox and contradiction, replaces static criteria with ideas of organic growth, and searches for the dialectical reconciliation of opposites. Perhaps the most familiar example of the use of paradox and contradiction is the German philosopher Georg Wilhelm Friedrich Hegel's idea of the dialectical development of history. Although Hegel considered himself an anti-Romantic, the Hegelian dialectic is very much a product of the Romantic age. Indeed, the tendency to think of nature, society, and truth as living processes emerging from the clash of opposites, to imagine progress as the dynamic reconciliation of oppositions and contradictions forms a basic mental habit of the period.

The differences between the Enlightenment and Romanticism are real and significant; not surprisingly, the notion that Romanticism was a rebellion against the Enlightenment is as old as Romanticism itself. Certainly, many Romantics saw themselves as rebels against Enlightenment, and it is easy to find examples of Romantic denunciations of Enlightenment rationality (see Figure 1). Indeed, it was a common belief in the early decades of the nineteenth century that the preceding century had been an age of shallow rationalism, naive belief in the power of reason to secure human happiness, and the false conviction that humans could better face the future stripped naked than clothed with the veils of faith, mystery, and tradition. If we can gain some distance from the Romantics' own presentation of their relationship to their immediate past, however, it becomes clear that Romanticism actually inherited certain aspects of the Enlightenment.

The most important of these aspects was the eighteenth-century campaign to liberate the individual from superstition, unexamined belief, and unjust political systems. Commitment to this intellectual, political, and social goal was, after all, the reason for the initial Romantic enthusiasm for the French Revolution. The Enlightenment conception of the individual—maximizing pleasure and avoiding pain, reasonable

Figure 1. *William Blake,* Isaac Newton, *1795*
The early eighteenth-century poet Alexander Pope once wrote, "Nature and Nature's Laws lay hid in night; God said, 'Let Newton be!'—And all was light." By contrast, Blake depicts the great genius of science sitting underwater, as if to suggest a permanent spiritual darkness. Newton appears as a menacing demigod, his geometer's compass taking the measure of the triangle, symbol of the Holy Trinity, as if Newton were vying against God the creator. Blake, an artist who celebrated multiplicity, wrote that Newton's vision was "Single," and this is suggested here by the rigid alignment of Newton's gaze with the compass arm.
Tate Gallery, London/Art Resource, N.Y.

and sensible in just measure, bearing rights by virtue of what is common among all individuals—differs sharply from the Romantic image of the individual as irreducibly unique but striving titanically for universality, autonomy, and self-expression. Yet, Romantic selfhood may be seen as a radicalization of eighteenth-century tendencies, a kind of prodigal child of the Enlightenment.

One can also see this emancipatory impulse at work, for example, in the situation of women. Although women's access to cultural activity continued to face many obstacles, the Romantic era accelerated a trend already set in motion in the later eighteenth century toward the loosening of traditional social conventions and small but significant expansions of women's opportunities as both producers and consumers of culture. This is especially notable in literature, where the Romantic writers Madame de Staël (see Document 14) and Mary Wollstonecraft Shelley (see Document 15) or the non-Romantic writer Jane Austen are the best remembered of a growing number of women writers, many of whom scholars are only now rediscovering. The same social forces seem to have contributed to subtle changes in gender relationships. The Romantic period witnessed an increasing informality in the relationships of men and women, as well as a new intensity in the concept and expectations of love: love as an expression of authenticity, the hope for fulfillment through love, the ideal of friendship between the sexes, and so forth (see Figure 2). At the same time, the intensity and complexity with which male Romantic artists explored the darker sides of love and sexuality suggest that even the modest transformations in

Figure 2. *Philipp Otto Runge,* We Three, *1805*
The German artist's painting of a married couple and the husband's brother suggests new ideas about love and friendship between the sexes that emerged during this period.
Hamburg Kunsthalle; painting destroyed by fire in 1931.

women's roles were accompanied by anxiety and ambivalence. The extent of these changes and their reach beyond small circles of educated women remain issues of debate.

Romantics drew intellectual resources from their Enlightenment predecessors. Among the first German Romantics, their conception of individual creative freedom rested heavily on the German Enlightenment philosopher Immanuel Kant and Kant's student Johann Gottlieb Fichte. "One cannot be critical enough," wrote the German poet and critic Friedrich Schlegel, echoing Kant's mid-eighteenth-century insistence that "Our age is, in especial degree, the age of criticism, and to criticism everything must submit."[3] In England, the poet William Wordsworth's conception of the creative process drew on the empiricist psychology of John Locke and the theory of the association of ideas developed by David Hartley in the early eighteenth century. In France, the writer François-René de Chateaubriand began as a rationalist skeptic, and even after the awakening of his faith in the late 1790s, the influence of the philosopher and writer Jean-Jacques Rousseau remains palpable. At its most extreme, the Romantic emphasis on the freedom of the individual could even produce an intensified variant of seventeenth- and eighteenth-century libertinism and free-thinking skepticism. Lord Byron, who pronounced it a "base / Abandonment of reason to resign / Our right of thought,"[4] was the very embodiment of this tendency in European Romanticism, a current that some contemporaries called "Demonic" or "Satanic."

Romanticism has often been presented as a rejection of Enlightenment rationalism in favor of the irrational, night's darkness, and the intuitive nonlogic of dreams. Undoubtedly we find many instances of such antirationalism; it is important to recognize, however, that the most frequent target of Romantic criticism was not reason but a limited and limiting conception of the human person. Romantics typically believed that the Enlightenment had wrongly elevated reason, over the other human faculties. In response, they emphasized the complexity and multidimensionality of the human personality, and they probed the ways in which passion, fantasy, imagination, and the unconscious operate. Such probings may have acted to dethrone the sovereignty of reason, but they contained an element of rationality, of reflective activity aimed at better understanding the human self. Another way to think of this is to recognize that the Romantics' search for unifying concepts and the reconciliation of opposites undoubtedly entailed a critical view of Enlightenment rationality, which in Romantic eyes seemed bent on dissecting the world. However, the development of dynamic, dialectical forms of thought may be seen as an attempt not to abandon reason altogether but to correct and expand the concept of reason inherited from the eighteenth century.

With regard to literature and the arts, we have become accustomed to viewing Romanticism as a rebellion against eighteenth-century taste. Here again, we will see how difficult if not futile it is to draw a rigid opposition between Romanticism and the eighteenth century. Eighteenth-century literature was dominated by Neoclassicism, an aesthetic doctrine centered on the emulation of ancient Greek and Roman art. This admiration was founded on the conviction that the Greeks and Romans had developed enduring models of artistic form that could best fulfill the goal of art. In defining art's goal, Neoclassicists followed a line of thinking almost as old as the West's discussion of art: The ideal of art is the "imitation" of Nature. As the great English neoclassical poet Alexander Pope instructed his readers,

> First follow NATURE, and your Judgment frame
> By her just Standard. . . :
> Unerring Nature, still divinely bright,
> One clear, unchang'd and Universal Light.

Pope's reasoning was circular, for in fact he believed that the rules enabling the artist to imitate nature were none other than the rules of nature itself, discovered already by the sages of ancient Greece and Rome. Thus, Pope asserted,

> Those RULES of old discover'd, not devis'd,
> Are Nature still, but Nature Methodiz'd;
> Nature, like Liberty, is but restrain'd
> By the same Laws which first herself ordain'd.[5]

Dominant as Neoclassicism was, the eighteenth century already contained countercurrents that challenged its norms. The cult of "sensibility" and "sentimentalism"—associated with the philosophical writings of the Earl of Shaftesbury as well as a host of poets from England's Oliver Goldsmith to Germany's Friedrich Gottlieb Klopstock—celebrated emotion, enthusiasm, sensitivity, and an intense love of nature, understood as the mirror of the human heart and not as the source of rational laws. Novelists like Samuel Richardson and Jean-Jacques Rousseau explored the uniqueness of the individual and lay their emphasis on the inner emotional and mental world. Antiquarian research into the history of poetry challenged the literary canon formed around classicist taste. This was particularly important in

England, where eighteenth-century literary histories by Thomas Percy and Thomas Warton placed the literary riches of the late Middle Ages and Renaissance in the hands of writers. The European-wide fame of the poems of Ossian, allegedly a third-century Gaelic bard, but in fact a fabrication by the Scottish poet James Macpherson in the 1760s, attests to a new fascination with nonclassical antiquity and myth. These various international currents helped stimulate the so-called *Sturm und Drang* (Storm and Stress), a German literary movement of the 1770s that transformed German literature and in turn had an enormous international influence. The German writers Johann Wolfgang Goethe's *The Sorrows of Young Werther* (1774) and Friedrich Schiller's *The Robbers* (1782) created characters that became primal models for the Romantic self: gifted, rebellious, sensitive, tempestuous, and tormented, emotional depth-charges dropped into a sea of stifling conformists.

Eighteenth-century aesthetic theory likewise raised new possibilities outside the framework of Neoclassicism. For example, the elaboration of the idea of the "picturesque" created a taste for a studied unruliness: hence, the enthusiasm for the deliberately wild "English" (as opposed to the rigorously symmetrical "French") garden; ruins, including fake ruins built for scenic effect; and certain landscapes deemed to fit the criteria. Even more important was the theory of the "sublime," that is, that which is overpowering, majestic, immense beyond human comprehension. As articulated in the Irish philosopher Edmund Burke's *A Philosophical Enquiry into the Origins of Our Ideas of the Sublime and Beautiful* (1757) and Immanuel Kant's *Observations on the Feeling of the Beautiful and Sublime* (1764) and *The Critique of Judgment* (1790), the idea of the sublime expanded the range of aesthetic experience from the smoothness, regularity, harmony, and graspable scale of the "beautiful" to the awesomeness and power of the "sublime." Sublimity subverted the measured values of Neoclassicism because it assigned an aesthetic worth to the obscure and ultimately unrepresentable vastness of nature. It was destined to become one of the central aesthetic categories of the Romantics, feeding their taste for towering mountains, raging seas, and the thought of infinity itself.

These eighteenth-century countercurrents reveal that Romanticism had roots that reached far into the Neoclassical period; they provide an important example of the difficulty, if not futility, of trying to identify precisely when the old period ended and the new one began. Still, although Romanticism drew on the new intellectual and artistic resources and possibilities that opened during the eighteenth century, the powerful radicalizing effects of the French Revolution brought greater sharpness and clarity to the Romantic attack on Neoclassicism. Indeed, the Neoclassical aesthetic doctrine of imitation and rules, along with the moderate, ordered, and tempered sensibility it advocated, collapsed before the Romantics' insistence that art is a medium of self-expression.

Having learned that the Romantics revolted against Neoclassicism, students are often perplexed when they encounter a Romantic embracing classical motifs or mythology. Against this puzzlement, it must be emphasized that *the Romantics did not reject classical antiquity.* Indeed, European intellectuals and artists since the Renaissance never stopped looking to the ancients; Romanticism certainly did not end this habit, but it did introduce new perspectives on the meaning of classical antiquity, how one was to emulate it, or what part of antiquity one privileged. The Romantics were far more inclined to celebrate the "primitive" and "robust" era of Homer than the polished civilization of Augustan Rome. Moreover, while some Romantics like the brothers Friedrich and August Wilhelm Schlegel actually dreamed of fusing the Classic and the Romantic, there were other examples of hardening battle lines, such as with the German Nazarene painters, whose fervent Catholicism was matched by a deep suspicion of pagan antiquity. However, the ongoing power of antiquity to fascinate and inspire is evident in the presence of classical motifs in Romantic painting, the mix of gothic and classical elements in much of the architecture of the era, or the use of Greek mythology by the German poet Friedrich Hölderlin or the English poets Percy Bysshe Shelley and John Keats.

The difference from the Neoclassical period, however, was that, for the Romantics, Classicism became one possibility within an increasingly pluralistic range of stylistic options. Classicism was no longer regarded as the cultural gold standard; rather, it was viewed as a variable currency that the artist might freely draw on when it served his or her needs. In short, the target of Romantic rebellion was not antiquity but Neoclassicism, that is, the attempt to prescribe a set of formal rules ostensibly drawn from classical antiquity, the claim for the normative status of an allegedly timeless set of aesthetic criteria. In this way, Romanticism broke the monopoly that classical models had come to exercise in European culture. Romanticism no longer measured artistic achievement against a permanent criterion of beauty. Rather, Romantic aesthetic criteria are intrinsically historical and subjective, and thus relativistic. Hence, August Wilhelm Schlegel could praise antiquity *and* argue that it no longer provided a compelling model for modern needs.

If the true point of art is self-expression, then there could be no prescribed relation between inner vision and external form. Relation had to be invented and, in this task, the Romantic assigned an unprecedented power and freedom to the imagination. As the English poet and artist William Blake said, "Nature has no outline, but imagination does."[6] The German painter Caspar David Friedrich urged the artist to "close your bodily eye, so that you may see your picture first with the spiritual eye. Then bring to the light of day that which you have seen in the darkness so that it may react upon others from the outside inwards. . . . The painter should paint, not only what he sees before him, but also what he sees in himself."[7] (See Figure 3.) Artistic rules, hierarchies of genres, and academic authorities could provide no reliable guidance for what must remain a personal quest. Indeed, they could become obstacles. Accordingly, the Romantic period placed a new value on originality and spontaneity. In Romantic literature, visual arts, and music, we see new impulses toward experimentation and stylistic innovation and, in many instances, a loosening and opening of forms. At the core of this artistic revolution stood the artist, conceived as a creative "genius." The "genius" is surely one of the great archetypes of the Romantic mind; this exaltation of the artistic genius greatly accentuated, indeed completed a transformation in the Western understanding of the artist that had begun in the age of the great Renaissance figure Leonardo da Vinci: away from the artist as master craftsman whose skills could be learned by diligent study and practice toward the artist as genius, possessed of heightened sensitivity, imagination, and titanic powers of creation, no longer bound by rules but free to create his or her own rules.

(Opposite) **Figure 3.** *Caspar David Friedrich,* Wanderer above the Sea of Fog, *ca. 1818*

In this enigmatic painting, the German artist Friedrich expresses both the Romantic ideal of individualism and the Romantic yearning for connection with God and cosmos. Friedrich loved to depict figures with their backs turned to us, peering into the world of the painting. Are we drawn into the image by identifying with the man surveying this majestic scene? Or does his turned back keep us out? Friedrich employs a strange perspective that makes it difficult to know where we "stand" in relation to the image, and the fact that this man is atop a mountain peak in his street clothes adds to the painting's uncanniness. What first might seem like a realistic picture emerges with closer inspection as an evocative statement about the superiority of the imagination over the visible and experienced world.

Bildarchiv Preussischer Kulturbesitz/Art Resource, N.Y.

REVOLUTION AS CULTURAL CATALYST: ROMANTICISM, 1795–1805

Artistic and intellectual movements never march in perfect tandem with political events. The roots of Romanticism run deeper than the outbreak of revolution in France in 1789, and we must be careful not to reduce Romanticism to a kind of reflex response to the French Revolution. Likewise, the reaction of artists and intellectuals to politics is rarely so direct that one can chart exact correlations between events and cultural expressions. Nonetheless, the excitement, hopes, and fears of the unprecedented events in France sent shock waves through all of Europe, jolting European intellectuals and artists into something fundamentally new. It is significant that the first generation of Romantics, figures like William Wordsworth and the English poet Samuel Taylor Coleridge, Friedrich and August Wilhelm Schlegel, Friedrich Wilhelm Joseph Schelling, and the German poet Novalis, were all born around 1770. Thus 1789 coincided with their individual transitions into adulthood. This moment of passage from adolescence to adulthood is one that we all undergo; only rarely does this individual experience occur simultaneously with world historical events that seem to parallel one's own sense of expanding personal liberation and possibility. "Bliss was it in that dawn to be alive, / But to be young was very Heaven!" recalled Wordsworth, in what is surely the most famous expression of this exhilaration. For the first generation of Romantics, the French Revolution marked a violent rupture in the old world in which they had been reared and educated. It was the disorienting but also liberating disintegration of the world they had known.

There can be little doubt that the French Revolution acted as a catalyst for the early Romantics. Wordsworth experienced the revolutionary excitement firsthand during two trips to France between 1790 and 1791. On returning to England, he had interactions with radical circles in London, figures like the philosophers and writers William Godwin and Mary Wollstonecraft, and dissenting Christian sects of the sort that had already shaped the millenarian radicalism of William Blake even before the outbreak of the Revolution.[8] Around 1795, the friends Samuel Taylor Coleridge and the English poet Robert Southey dreamt of founding an ideal community of equal men and women in America. In Germany, Friedrich Schlegel claimed that "everyone was caught up in this process of fermentation, whether he liked it or not, yielding to it or struggling against it."[9] He insisted in 1793–1794 that the "moment appears in fact ripe for an aesthetic revolution," and, by 1795, he was capable of writing a spirited defense of republicanism and the Rousseauean idea of the General Will.[10] Legend has it that the three young friends Schelling, Friedrich Hölderlin, and the German philosopher Georg Wilhelm Friedrich Hegel planted a liberty tree at the Tübingen seminary where they were students together. The atmosphere of radical upheaval also helps to explain the power that the philosopher Johann Gottlieb Fichte had over the first group of German Romantics who gathered around the Schlegel brothers in the small university town of Jena. A student of Immanuel Kant, Fichte preached a radical doctrine of the human self as an infinitely striving subjectivity that overcomes every boundary it confronts. "My system is the first system of freedom," claimed Fichte, drawing an exact parallel to the political revolution under way in France.

Unbridled enthusiasm for the Revolution turned out to be short-lived, as the Revolution veered from its initial promise of human liberation, to the Jacobin Terror (1793–1794), to the ambivalent republicanism of the Directory (1795–1799), and, finally, to Napoleon Bonaparte's coup d'état (1799). As the Revolution grew bloodier and became embroiled in international warfare, the Romantics grew disillusioned. This pattern of disillusionment did not follow identically the course of events in France. Romantic enthusiasm did not end with the first drop of the guillotine blade. In Germany, Friedrich Schlegel defended elements of the Revolution well after the Jacobins had fallen from power, while the poet Novalis strove to reconcile republicanism and monarchism in "Faith and Love" (1798), a text dedicated to the new Prussian king, Friedrich Wilhelm III. In England, William Blake never renounced his commitment to political, racial, and sexual equality. Wordsworth certainly left behind his radicalism by the mid-1790s, but his poetry continued to uphold the dignity and rights of marginalized and oppressed people. Furthermore, in "Preface to *Lyrical Ballads*," Wordsworth could still link "revolutions" in literature to broader revolutions in society. (See Document 3.) By the time Wordsworth and Coleridge published their pathbreaking poetry collection *Lyrical Ballads* (1798), however, they had both turned away from the Revolution, in part because of conflicts in loyalty posed by the outbreak of war between France and Britain in 1793 and in part because of the excesses of the Jacobins. Neither Coleridge nor Wordsworth simply abandoned hopes for social improvements, but they rejected violent means and, gradually, as their conservatism deepened, they came to doubt human reason's capacity to build a more just world. According to Wordsworth's account in his great autobiographical epic poem *The*

Prelude; or, Growth of a Poet's Mind (1805), the collapse of his revolutionary faith threw him into a crisis that was only resolved when he found sources for a more "permanent" faith in Nature.[11]

The beginning of the greatest phase of creativity in English and German Romanticism coincides with the onset of this disillusionment. Noting this coincidence, scholars have sometimes presented Romanticism as a flight from politics into imagination, a massive displacement of energy and emotional investment from the world of society and politics onto nature or a transcendental level of spiritual freedom. It is, however, more accurate to stress that this phase of Romanticism, which lasted from roughly 1798 to 1805, drew much of its creative power from a potent interplay between liberation and disorientation, enthusiasm and dismay, hope and disappointment. Hence, utopian idealism and apocalyptic visions lingered in Romantic thinking even after the hopes of realizing those goals in the political world had faded. In a culture that was still deeply Christian in its habits of thought, the initial hope that the Revolution would usher in a new epoch of freedom could easily blend with Christian images of salvation and the coming of a new millennium, in which the "true" message of Christianity—its democratic, egalitarian ethic—would be realized in the world. The Jacobin Terror, the spread of warfare, and the French regime's attempts to create a surrogate religion of reason and republican virtue made it harder to sustain the belief that this kingdom of God on earth would be won by political action. The failure of that faith in the power of politics could lead poets and intellectuals to transfer their quest for freedom from revolution to the mind's own experience of the world. It could lead one to hope for a more fundamental revolution—one that would reestablish unity among humans, nature, and God—that would now be won within consciousness itself, with imagination as the tool that would change the way we see the world.[12]

This exalted estimation of the powers of art and imagination was a crucial dimension of the Romanticism of the late 1790s and early 1800s. Yet, belief in a millennial transformation through the power of art coexisted with aspects that undercut and challenged it. Even in their highest flights of exaltation, moments of doubt could cast shadows across the Romantic vision. Hence, in "Tintern Abbey" (1798) (see Document 4), Wordsworth raises the possibility that the visionary experience might be a "vain belief," although he apparently does not think it loses significance if it is. Such moments of doubt appear in the poetry of Coleridge and Wordsworth with increasing frequency after 1800, and those moments become compounded by a despairing sense that their visionary powers are on the decline. At the opposite end of the spectrum from Wordsworth's intense sincerity, we have Friedrich Schlegel, whose theory of "irony" constantly shuttles back and forth between grand vision and its impossibility, between unity and fragmentation (see Document 6); at most, in Schlegel, everything is kept aloft by the ironist's quick motion, which is always the case in good juggling. In short, even in the highest moments of Romanticism, the attempt to formulate a stable position or outlook contended with conflicting impulses.

Exacerbated polarity belonged essentially to the mindset of the first generation of German and English Romantics. August Wilhelm Schlegel claimed in 1798 that the "Romantic sensibility as a whole exists in contrasts."[13] Blake wrote, "Without contraries is no progression. Attraction and repulsion, reason and energy, love and hate, are necessary to human existence." That, fittingly enough, comes in a work titled *The Marriage of Heaven and Hell* (1790–1793); Blake's *Songs of Innocence* (1789) and *Songs of Experience* (1794) bear the subtitle "The Two Contrary States of the Human Soul." Coleridge's deepest conviction rested on what seems a paradox: "Everything has a Life of its own, we are all *one Life*."[14] Friedrich Schlegel enjoyed the tensions and revelations created by combining opposites. This was the essence of his concept of irony, which he described as "an absolute synthesis of absolute antitheses, the continual self-creating interchange of two conflicting thoughts."[15] Of his own frame of mind, Schlegel wrote, "It is equally fatal for the mind to have a system, and to have none. One will simply have to decide to combine the two."[16]

The Romantics connected this interest in contradiction and polarity to an analysis of their own historical period, which they judged to be divided and dualistic. For all contemporaries, the great political conflict of the age represented an obvious source of division; but Romantics saw other causes as well. Particularly in England, where the Industrial Revolution had already transformed life in ways not yet seen on the continent, the Romantics regarded the "Satanic mills" of industry and the growth of cities as sources of division. Modern commercial society destroyed older bonds of loyalty and obligation between people, enriching a few, but thrusting many into poverty. Both the destruction of the rural countryside and the mushrooming growth of industrial cities pointed to a growing alienation of modern society from nature. The Romantics applied a similar diagnosis to the Enlightenment. It was, as we saw, a common belief of Romanticism that the Enlightenment had fallen under the spell of a limited conception of reason as a faculty that weighs, calculates, and parcels out, thus not only dividing humanity from emotion and intuition but also hindering the development of a more comprehensive and flexible rationality capable of both analysis and synthesis. August Wilhelm Schlegel even presented the entire Christian epoch as intrinsically dualistic, with Christian consciousness divided between the "here" and the "beyond," the flesh and the spirit, the Fall and the Redemption. (See Document 10.)

Again, we must recall that the focus on duality and contradiction stood in a dynamic relation to the Romantic quest for harmony and synthesis. Even if the Romantics recognized the divisions and fractures of the modern world and even if they reveled in the creative tensions generated by the marriage of opposites, nonetheless, they fundamentally believed that all contradictions are ultimately contained within a great totality. The overwhelmingly powerful impulse of Romanticism was to search for a principle that would unify all phenomena. Coleridge dreamed of knowing something *"great—something one and indivisible."*[17] In 1795, the most important of the German Romantic philosophers, F. W. J. Schelling, put the search for a unifying principle in stark terms: "Either our knowledge must be totally without reality—an eternal circling, . . . a chaos, . . . or—There must be a last point of reality, on which everything depends, from which all permanence and all form of our knowledge proceeds."[18] This was a typical conclusion reached by the Romantics: The world, society, we ourselves have become divided, torn. Points of connection and integration must be found; that which is in conflict must be reconciled. For the Romantics, this was the key to the regeneration of human potential. The dream of unity within a great totality ultimately fueled Romantic ideas about nature, divinity, and society.

It would be wrong, though, to think that the goal of the Romantic was so fully to identify with a mighty whole that his or her own individuality would disappear. After all, the assertion of individual freedom and self-expression belong intrinsically to the Romantic sensibility. Were the individual truly to be absorbed into the totality, then the very source of the world's energy, the clash of opposites, would be lost. Hence, the pursuit of harmony and synthesis did not presuppose an endpoint, a moment of arrest or closure; it was, rather, conceived as an open-ended task, a process driven by the ongoing productive interactions of contrary elements. True to this spirit, the Romantic believed that the "universal" and the "individual self" must both be pursued with equal fervor; or, paradoxically, to pursue the individual

self leads to the revelation of the universal, while the truth and fulfillment of the individual self lies in its relation to the whole. No one
expressed this reciprocal exchange better than Novalis, who was perhaps the closest thing to a true mystic among all the Romantics. "We
dream of a journey through the universe. But is the universe then not
in us? . . . We do not know the depths of our spirit. Inward goes the
secret path. Eternity with its worlds, the past and the future, is in us or
nowhere." But Novalis was careful to emphasize "how relative the
activities of going outside oneself and returning to oneself are. What
we call going into ourselves is really going outside ourselves."[19] In a
similar spirit, Wordsworth's *The Prelude* bears the subtitle *Growth of a
Poet's Mind*; but Wordsworth believed that this lengthy poetic chron-
icle of his own development, far from being an epic exercise in navel-
gazing, revealed that the deeper his subjectivity became, the more he
opened to the world.

In its highest form, the Romantic quest for integration and wholeness directed itself toward nature and divinity, although in truth,
nature and God were frequently viewed as virtually identical. To grasp
the novelty of the Romantic idea of nature, recall that Newtonian
physics depicted nature as a self-regulating system of laws, and under
the impression of this idea, many Enlightenment thinkers espoused
"Deism," the belief in the "clock-maker" God who designed the universe, created laws for its operation, and then withdrew from His creation. Eighteenth-century thinking about nature was, in fact, seldom
this barren, but the Romantics rarely paid attention to the nuances
and conflicting tendencies in Enlightenment thought. What they perceived in the Enlightenment was an overwhelming tendency to reduce
nature to a machine governed by unalterable laws, to see only the
things of the visible world without sensing the creative life force and
spiritual power that animate all of nature.[20] Romantic nature, by contrast, is in continual process, a world in a perpetual state of becoming.
The machine no longer supplies an acceptable metaphor; the dominant metaphor of Romanticism is the organism.

Organism suggests, first, unity, that which is "at one with itself . . .
and not torn into plurality," as the German poet and philosopher Karoline von Günderrode wrote. For Günderrode, as for many Romantics,
the principle of unity starts with the integral wholeness of the singular
being and expands into a conception of life, world, and cosmos as a
unity, "life as a whole." (See Document 8.) Second, organism implies
that the interrelations of parts within the whole are too complex to be
reduced to laws of mechanical causality. The rejection of mechanism

did not necessarily mean the abandonment of the search for natural law, but the quest shifted to laws of development. Romantic thinking tended to trace development to an organism's core impulse or drive to fulfill its potential. The acorn is the oak tree in *potentia*; "the child is the father of the man," as Wordsworth famously said. This idea of growth transformed the moral category of *human striving* into the very principle of nature itself. As with humanity, so too with nature, all things are infinitely striving toward a higher state. The Romantic philosophy of nature sees meaning and purpose everywhere in nature.

For thinkers rooted in a Christian culture, it was perhaps inevitable that the Romantic generation should link the dynamic, purposeful development of nature to God as the animating spiritual presence in all of nature. In visionary language, Wordsworth speaks of "the one interior life / That lives in all things, . . . In which all beings live with God, themselves / Are God, existing in one mighty whole."[21] This pantheistic belief that God is everywhere in nature revitalized a much older idea that nature is a great web of meaningful correspondences. "Every portion of the universe appears to be a mirror, in which the whole creation is represented," wrote Madame de Staël.[22] Novalis begins his novel *The Novices of Saïs* (1802) with reference to "that marvelous secret writing that one finds everywhere, upon wings, eggshells, in clouds, in snow, crystals and the structure of stones, on water when it freezes, on the inside and outside of mountains, of plants, of animals, of human beings, in the constellations of the sky, on pieces of pitch or glass when touched or rubbed, in iron filings grouped about a magnet, and in the strange conjunctures of chance."[23] An early chapter of *The Prelude* tells of the young Wordsworth's awakening sense of the symbolic resonances of the world; one of *The Prelude*'s climactic moments comes during Wordsworth's passage through the Alps, when the sublime landscape appears to him

> like workings of one mind, the features
> Of the same face, blossoms upon one tree,
> Characters of the great apocalypse,
> The types and symbols of eternity,
> Of first, and last, and midst, and without end.[24]

This sense that the world resonates with hidden meaning explains one of the dominant metaphors of the Romantics, nature as a "Hieroglyph of the divine."

The idea that the world is a symbolic landscape is much older than Romanticism, as is the metaphor of the Hieroglyph. But a short poem by the German poet Joseph von Eichendorff suggests what is new in the Romantic version of this age-old notion:

> A song sleeps in all things,
> Which are dreaming on and on,
> And the world rises up to sing,
> If only you speak the magic word.

Eichendorff expresses a widely held Romantic idea, namely that because humans are the only natural beings that possess consciousness, they play the vital and unique role of giving words to the meaning of the world. As Coleridge writes, "we receive but what we give, / And in our life alone does Nature live."[25] If all of nature strives toward higher form, then it is humanity which fulfills this striving, because the human mind alone can lift nature to spirit. The core Romantic vision does not focus on nature in its endless variety or its brute givenness; it focuses on the spiritual, transcendent meaning of the world. We see here that the Romantic vision really centers on the human in its role as the active mediator between nature and spirit, world and God. This belief in the unity, or at least the communication of the human mind with nature and God furnishes yet another—perhaps the fundamental—basis for the Romantic exaltation of the artist and artistic creation. For the Romantics saw imagination as that mental faculty that could actively forge new unities from the diversity of experience, reinvest the world with spirit, and reunite the visible and the invisible.

This vision is inherently unstable. The Romantics grasped for totality, but the whole is infinite and can never be grasped. Alongside the Romantics' exorbitant claims for the creative powers of the human imagination runs an acute—and unprecedented—recognition of the limits of our capacity to represent reality. "For the sum total of human powers," wrote Novalis in his novel *Heinrich von Ofterdingen* (1802), "there is a definite limit of poetic representation beyond which representation cannot maintain the necessary density and formative power but degenerates into an empty, deluding chimera."[26] Percy Bysshe Shelley's "A Defence of Poetry" (Document 16) registers a despairing suspicion that by the time the poet begins to write, the flames of inspiration have waned, making even the most glorious poetry "a feeble shadow of the original conceptions of the poet." A similar despair could fuel fantasies about humanity's increasing distance from an original divine revelation in which words had perfectly mirrored things. In the Romantic view, the highest task of human creativity is to communicate with the totality that lies all about us; but this is an enterprise that will, in a certain sense, always fail. For as Friedrich Schlegel wrote, "All beauty is allegory. One can only express the highest allegorically, precisely because it is inexpressible."[27] In the first great phase of Romanticism, no Romantic doubted that there is a totality toward which the self should strive; that it will remain mysterious and elusive did not undermine the dream of reaching it. Indeed, precisely this dynamic interchange between possibility and impossibility seems to underpin the Romantics' sense of the moral grandeur of their own striving spirit, what Friedrich Schlegel called "the unformed colossalness of the moderns."[28]

TRANSITIONS IN ENGLISH AND GERMAN ROMANTICISM

This highly charged vision of nature, God, and humanity continued to resonate in the subsequent history of European Romanticism. Nonetheless, the initial form of this Romantic vision clearly began to fade shortly after 1800. After a few years of fervent enthusiasm, a feeling of crisis set in. Coleridge reached a point where he felt that his poetic muse had utterly abandoned him; though he continued to write poetry, his later period is defined more by his works in literary theory and political philosophy and by an overarching conservatism that differs profoundly from his brief radical phase. Wordsworth's *The Prelude*, begun in 1798 and completed in 1805, marked a pinnacle of achievement that he would never again reach. What is more, he gradually abandoned the convictions that had animated his work during that highly creative period. Indeed, in the ensuing years, Wordsworth revised many of his earlier poems, including *The Prelude*, from which he removed references to the pantheism that had been his most powerful image of humanity's place in the world. Coleridge, who became a firm supporter of Anglican orthodoxy, later identified "the vague misty, rather than mystic confusion of God with the world & the accompanying nature-worship" as "the trait in Wordsworth's poetic works I most dislike."[29] In his later philosophical writings, Coleridge criticized his own youthful lapse into pantheism and sought to realign his thought with a more orthodox concept of God and a drastically more modest concept of human imagination.

In Germany, F. W. J. Schelling backed away from his pantheistic philosophy of nature; even if he never became an orthodox Christian, he came to espouse the notion of a transcendent, personal God separate from the created world.[30] Novalis died before he might have abandoned his initial ideas, and Friedrich Hölderlin went mad. Friedrich Schlegel's move away from his early, radical phase took a dramatic form when he and his wife Dorothea converted to Catholicism in 1808. Looking back at his career in 1817, Schlegel wrote,

> In my life and philosophical apprenticeship there has been a constant search after eternal unity . . . and an attaching to something external, a historical reality or a given ideal. . . . There was an attaching to the orient, to the German, to freedom in poetry, finally to the church, as everywhere else the search for freedom and unity was in vain. Was this attaching not a search for protection, for a final foundation?[31]

As Schlegel's path shows, the open-ended searchings of early German Romanticism yielded to an increasingly strong desire to anchor the self to the pillars of the Church, the nation, tradition, and history.

The next phase of German Romanticism, often called "High Romanticism" (*Hochromantik*) as distinct from the "Early Romanticism" (*Frühromantik*) of the late 1790s, was much more rooted in orthodox religion. Joseph von Eichendorff, for example, was a devout Catholic, and the poet Clemens Brentano increasingly returned to his native Catholic faith. The group of German painters who came to be known as the Nazarenes turned from Protestantism to Catholicism and looked to the Middle Ages for artistic inspiration. They moved to Rome, heart of Catholic Europe, with the intention of dedicating their artistic work to a general cultural and social regeneration through the revival of belief. With this shift to revealed religion and Church tradition, some of the dizzying excitement of the initial years of German Romanticism faded. However, the animating concerns of the 1790s did not simply disappear. Rather, they were reinterpreted within more orthodox frameworks. So, for example, Friedrich Schlegel did not abandon the notion of art as a process of "becoming," but his later work attempts to understand this within the terms of Christian eschatology. Nor did nature cease to be a hieroglyph of divine purpose, but, as in Eichendorff's case, nature became more like the tablet on which the divine message is inscribed and less like the message itself. Likewise, the Nazarene painters' turn to medieval Christianity was not a naïve attempt to restore the Middle Ages; rather, it was undertaken within the general parameters of the Romantic understanding of history as a river flowing in one direction only. That is, the Nazarenes had a strong historicist awareness of the stream forever bearing the present away from the past. Their medievalism was a stylistic and political choice that remained within the general horizon of Romanticism's initial understanding of artistic freedom.[32]

The same ambiguous continuity can be seen in Wordsworth and Coleridge, whose retreat from their initial vision did not prevent them from spending the rest of their lives circling around the philosophical and artistic questions raised during the heady years of the late 1790s. Those issues remained important for a younger generation of English Romantics as well, especially for Percy Bysshe Shelley. Despite his deep hostility toward religion, much of Shelley's greatest poetry explores the question of spirit in nature, although in contrast to the young Wordsworth and Coleridge, Shelley's sensibility is much more torn by skepticism, as is evident in "Mont Blanc" (Document 17).

As with the period of its emergence, Romanticism's subsequent history remained closely bound to the broader events that kept Europe in a state of unrest. In 1799, Napoleon Bonaparte seized power in France and, from his seat of power, he intensified France's military campaigns. His defeat of Austria in 1800 and, above all, his conquest of Prussia in 1806 had an indelible impact on German Romanticism. The initial sensibility of the German Romantics had mixed a concern for historical and national specificity with an intrinsically cosmopolitan vision of humanity's growth. An excellent example of this is Novalis's essay "Christianity or Europe: A Fragment" (1799), in which the poet dreams of a European culture reunified by a new universal Christian faith. (See Document 2.) Within a few years, however, as Germans suffered the humiliation and trauma of defeat and occupation, the search for communal integration had become firmly anchored in the idea of nationalism. Given the devastating course of German nationalism in the twentieth century, we must stress that German Romantic nationalism was defensive and mainly focused on culture; on the European continent, it was the French who were bent on imperial expansion and mastery in the name of the nation. The Germans were by no means alone in their nationalism. Indeed, the history of Romanticism in every European country became closely associated with the rise of nationalist sentiment. The English Romantics, particularly of the first generation, were no exception.

The nationalist turn in Germany meant a sharpened reaction against all things French, a sentiment that had not been strong in the first wave of German Romanticism. Where the characteristic literary productions of the circle gathered around the Schlegel brothers in Jena in the late 1790s include experiments in mixed genres, textual fragments, and aphorisms, the nationalist phase brought historical studies of the German Middle Ages, philological treatises on the history of the German language, and efforts to collect German folktales, such as the great undertaking of Jacob and Wilhelm Grimm, which led to the volume known in English as Grimms' *Fairy Tales*. In Germany, the first cohort of Romantics, those born around 1770, shared this turn toward orthodox revealed religion, historical tradition, and the nation with their younger contemporaries, those born in the 1780s and 1790s.

In England, by contrast, we see signs of generational conflict between initial Romantic figures like William Wordsworth and Samuel Taylor Coleridge and the great figures of the next generation (Percy Bysshe Shelley, Lord Byron, and John Keats). The oldest of this latter group, Byron, was one year old when the French Revolution began. The formative experience for Keats, Shelley, and Byron was not the exhilarating early years of the Revolution, but, rather, a British culture dominated by an atmosphere of conservatism, xenophobia, nationalism, and religious orthodoxy as Britain waged war against France from 1793 to the final defeat of Napoleon in 1815. During these years, the government spied on artists, occasionally suspended habeas corpus, and tried working-class radicals for sedition. The government divided its energies between fighting foreign wars and suppressing dissent within Britain, and this domestic repression continued even after the defeat of France. For Shelley, the French Revolution remained "the master theme of the epoch in which we live," as he claimed in an 1816 letter to Byron;[33] however, for this younger generation of Romantics, the Revolution was a betrayed memory. Both Shelley and Byron chose self-exile on the continent rather than life in Britain.

Undoubtedly, despite these generational tensions, similarities existed between the older and younger Romantics, including the critique of industrialism, utilitarianism, and egotistical individualism, as well as belief in the power of imagination, the sublimity of nature, the yearning for transcendence, and the wavering between visionary hope and apocalyptic despair. Nonetheless, the second generation defined itself to a considerable extent against the older Romantics. In the Preface to his play *The Revolt of Islam* (1817), Shelley chastised the period for its "gloom and misanthropy," and he complained that the literature of the age had become tainted with the "hopelessness of the minds from which it flows." Shelley became, at an early age, an atheist and a self-professed republican. He met his future wife, Mary Wollstonecraft

Godwin, in 1814, having searched out her father, William Godwin, who had dominated English radicalism in the mid-1790s but had faded into obscurity in the reactionary times of the early 1800s. Byron's commitments ran in a decidedly liberal direction, culminating in his participation in the Greek War of Independence, where he died at Missolonghi in 1824. To a greater extent than Shelley, Byron cultivated a sharp stylistic break from the first generation of Romantics, developing a satirical style that self-consciously echoed the eighteenth-century writers Voltaire and Alexander Pope. Even Keats, often seen as the most ethereal of all the English Romantics, expressed democratic views and championed freedom fighters like the Polish rebel Thaddeus Kosciusko. Moreover, Keats turned back to the imaginative resources of ancient Greek mythology, sharing with Byron and Shelley a preference for pagan sensualism over Christian asceticism. What might have become of these younger figures is speculative, for all three were dead by 1824, the oldest, Byron, having reached the age of thirty-six.

FRENCH ROMANTICISM

In the early 1800s, the publication of François-René de Chateaubriand's *The Genius of Christianity* (1802; see Document 7) and Étienne Pivert de Senancour's novel *Oberman* (1804) suggest the emergence of the new sensibility in France. It is hardly surprising that we see French parallels to the Germans and the English, given that the writings of Jean-Jacques Rousseau had inspired all European Romantics. It is striking, however, that the real flowering of French Romanticism belongs to the 1820s and 1830s. This delay seems to be explained by the upheavals of the Revolution and the Napoleonic period and, above all, by the deeply rooted strength of Neoclassicism in France. Those roots were, if anything, strengthened by French revolutionaries, who imagined their own republic as a revival of ancient civic virtue. Neoclassicism was, indeed, so closely associated with France that in the German lands, the Romantic stylistic revolt against Neoclassicism easily became identified with the armed resistance to Napoleon. It is ironic that the revolutionary decade provoked a break with Neoclassical aesthetic norms in England and Germany, while in France, as Karl Marx once remarked, "the Revolution of 1789–1814 draped itself alternately in the guise of the Roman Republic and the Roman Empire."[34] Napoleon shared the classical aesthetic tastes of the revolutionaries of the 1790s, and his official preferment ensured that Romanticism remained marginalized in French culture so long as he was in power. Chateaubriand briefly backed Napoleon, but once he turned against the emperor, he was censored; as for the Swiss-born Madame de Staël, whose liberal views were well-known, it was once remarked, "Bonaparte had so persecuted her that people said that in Europe one had to count three Great Powers: England, Russia, and Mme. de Staël."[35] Staël's *De l'Allemagne* (*On Germany*), a three-volume discussion of the German Romantic movement, provoked Napoleon not only because of its support for Romantic aesthetics, but because it contained veiled attacks on his despotic rule as well as on French claims to cultural supremacy. In 1810, Napoleon's troops destroyed the entire first printing of Staël's book, which explains why she published French and English editions of the book in England in 1813.

When Napoleon was finally defeated at the Battle of Waterloo in 1815, the path lay open for the restoration of the monarchy in France. With the crowning of Louis XVIII, interest in Romanticism quickly grew among younger French intellectuals and artists. The subsequent history of French Romanticism is largely the story of a succession of social circles of artists, writers, and intellectuals, as well as a pattern of shifting political allegiance, from royalism to liberalism to, in some cases, socialism. Even though English and German Romanticism always contained a political component in the broad sense of addressing matters bearing on national identity and social relations, French Romanticism was explicitly, combatively political. Although French Romanticism may have been more a response to the traumas of the Revolution than to its promises, it mirrored the highly politicized nature of postrevolutionary French society.

The novelist Victor Hugo's early career illuminates the course of French Romanticism as he passed from support of the monarchy and the Catholic Church to liberalism and a concern for the socially downtrodden. In 1816, at the tender age of 14, Victor Hugo had declared his ambition "to be Chateaubriand or nothing."[36] In 1819, along with his two brothers, Hugo created the journal *Le Conservateur littéraire*. The Hugos' journal, which lasted until March 1821, strongly supported the restored monarchy and emulated Chateaubriand in advocating the rediscovery of Christianity and the medieval roots of modern France. In 1823, a new journal, *La Muse française*, animated by Hugo and several friends, continued to support royalism and Catholicism but was also more explicit in championing Romantic ideas about the essential mission of poetry. This group believed that Christian poetry offered an adequate answer to the ordeals of the revolutionary and Napoleonic years, with the poet as the guardian of the vitality of beliefs and institutions. Royalist Romanticism defended traditional values, but it always saw itself as a militant force, advocating renovation, not restoration. This aspect ensured that many royalists would come to distrust the Romantic impulse, for it had an uncontrollable dynamism that threatened the cultural and political project of the restored Bourbon monarchy. In certain ways, the activism of royalist Romanticism thus foreshadowed the emergence of a liberal, humanitarian Romanticism in the middle years of the 1820s.

By the later 1820s, many Romantics, including Victor Hugo, had become disillusioned by the ineptitude of the restored Bourbon monarchy and the evident stagnation of French society. Romantics found new vigor in rebuffing traditionalists like the "immortals" of the Académie Française, that literary body charged with defending the purity of French language and culture, who denounced Romanticism as an insidious foreign intrusion. Hugo's preface to his play *Cromwell* (1827; Document 20) vigorously defends the "liberty of art against the despotism of systems of codes and rules";[37] shortly before a new revolution brought down the restored Bourbon monarchy in July 1830, Hugo could write in the preface to *Hernani:* "Liberty in the arts, liberty in society, *voilà*, that is the double goal."[38] This identification of the ideal of free artistic expression with the political goal of political liberty was at the very heart of the liberal turn in French Romanticism. Indeed, when revolution broke out in July 1830, Romantics like Hugo were eager supporters, ready to draw direct links between the Romantic revolution in the arts and the struggle for political liberty and social equality.

EUROPEAN ROMANTICISM

English and German Romanticism had already lost much of their energy when Romanticism began to spread to all parts of Europe in the late 1810s and 1820s. Nonetheless, the shape of European Romanticism was crucially determined by the dissemination of ideas from the core contexts of Germany, England, and France. Madame de Staël's *De l'Allemagne* (*On Germany*) played an inestimable role in spreading the ideas of the German Romantics throughout Europe. In French translation, August Wilhelm Schlegel's *Lectures on Dramatic Art and Letters* (see Document 10) reached a Europe-wide audience; an English edition published in Philadelphia ensured Schlegel an

American readership as well. Schlegel's distinction between the "Classic" and the "Romantic" crops up in England, France, Spain, Italy, Scandinavia, indeed, in every national context, including Russia, where the great poet Alexander Pushkin picked up on Schlegel's identification of the origins of Romanticism in medieval Christendom. Lord Byron had a continent-wide impact, providing all of Europe with his poetry and with himself, regarded by his fans as the living embodiment of the archetypal Romantic. For example, during a crucial phase of Pushkin's creative life, Byron was his major model, although by the time he wrote his masterwork *Eugene Onegin* (1833), Pushkin had achieved enough distance to analyze rather than wallow in Byronic *Weltschmerz* (world-weariness). Great and singular as Pushkin was, he was in a large company in finding inspiration in the Byronic hero. The Russian Mikhail Lermontov's *A Hero of Our Time* (1840), the Frenchman Alfred de Musset's *The Confession of a Child of the Century* (1835), and the Italian Giacomo Leopardi's poetry are just some of the works that testify to Byron's impact. Victor Hugo had a lesser, though still substantial resonance. In Spain, Hugo's preface to *Cromwell* helped stimulate the liberal Romanticism of the 1830s. In the same years, French Romantic concern with the plight of the oppressed and impoverished inspired the Spanish writers Mariano José de Larra and José de Espronceda to create social-revolutionary works critical of the inequities of their society.

The themes and polarities that we saw in the first generation of German and English Romanticism returned in the Romantic literature, music, art, and thought that emerged throughout Europe from 1815 through 1840. However, whereas those founding figures of German and English Romanticism had generally grown quite reactionary by the 1810s, the dominant political tenor of the Romanticism that spread throughout Europe was liberal. This may be because much of Europe learned of Romanticism through Madame de Staël, whose political campaign against Napoleon had motivated her to portray German Romanticism as a progressive, liberal movement. It may also be because the defeat of Napoleon and the attempt to restore the ancien régime exposed the deep gulf between the emancipatory hopes awakened by the revolutionary period and the unwillingness of restored monarchic regimes to recognize the validity of even the most modest of these hopes.

Indeed, although Napoleon's banishment to the distant island of St. Helena and the restoration of the monarchies that had fallen to the Revolution were greeted by many Europeans, including many intellectuals and artists, as the promise of a new era of tranquility, the peace established by the Congress of Vienna in 1815 was accompanied by government repression and rigid censorship across Europe, from England to central and eastern Europe, where the Holy Alliance of Prussia, Austria, and Russia consecrated itself to the defense of monarchy and religion; the attempt to restore the order and social hierarchies of the ancien régime was overshadowed by indications that the aspirations of the Revolution had not disappeared. Thus, the 1820s witnessed the Chartist movement in England, the Decembrist conspiracy in Russia, the emergence of new liberal forces in France, the struggles of Spanish liberals against the restored Bourbon throne, nationalist conspiracies in Italy against Austrian control, a wave of "Philhellenism" aroused by international sympathy for the Greeks in their struggle for independence from the Ottoman Empire, and another wave of international sympathy for liberal Poles in their ill-fated November 1830 uprising against the Russian overlords whose control over much of Poland had been reestablished by the Congress of Vienna.

Even though German figures had provided many of the intellectual resources of European Romanticism, the French turn toward liberal Romanticism more closely resembles the experience of numerous other national contexts. In Spain, many of the leading Romantics were liberals who returned to Spain in 1833 after being driven into exile by a French invasion in 1823 that had restored King Ferdinand to absolute power. As in France, Spanish liberals had been initially skeptical of Romanticism precisely because they had judged it conservative; in exile, many liberals changed their mind when they encountered the progressive, socially critical Romanticism of Lord Byron and Victor Hugo. In post-Napoleonic Italy, where the Congress of Vienna had placed much of the north under Austrian control and returned other regions to the stifling rule of local autocrats, Romantics like the poet Giacomo Leopardi and the novelist and poet Alessandro Manzoni were committed liberals, while Giuseppe Mazzini, the leading advocate of an Italian national republic, was a committed Romantic. In Poland, the 1830 uprising against Russia galvanized Romantics like the poet Adam Mickiewicz. In Russia, the poet and novelist Mikhail Lermontov was exiled to the Caucasus region, just like Grigorii Pechorin, the rakish hero of his novel *A Hero of Our Time*. From 1820 to 1826, Alexander Pushkin too was banished to the south of Russia for a series of provocative poems, including his "Ode to Freedom," with its opening lines, "Tremble, o tyrants of the world / And you . . . o fallen slaves, arise!" Though Pushkin did not participate in the 1825 Decembrist conspiracy, he came under suspicion because so many of the arrested Decembrists possessed copies of his poems. True to the diversity and polarities that we have repeatedly encountered, there were politically conservative Romantics in each of these national contexts, but the dominant tendency was to connect the assertion of artistic and intellectual freedom with the struggle for political rights and liberty.

ROMANTIC NATIONALISM

In many parts of Europe, liberal Romanticism mixed easily with nationalist enthusiasm. Here, we can see Napoleon's paradoxical effects on European culture and politics. On the one hand, his attempt to dominate Europe stimulated nationalist resistance movements not just in Germany but in many other parts of Europe as well. (See Document 11.) On the other hand, the withdrawal of the foreign aggressor Napoleon left a simmering desire for national unity and self-determination that the Restorationist monarchies could suppress but not erase. This desire was intensified by the fact that in many regions of Europe—in cases like Germany, Poland, Italy, and Russia—the nation was more a goal to be achieved than a reality of political and cultural life. That is, in early nineteenth-century Europe, nationalism consisted mainly of a cultural and ideological project aimed at constructing the very idea of the nation, fostering people's identification with the "nation," and building political unity on the national principle. In the process of creating nationalist sensibilities that more or less persist to this day, Romantic intellectuals supplied crucial philosophical and historical arguments. Likewise, writers and artists created images that galvanized national sentiment, as in Eugène Delacroix's personification of Greece's heroic suffering (see Figure 4).

The aspect of early nineteenth-century nationalism that can be hardest to recapture from our vantage point is its utopian dimension. After all, the history of the twentieth century has taught us to regard nationalism as inherently dangerous, linked to fantasies of superiority and the insidious and violent dynamics of inclusion and exclusion. Far from sharing these misgivings, Romantic nationalists were inclined to believe that nations could harmoniously coexist; perhaps even stranger to our ears, they tended to believe that the nation is the best vehicle for the achievement of true human universality. Readers should recognize here a structure of thought that we have already encountered, namely, the Romantic belief that true individuality will

Figure 4. *Eugène Delacroix,* Greece on the Ruins of Missolonghi, *1826*
The French painter presents an allegory of Greece's suffering in its war of
independence against the Turks and also evokes the death of Lord Byron at
Missolonghi in 1824.
Réunion des Musées Nationaux/Art Resource, N.Y.

reveal the universal, and, conversely, that true universality will contain a rich diversity of individual forms. The most influential novelist of the period, the Scottish Walter Scott provides an emblematic instance of this belief when he wrote: "The degree of national diversity between different countries is but an instance of that general variety which Nature seems to have adopted as a principle through all her works."[39] Scott assumes that nature is meaningful, indeed providential, insofar as "Nature" has a singular purpose to be fulfilled precisely through the diversification of life forms. Scott and his contemporaries did not automatically associate this diversification with conflict; to the contrary, many associated diversity with peace. It took a different conception of nature, that of the English naturalist Charles Darwin, to irrevocably shift our thinking about natural diversity from a model of harmony to a model of competition. And it was the Darwinian concept of nature—not the Romantic one—that fed into the competitive nationalist ideologies of the later nineteenth century.

Compared to late nineteenth-century nationalism, early nineteenth-century nationalism was much more politically ambiguous. Was nationalism a position of the left or of the right? Johann Gottfried von Herder, the eighteenth-century German whose writings on culture, history, and group identity have led some to name him the "father" of nationalism, was in fact something of an anarchist; he was against state power, seeing states as hindrances to the flourishing of cultural diversity. By the end of the nineteenth century, it would have been almost inconceivable to be a nationalist *and* an antistatist, because nationalism had by then become inseparable from the idea of the nation-state. Furthermore, by 1900, nationalism had become associated with right-wing politics, while progressive politics was identified with the international workers' movement. In the early nineteenth century, by contrast, the political meaning of nationalism was still unsettled. Certainly, it had already departed from Herder. The French Revolution had defined the "nation" politically, as the source of political sovereignty, and there was no retreating from this new idea that a nation should find embodiment in a political state. However, contemporaries drew quite different conclusions from this basic point.

Hence, we find Romantic nationalists like the conservative German economist Adam Müller, who envisioned a harmonious national community based on the organic solidarity of traditional social hierarchies, age-old institutions, and the unity of church and state (see Document 12), while others, like the liberal Giuseppe Mazzini, envisioned a national community bound not only by its history but also by its allegiance to democratic institutions and the linkage between individual rights and national self-determination (see Document 21). Despite the dramatic differences separating these political tendencies, the established powers viewed both with considerable suspicion. After all, all Romantic nationalists followed the same basic logic: The people, not the monarch or the aristocracy, form the primordial foundation of the state; therefore, sovereignty resides finally in the people, not the monarch; thus, kings rule for the benefit of the people. Even for those nationalists who tried to reconcile their belief in the people with the supremacy of the king, these beliefs implied a new relationship between the ruler and the people, one that threatened the attempt to restore the order and hierarchy of the ancien régime. For liberal and democratic nationalists, this meant a politics of opposition to the European order which the Congress of Vienna had restored in 1815; in return, states censored and sometimes persecuted nationalists, especially of the liberal-democratic sort.

Under the pressure of these tensions, the "nation" became a major theme of European Romantic art and thought in the period from Napoleon's defeat to the revolutions of 1848 in Sicily, Italy, France, Germany, and the Austrian Empire. The examples of this are legion. In emulation of Walter Scott, whose historical novels were the most popular literature of the era, writers in every European country turned to their own national histories in search of subject matter. In the visual arts and music, we see a strong turn toward subjects drawn from national history and mythology, folkloric elements, and the national landscape. Many painters in the period drew inspiration from past episodes claimed for the national history. The Napoleonic wars furnished material for many images of heroic resistance against the French or, in France itself, of images of Napoleon and the campaigns of the French army. Artists reached further into the past, especially to the Middle Ages; true to the Romantic interest in mythology, they also turned for inspiration to national myths, such as the Nibelungen saga, which depicted the legendary heroes and pagan gods of pre-Christian northern Europe. The *Nibelungenlied*, a medieval epic poem based on that body of Germanic and Nordic myth, fascinated the German Romantics; it in turn inspired Richard Wagner's four opera cycle, *The Ring of the Nibelung* (1869–1876), and, at a farther remove, J. R. R. Tolkien's *Lord of the Rings* (1954–1955). The Romantic interest in folklore and peasant life led to an explosion of paintings depicting rural folk. Such paintings frequently mix ethnographic precision with sentimental yearning for the allegedly simple and authentic country life. The interest in traditional costumes and folkways evident in such genre paintings found a musical equivalent in composers' interest in ethnic coloration and folk motifs. Composers took up melodies considered native to their national tradition or inserted snatches of foreign melody, as the case demanded, perhaps a Scottish air for local color or a Moorish or Chinese melody to evoke the "Orient."

As with painting and literature, so too in music, this practice pointed to the importance given to the "Characteristic," Romanticism's emphasis on the idiosyncratic rather than typical, the exception rather than the rule, even at the cost of sacrificing melodic unity to coloristic effects. The collection of folk music became an important activity in this period, undertaken with equal passion in England by the poet John Clare and in Germany by collectors like Ludwig Erk, Clemens Brentano, and Achim von Arnim. Folk melodies in turn found their way into the compositions of major composers like Hector Berlioz, Carl Maria von Weber, Franz Liszt, and Mikhail Ivanovich Glinka. This was true even of Ludwig van Beethoven, despite the author and critic E. T. A. Hoffmann's enduring image of him as the consummate creator of a transcendental music that has only the infinite for its object. (See Document 13.) In the nationalist mood of the period, the initial association of folk music with the "lower classes" quickly passed over into an association with the "nation." The complex historical reality of such musical pieces, which may have originated in a specific region or group or may even have migrated from elsewhere, was generally suppressed in favor of the belief that a nation expresses its spiritual substance in certain basic melodies.

Musical composers even tried to evoke the features of national landscape. Perhaps the most famous of such efforts comes after the Romantic period proper, the Czech composer Bedřich Smetana's *Má Vlast* (My Fatherland) from 1879, a symphonic poem that tries to capture the Czech landscape and the Moldau River running through it. Landscape was, of course, much more central to painting than to music. Landscape painting acquired new prestige in the early nineteenth century largely through the association of landscape and national identity. The Prussian liberal nationalist painter Caspar David Friedrich broke with convention when he refused to follow the customary path of all European artists on a journey to Italy and instead painted only the German landscape. Friedrich's paintings are rich in national symbols, from the "old-German" hats and cloaks worn by many of his figures to Gothic ruins to the prominence of the "German" oak tree in many of his compositions. English painter John Constable's depictions of the Suffolk countryside where he spent his childhood suggest an equally strong emotional attachment to a local landscape, even if his style is decidedly different from Friedrich's. Constable's painting *Hay Wain* was displayed in the Paris Salon of 1824 and helped to stimulate the formation of the Barbizon School, whose naturalistic depictions of the French landscape expressed nationalist attachments. In most countries in Europe, one sees similar nationalist impulses in landscape painting, for example, the Danish artists grouped around the painter Christen Køpke or the Swiss painters Alexandre Calame, Karl Gerardet, and François Diday, whose images of the Alps created the ultimate symbols of Swiss national identity.

As many of these examples suggest, artistic interest in the nation dovetailed with a powerful new fascination for history. Reciprocal effects emerged between artists' engagement with history and the writing of history proper. Historians like the Frenchman Augustin Thierry set out to create historical narratives as compelling as the fictions of Walter Scott, and Thierry emphasized the crucial role of imagination in all historical writing. Even the Prussian Leopold von Ranke, often seen as the father of "scientific" history, repeatedly claimed that history is both a science and an art. Jules Michelet, perhaps the greatest French historian of the nineteenth century, created historical narratives that are still page-turners. If Michelet was a great practitioner of history as literary art, he was also a consummate nationalist historian. A committed republican, his subject, again and again, was the French people in its struggle for freedom. The driving force of history, for Michelet, is not the great man but the mass. "Shouldn't the individual be symbolic of the community?" he asked, in a deeply Romantic vein.[40] The hero of Michelet's magisterial histories of France and of the French Revolution is not the individual but the "people." (See Document 22.)

The Romantic era in fact initiated a crucial transformation in European thinking about history. As we have already seen in the historical relativism of Romantic aesthetic standards, Romanticism expressed a new appreciation of the individual specificity of historical epochs and the need to evaluate the past in terms that are sensitive to historical difference. Moreover, it became a common belief of the period that history provides a key form of understanding for almost every phenomenon. Guided by this idea, the Romantic period witnessed efforts to create historical disciplines from almost every branch of human knowledge, from the study of nature to law, economics, linguistics, theology, and philosophy. The Romantic emphasis on the interactions of diversity and unity, the organic metaphor, the stress placed on processes of growth and becoming, all contributed to the emergence of this "historicist" sensibility. The experience of revolutionary upheaval may have given a paradoxical impetus to this strong interest in history and, in some cases, deep nostalgia for the past. On the one hand, the Revolution gave everyone touched by it the sense of living in history, of being involved in "world-historical events," to use a loaded phrase invented in those years; on the other hand, the Revolution represented a *caesura*, a break between "then" and "now," which distanced the present from a past that could be accessed only through an act of will and imagination.

CONCLUSION

The end of the Romantic period in Europe is perhaps even more difficult to pinpoint than its beginnings. By the 1820s, English and German Romanticism had lost much of their energy and had blended almost seamlessly with a less transcendentalist and more prosaic sensibility. The critics of Romanticism gained considerable ground, particularly in Germany, where in the 1830s and 1840s the so-called Young German writers and Young Hegelian philosophers rejected Romanticism in the name of social realism in the arts and political activism in philosophy. Having experienced its heyday in other parts of Europe during the 1820s and 1830s, the Romantic temperament received a hard blow from the experience of the revolutions of 1848. Among the revolutionaries of 1848, when political ideals faced political realities, national self-interest trumped international brotherhood; and liberalism shattered on the difficulties of building political coalitions that would surmount class divisions between the middle class and the working class. The collapse of such dreams ushered in a more hardheaded era. Nationalism began its journey toward an almost exclusive association with right-wing politics; liberal idealism was discredited; Romantic socialism's vision of social harmony lost its persuasive power and yielded to a socialism based on class conflict and the "scientific" analysis of capitalism. The soaring idealism and grand hopes of Romanticism seemed naïve and out of place in a culture that increasingly granted primacy not to the poetic but to the scientific mind.

If one can say that the Romantic era came to a close with the revolutions of 1848, the impact of Romanticism endured. In its rebellion against Neoclassicism, Romanticism broke the hold of allegedly universal, timeless artistic standards; it emphasized the historical relativity of our definitions of beauty and the paramount importance of self-expression through artistic creation. The notion that the arts could or should be subjected to rules lost its grip on European culture. The result was an enormous expansion in the range of styles and artistic practices, as well as a dynamic process of artistic innovation and experimentation. At the same time, the Romantic era opened a characteristic debate about artistic standards and quality that has accompanied modern culture ever since. To what should an artwork correspond? The decline in the guiding power of rules—or, at least, the decline in the *belief* that rules exist and can be discovered and implemented—brought an unprecedented difficulty to the task of judging art. "Yes, but is it art?" has become an all-too-familiar question posed to any new and challenging work. Yet far from having a crippling effect, modern culture seems to draw much of its sustaining energy from the repeated dynamic exchange between the art object as provocation and the perennial debate it opens about the very status of art itself.

In our search for criteria by which to judge art, we still frequently return to the Romantic idea that artistic value derives not from "beauty" but from the originality of vision, the power of self-expression, or the authenticity of the search for self-expression that we believe can be traced in an artist's works. It became a commonplace of the Romantic period to insist that genius creates its own rules as it pursues its self-appointed goals. Even if we have abandoned many of Romanticism's theological, quasitheological, or metaphysical ideas about art, the exalted image of individual genius as a force of creation continues to resonate in our culture. These Romantic ideas about the exceptional individual were, in turn, tied to more general ideas about the human being. The Romantic era intensified the sense of the individuality and uniqueness of each person. It placed a new value on the inner life of the individual, and articulated a new appreciation of the complex interplay among reason, emotion, and fantasy that constitutes this inner life. It made new claims that the purpose of an individual life should be to search for an adequate expression of the self, a personal path leading to fulfillment.

Romanticism thereby forms one of the main tributaries feeding into the great discourse of personal authenticity that flows through modern culture. At the same time, critics of Romanticism have argued that this quest for personal fulfillment produced a specifically modern form of hedonism in which the self is caught in an endless cycle of desire, pursuit, and attainment, followed by disappointment and displacement of desire onto a new object. Hegel called this a "bad infinity"; recent times have seen efforts to link this narcissistic Romantic cycle to the emergence of modern consumer society.[41] Whatever one makes of such arguments, it is necessary always to recall the dialectical and contradictory nature of Romanticism itself. Romanticism may have contributed a dose of narcissistic self-absorption to the modern personality; but, from another perspective, the very notion of authentic, immediate, and uncompromised engagements with nature, society, and the self has provided critical resources whereby intellectuals and artists have repeatedly challenged complacent claims that society has actually attained a condition of authenticity and fulfillment. Moreover, Romanticism introduced characteristic tensions in the modern understanding of the problem of authenticity. Is inauthenticity the result of our distance from our own inner resources or is it the product of our alienation from something greater than ourselves? Is authenticity to be sought by cultivating and enhancing our individual potentiality or by seeking involvement and immersion in the whole, whether that is understood as community, nation, nature, or God? Modernity has certainly been marked by experiments on both sides of this divide, from New Age spiritualism's invent-your-own-religion to the periodic revivals of orthodox religiosity, from rebellious individualism to communitarianism to the persistent fantasy of integral nationalism. Finally, Romanticism articulated both the dream of fulfillment and its inherent impossibility. In this sense, disappointment is not an accidental by-product of the Romantic quest but an integral dimension of Romanticism's understanding of the world and of human possibilities.

The centrality of contradiction and polarity in the Romantic sensibility is evident in the selected readings that follow. The concerns with the self, nature, society, nations, history, and God that these texts express do not add up to a doctrine or formula. Rather, they reveal the urgent questions of a period that had the privilege or misfortune of knowing itself to be a period of transition. In a certain sense, this reminds us that Romanticism lived and died with the great age of revolutions stretching from 1789 to 1848. Yet, since that tumultuous epoch, what age has not been an age of transition and which generation has not felt itself to be in the middle of transition? This may help to explain why the new questions that Romanticism posed and the old questions it recast have never ceased to be provocative and engaging. Indeed, the themes and perspectives of the Romantic period became enduring features of modern culture even as they metamorphosed in later periods and other circumstances and met resistance from other cultural impulses and ideas. It is hoped that the selections in this book will provide readers with resources for evaluating the richness and complexity of the Romantic period itself, as well as the continuing resonances of Romanticism in our own culture.

NOTES

[1] Lord Byron, "Manfred: A Dramatic Poem," *Poetical Works*, ed. Frederick Page (Oxford: Oxford University Press, 1970), act III, scene I, 1, lines 70–71.

[2] Frank Paul Bowman, "The Specificity of French Romanticism," in *The People's Voice: Essays on European Romanticism*, ed. A. Ciccarelli et al. (Melbourne: Monash University, 1999), 74.

[3] Friedrich Schlegel, "Athenaeum Fragmente no. 281," *Kritische Friedrich-Schlegel Ausgabe*, vol. II, ed. E. Behler et al. (Munich: F. Schönigh, 1958–); Immanuel Kant, *Critique of Pure Reason*, trans. Norman Kemp Smith (New York: St. Martin's, 1961), 9.

[4] Lord Byron, "Childe Harold's Pilgrimage," *Poetical Works*, Fourth Canto, CXXVII.

[5] Alexander Pope, "An Essay on Criticism," *Poetical Works*, ed. Herbert Davis (Oxford: Oxford University Press, 1965), 1, 88–91

[6] William Blake, "The Ghost of Abel: To Lord Byron in the Wilderness," *Blake: Complete Writings*, ed. Geoffrey Keynes (London: Oxford University Press, 1972), 779.

[7] C. D. Friedrich, *Briefen und Bekenntnissen*, ed. Sigrid Hinz (Berlin: Henschelverlag, 1968), 92, 128.

[8] No evidence exists that Wordsworth had interactions with Blake.

[9] Schlegel, *Kritische Friedrich-Schlegel Ausgabe*, vol. VI, 394.

[10] Friedrich Schlegel, *Friedrich Schlegel 1794–1802: Seine prosaischen Jugendschriften 1794 bis 1802*, vol. I, ed. J. Minor (Vienna: C. Konegan, 1906), 121.

[11] See especially *The Prelude; or, Growth of a Poet's Mind*, ed. Ernest de Selincourt (London: Oxford University Press, 1928), book XI.

[12] For the most influential version of this thesis, see M. H. Abrams, *Natural Supernaturalism: Tradition and Revolution in Romantic Literature* (New York: Norton, 1971).

[13] Quoted in Gerhard Schulz, *Romantik: Geschichte und Begriff* (Munich: C. H. Beck, 1996), 66–67.

[14] Samuel Taylor Coleridge, letter to John Thelwall, September 10, 1802, *The Collected Letters of Samuel Taylor Coleridge*, vol. II, ed. L. Griggs (Oxford: Clarendon Press, 1956), 459.

[15] Friedrich Schlegel, *Friedrich Schlegel's* Lucinde *and the Fragments*, ed. P. Firchow (Minneapolis: University of Minnesota Press, 1971), 176.

[16] Friedrich Schlegel, *Philosophical Fragments*, ed. P. Firchow (Minneapolis: University of Minnesota Press, 1991), 24.

[17] Samuel Taylor Coleridge, letter to John Thelwall, October 14, 1797, *The Collected Letters of Samuel Taylor Coleridge*, vol. I, 349.

[18] F. W. J. Schelling, *Sämmtliche Werke*, vol. I (Augsburg: J. G. Cotta'scher Verlag, 1856), 162.

[19] Novalis, "Pollen," in *The Early Political Writings of the German Romantics*, ed. F. Beiser (New York: Cambridge University Press, 1996), 11, 17.

[20] See, for example, Novalis's image of the "grist mill" in Document 2.

[21] William Wordsworth, "MS. Drafts and Fragments," in *The Prelude, 1799, 1805, 1850*, ed. Jonathan Wordsworth et al. (New York: Norton, 1979), 496.

[22] Madame de Staël, *Germany*, vol. II, trans. O. W. Wight (Boston: Houghton Mifflin and Co., 1859), 218.

[23] Novalis, *The Novices of Saïs*, trans. R. Manheim (New York: Valentin, 1949), 1.

[24] William Wordsworth, *The Prelude*, book VI, 1, 568–572.

[25] Samuel Taylor Coleridge, "Dejection: An Ode," *The Complete Poetical Works of Samuel Taylor Coleridge*, vol. 1, ed. Ernest Hartley Coleridge (Oxford: Oxford University Press, 1975), 1, 47–49.

[26] Novalis, *Heinrich von Ofterdingen*, trans. P. Hilty (New York: Frederick Ungar, 1964), 114.

[27] Friedrich Schlegel, *Dialogue on Poetry and Literary Aphorisms*, ed. E. Behler (University Park: Pennsylvania State University Press, 1968), 89–90.

[28] Friedrich Schlegel, *Literary Notebooks 1787–1801*, ed. Hans Eichner (Toronto: University of Toronto Press, 1957), 46.

[29] Samuel Taylor Coleridge, *Letters, Conversations, and Recollections of S. T. Coleridge*, ed. Thomas Allsop (New York: Harper & Brothers, 1836), 71.

[30] I have discussed the later period of Schelling's thought and its impact on German intellectual life in *Marx, the Young Hegelians and the Origins of Radical Social Theory: Dethroning the Self* (Cambridge: Cambridge University Press, 1999).

[31] Quoted in F. Beiser, *Enlightenment, Revolution, and Romanticism: The Genesis of Modern German Political Thought, 1790–1800* (Cambridge, Mass.: Harvard University Press, 1992), 262.

[32] See Cordula Grewe, "Reenchantment as Artistic Practice: Strategies of Emulation in German Romantic Art and Theory," *New German Critique* 94 (Winter 2005): 36–71.

[33] Shelley, letter to Lord Byron, September 8, 1816, *The Letters of Percy Bysshe Shelley*, vol. 1, ed. Frederick L. Jones (London: Oxford University Press, 1964), 504.

[34] Karl Marx, *The Eighteenth Brumaire of Louis Napoleon* (New York: International Publishers, 1963), 1.

[35] Madame de Chastenay, quoted in J. C. Isbell, *The Birth of European Romanticism: Truth and Propaganda in Staël's* De l'Allemagne, *1810–1813* (Cambridge: Cambridge University Press, 1994), 6.

[36] Victor Hugo, quoted in Adèle Hugo, *Victor Hugo raconté par un témoin de sa vie*, ed. Evelyne Blewer et al. (Paris: Plon, 1985), 297.

[37] Victor Hugo, "Préface à *Cromwell*," *Oeuvres Complètes*, vol. 3, ed. Jean Massin (Paris: N. Fortin et ses Fils, 1967), 77.

[38] Victor Hugo, "Préface à Hernani," *Oeuvres Complètes*, vol. 3, 922.

[39] Walter Scott, "Letters from Malachi Malagrowther, Esq. on the Proposed Change of Currency," in *The Miscellaneous Prose Works of Sir Walter Scott*, vol. I (Edinburgh: R. Cadell, 1847), 749.

[40] Jules Michelet, *Mother Death: The Journal of Jules Michelet*, trans. E. K. Kaplan (Amherst: University of Massachusetts Press, 1984), 58.

[41] Colin Campbell, *The Romantic Ethic and the Spirit of Modern Consumerism* (Oxford: Blackwell, 1987).

PART TWO

The Documents

1

WILHELM HEINRICH WACKENRODER

Of Two Wonderful Languages and Their Mysterious Power

1797

Wilhelm Heinrich Wackenroder (1773–1798) was the son of a senior civil servant, whose artistic and intellectual temperament conflicted with family expectations that he would pursue a practical career. His short life was closely tied to his friend the writer Ludwig Tieck, with whom he studied at the Berlin gymnasium and the universities of Erlangen and Göttingen. Forced to return to Berlin in 1794, Wackenroder began a civil service career but dedicated his energies to numerous literary projects, including a series of musings on literature, painting, and religion written in the voice of an imaginary friar. Tieck persuaded Wackenroder to publish these musings, along with contributions by Tieck, which appeared anonymously as Outpourings of an Art-Loving Friar *(1797).*

Wilhelm Heinrich Wackenroder, "Of Two Wonderful Languages and Their Mysterious Power," *Outpourings of an Art-Loving Friar*, trans. Edward Mornin (New York: Frederick Ungar, 1975), 59–62.

When Wackenroder died of typhoid fever at age 24, Tieck published a continuation of the Outpourings *under the title* Fantasies on Art *(1799). It was a fitting memorial to a friendship based on an intense exchange of ideas and a shared passion for art and literature. One of the earliest expressions of the Romantic sensibility in Germany, the* Outpour-ings *express many of German Romanticism's core features: an intensely emotional tone, a sense of mystery, a yearning for transcendence, the belief that the visible world is a hieroglyph of the invisible, and a pious reverence for art. In this excerpt, Wackenroder presents "Nature" and "Art" as the means by which humans are able to grasp the divine in creation and in themselves. For Wackenroder, nature and art possess reve-latory powers even greater than those of orthodox revealed religion. In transferring a key religious function into the domain of aesthetic prac-tice, he establishes the basis for the Romantic idea of* Kunstreligion *(re-ligion of art). Already at the very beginning of Romanticism, we encounter ambiguities that run through much of Romanticism's subse-quent thinking about the relationship between art and religion: Is art a secular alternative to religion? Is it a surrogate religion in an age when traditional faith is in crisis? Or, is art another way to access the divine, one that is neither secular nor merely a continuation of traditional piety?*

The language of words is a precious gift of Heaven, and it was to our everlasting benefit that the Creator loosed the tongue of our first ancestor so that he might name all the things which the Almighty had put in the world around him, and all the spiritual images which He had implanted in his soul and so enrich his spirit by endlessly combin-ing this wealth of names. By means of words we have dominion over all of nature; by means of words we acquire with ease all the treasures of the earth. Yet words cannot call down into our hearts the invisible spirit which reigns above us.

We gain power over worldly things by naming them; but if we hear of God's boundless goodness or of the virtues of the saints—subjects which should overwhelm our whole being—our ears merely ring with empty sound and our spirits are not uplifted as they should be.

Yet I know of two wonderful languages through which the Creator has granted man the means of grasping and comprehending the Divine in all its force, at least (not to appear presumptuous) insofar as that is at all possible for poor mortals. These languages speak to our inner selves, but not in words; suddenly and in wondrous fashion they invade our whole being, permeating every nerve and every drop of blood in our veins. One of these wonderful languages is spoken by God alone; the other is spoken only by a few chosen men whom He has anointed as His favorites. They are: Nature and Art.

Since my early youth, when I first encountered God our Heavenly Father in our ancient books of holy scripture, I have always looked to Nature for the fullest and clearest explanation of His being and His attributes. The rustling of treetops in a forest or the rolling of thunder told me mysterious things about Him which I cannot put into words. A lovely valley enclosed by fearsome crags, or willows reflected in a smooth-flowing stream, or a meadow, green and serene, beneath a clear blue sky—ah! these things thrilled me more wonderfully, infused my heart more deeply with the infinite power and bounty of God, and purified and exalted my soul far more than words can ever do. Language, it seems to me, is too worldly and clumsy a tool to convey things of the spirit as well as material things.

I find in this great cause to praise the power and benevolence of the Creator. He has surrounded us mortals with an infinite variety of things, each of which has its own reality and none of which we can understand or comprehend. We do not know what a tree is, or what a meadow is, or what a rock is; we cannot talk to them in our language and we are capable of communication only among ourselves. And yet the Creator has instilled in us such a marvellous sympathy for these things that they fill our hearts in unknown ways with feelings or sentiments or whatever we may wish to call those intimations which not even the most precise words can convey to us.

The worldly-wise have been led astray by an otherwise admirable love of truth. In their desire to uncover the secrets of Heaven and to bring them down to earth and cast earthly light upon them, they have banished from their breasts those vague feelings which they once had for them, and they have justified this procedure quite vehemently.— Can puny man explain the secrets of Heaven? Can he drag into the light of day what God has veiled in darkness? Can he in his arrogance dismiss those indistinct feelings which descend to us from Heaven like angels in disguise?—I honor them in deep humility; for it is only by divine grace that these genuine witnesses of truth come down to us. I fold my hands in adoration.

Art is a language quite different from nature, but it too, in similar mysterious and secret ways, exercises marvellous power over the human heart. Art speaks through pictorial representations of men;

that is, it employs a hieroglyphic language whose signs we recognize and understand on sight. But in the figures which it presents, the spiritual and the sensuous are merged in such an effective and admirable fashion that the whole of our selves and every fiber of our being is doubly moved and shaken utterly. It would be no exaggeration to say that many paintings portraying Christ's Passion or the Holy Virgin or the lives of the Saints have purged my soul more pure, and inspired more divinely virtuous sentiments in my heart than systems of moral philosophy or pious sermons ever have. One work among others which I still recall with emotion is an exquisite painting of Saint Sebastian standing naked and bound to a tree while an angel draws the arrows from his breast and another angel descends from heaven with a garland of flowers for his head. To this painting I owe the most profound and lasting Christian sentiments, and even yet I can scarcely recall its details without tears coming to my eyes.

The teachings of the wise stir only our intellects, only one half of our selves. But the two wonderful languages whose power I here proclaim touch our senses as well as our minds, or rather (I cannot express the thought otherwise) appear in the process to merge every part of our being (so mysterious to us) into one single new organ of perception, which in this twofold way grasps and comprehends heavenly mysteries.

One of these languages, which the Almighty Himself speaks from everlasting to everlasting—eternal, infinite Nature—, raises us through the immensities of space into the presence of God Himself. Art, however, which by the meaningful combination of colored earth and a little moisture recreates the human shape in ideal form within a narrow, limited sphere (a kind of creative power which was vouchsafed to mortals)—art reveals to us the treasures of the human breast, turns our gaze inward, and shows us the Invisible, I mean all that is noble, sublime, and divine in human form.

When I leave the consecrated chapel of our cloister where I have been meditating upon Christ on the cross and step out into the open air where the sun shines down from a blue sky, enveloping me in its warmth and vitality, and when the beauties of the landscape with its mountains, streams, and trees impinge upon my vision, then I see a unique and divine world unfolding before me and feel great things stirring strangely in my breast. And when I leave the outdoors and enter the chapel again, and with earnest fervor contemplate the painting of Christ on the cross, then I see another unique but different divine world unfolding before me and feel great things stirring in my breast in a similarly strange yet different fashion.

Art depicts man in his most perfect form. Nature—at least as much of it as is visible to our mortal eye—is like a fragmentary oracular utterance from the mouth of the Divinity. If one may speak so familiarly of such things, one might perhaps say that in a sense the world of nature or the entire universe is to God what a work of art is to man.

2

NOVALIS

Christianity or Europe: A Fragment

1799

Novalis (1772–1801), the pen name for Friedrich von Hardenberg, was born into an extremely pious but impoverished aristocratic family. After studying law, Novalis began his career as an administrator in the royal saltworks of Saxony. His most productive literary period began in 1797 when he joined the Romantic circle clustered around the Schlegel brothers in the university town of Jena and lasted until his death from tuberculosis in 1801. In a remarkable burst of creativity, Novalis produced two long novel fragments, the greatest poetry of the Jena Romantics, and a body of theoretical-philosophical writings. Inspired by Johann Gottlieb Fichte's philosophy, Novalis saw the poet as a kind of magus, whose poetic word transforms the world into a product of imagination. This imaginative power to poeticize the world and unite nature, spirit, soul, finitude, and infinity, forms the base of what Novalis called "magical idealism."

"Christianity or Europe" caused a scandal within the Jena group. Upon Johann Wolfgang Goethe's advice, August Wilhelm and Friedrich Schlegel decided not to publish the essay in their journal Athenaeum.

Novalis, "Christianity or Europe: A Fragment," *The Early Political Writings of the German Romantics*, ed. and trans. Frederick Beiser (New York: Cambridge University Press, 1996), 59–79.

The Jena circle's fear was that it would be misunderstood as an expression of reactionary nostalgia for the Catholic Middle Ages. However, the historical narrative that Novalis constructs—from medieval Christendom through the Protestant Reformation and the Scientific Revolution to the Enlightenment and the Revolution—does not circle back to the past. Rather, it arrives at a present moment in which the violent clash of revolution and reaction, unbelief and faith, reason and intuition has reached a fatal deadlock that calls for a new reconciliation respecting both sides. By 1826, when the essay was published in its entirety, the conservative political climate virtually ensured that it would be read as an antirevolutionary, orthodox, and pro-Restorationist tract. Yet, far from offering a clear message, the text raises many questions. Is Novalis nostalgic or utopian, reactionary or revolutionary? Is his vision of a coming faith really still "Christian"? Are the Middle Ages offered as a solution or as a poetic metaphor?

Those were beautiful, magnificent times, when Europe was a Christian land, when *one* Christianity dwelled on this civilized continent, and when *one* common interest joined the most distant provinces of this vast spiritual empire. Without great worldly possessions *one* sovereign governed and unified the great political forces. Immediately under him stood one enormous guild, open to all, executing his every wish and zealously striving to consolidate his beneficent power. Every member of this society was honored everywhere. If the common people sought from their clergyman comfort or help, protection or advice, gladly caring for his various needs in return, he also gained protection, respect and audience from his superiors. Everyone saw these elect men, armed with miraculous powers, as the children of heaven, whose mere presence and affection dispensed all kinds of blessings. Childlike faith bound the people to their teachings. How happily everyone could complete their earthly labors, since these holy men had safeguarded them a future life, forgave every sin, explained and erased every blackspot in this life. They were the experienced pilots on the great uncharted seas, in whose shelter one could scorn all storms, and whom one could trust to reach and land safely on the shores of the real paternal world. The wildest and most voracious appetites had to yield with honor and obedience to their words. Peace emanated from them. . . .

This mighty peace loving society ardently sought to make all men share its beautiful faith, and sent its disciples to all parts of the globe to preach the gospel and to make the heavenly kingdom the only kingdom on earth. With justice, the wise head of the church resisted impudent developments of the human powers, and untimely discoveries in the realm of knowledge, that were at the expense of the sense for the divine. Thus he prevented the bold thinkers from maintaining publicly that the earth is an insignificant planet,[1] for he knew all too well that, if people lost respect for their earthly residence and home, they would also lose their respect for their heavenly home and race, that they would prefer finite knowledge to an infinite faith, and that they would grow accustomed to despising everything great and miraculous and regard it as the dead effect of natural laws.

All the wise and respected men of Europe assembled at his court. All treasures flowed there; destroyed Jerusalem was avenged and Rome itself had become Jerusalem, the holy residence of divine government on earth. Princes submitted their disputes before the father of Christendom and willingly laid down their crowns and splendor at his feet; indeed, they saw it as their glory to be members of this holy guild and to close the evening of their lives in divine meditation within lonely cloistered walls.[2] The mighty aspirations of all human powers, the harmonious development of all abilities, the immeasurable heights reached by all individuals in all fields of knowledge and the arts, and the flourishing trade in spiritual and earthly wares within all of Europe and as far as the distant Indies—all these show how beneficial, how suitable to the inner nature of man, this government and organization were.

Such were the beautiful chief characteristics of these truly catholic and truly Christian times. But for this splendid realm mankind was not mature or educated enough. It was a first love, which died under the pressure of commercial life, whose devotion was repressed by selfish concerns, and whose bond was later denounced as deceit and delusion and then judged according to later experience. Thus it was for ever destroyed by a large number of Europeans. Accompanied by destructive

---

The notes in this selection are partly adapted from Frederick Beiser's notes in the Cambridge University Press edition of Novalis's "Christianity or Europe: A Fragment."

[1]Novalis alludes to the astronomers Copernicus (1473–1543) and Galileo (1564–1642).

[2]A reference to Charles V, German emperor (r. 1519–1556), who lived after his abdication until his death (1558) in a Spanish cloister.

wars, this great inner schism was a remarkable sign of how harmful culture—or at least how temporarily harmful culture of a certain level—can be for the spiritual sense. That immortal sense can never be destroyed; but it can be dimmed, paralyzed, or repressed by other senses.

A longer association of men diminishes their inclinations toward, their faith in their race; and it accustoms them to applying their thought and effort to acquiring the means of material comfort. Needs, and the arts of satisfying them, grow more complicated; greedy man then requires so much time to know and acquire skill in these arts, that he no longer has time for the quiet collection of mind for the attentive consideration of the inner world. Should a conflict arise, his present interest seems to mean more to him; and so withers the beautiful blossoms of his youth, faith and love, giving way to the bitter fruits of knowledge and possession. . . . Here we have to deal with times and periods, and is not oscillation, an alternation of opposed tendencies, essential to them? Is not a limited duration proper to them, a growth and decay part of their nature? And is not resurrection, a rejuvenation in new vital form, to be expected with certainty of them? Progressive, constantly expanding evolution is the very stuff of history.

What does not now reach perfection will do in a future attempt, or in another later one. Nothing in the grasp of history is transient; from innumerable transformations it always proceeds anew to ever richer forms. Christianity once appeared with full power and splendor; its ruins, and the mere letter of its law, ruled with ever increasing impotence and mockery until a new world inspiration. Infinite inertia lay heavily on the complacent guild of the clergy. They stagnated in the feeling for their authority and material comfort, while the laity snatched from them the torch of experience and learning, surpassing them with great strides on the path of education. Forgetting their proper mission to be the first among men in spirit, knowledge and education, their lower desires went to their heads. The banality and baseness of their attitude became all the more offensive because of their clothing and calling. Thus respect and trust, the basis of this and any empire, gradually collapsed, destroying this guild and silently undermining the real authority of Rome long before the powerful insurrection. Only prudent, and therefore merely expedient, measures held the corpse of the old constitution together and preserved it from a too hasty dissolution. Among such measures was, for example, the abolition of the right of priests to marry. Such a measure, had it been applied to the similar profession of soldiers, could have given it a formidable coherence and prolonged its life. What was more natural than that a fiery agitator should preach open rebellion against the despotic letter of the previous constitution, and with such great success because he was a member of that guild.[3]

The insurgents rightly called themselves Protestants, for they solemnly protested against any pretension to rule over conscience by an apparently tyrannical and unjust force. For a while they reclaimed their once tacitly surrendered right to investigate, determine and choose their religion. They also established a number of correct principles, introduced a number of laudable things, and abolished a number of corrupt statutes. But they forgot the necessary consequences of their actions: they separated the inseparable, divided the indivisible church, and impiously divorced themselves from the universal Christian union, through and in which alone genuine lasting rebirth was possible. A condition of religious anarchy should be no more than transitional, for the basic need for a number of people to devote themselves to this high vocation, and to make themselves independent of secular power in regard to these concerns, remains pressing and valid.

Establishing consistories and retaining a kind of clergy did not satisfy this need and was not a sufficient substitute. Unfortunately, the princes intervened in this split, and many used the dispute to consolidate and expand their sovereign power and revenue. They were happy to rid themselves of that higher influence and took the new consistories under their paternal protection and direction. They were zealously concerned to prevent the complete reunion of Protestant churches. With religion sacrilegiously enclosed within the boundaries of the state, the foundation was laid for the gradual undermining of the religious cosmopolitan interest. Religion thus lost its great political influence as a peacemaker, its proper role as the unifying, characteristic principle of Christianity. The religious peace was concluded according to completely mistaken and sacrilegious principles and, through the continuation of so-called Protestantism, something completely contradictory was declared—namely, a permanent revolutionary government.[4]

---

[3]An allusion to Martin Luther (1483–1546), who was an Augustinian monk when he launched his critique of the Catholic Church.

[4]A reference to the Peace of Augsburg (1555), which gave equal rights to the Protestant and Catholic churches and granted princes the right to determine the religion of their subjects. Novalis implies a link between the Protestant Reformation and the French Revolution by alluding to the French National Convention's 1793 declaration that the Revolution was permanent.

However, Protestantism is by no means based solely on this pure concept.[5] Luther generally treated Christianity in an arbitrary manner, misunderstood its spirit, and introduced another law and another religion, namely the universal authority of the Bible. In this manner another alien, earthly science—philology—interfered with religious concerns, and its corrosive influence has been unmistakable ever since. From the dark feeling of his error, a large part of the Protestants elevated Luther to the rank of an evangelist and canonized his translation.

This decision was fatal for the religious sense, since nothing destroys its sensibility as much as the dead letter. Previously, this could never have been so harmful, because of the broadness, flexibility and richness of the catholic faith, because of the esoteric stature of the Bible, and because of the holy might of the councils and pope. But now that these antidotes were destroyed, and the absolute popularity of the Bible maintained, the meagre content of the Bible, and its crude abstract scheme of religion, became even more obviously oppressive. It made the revival, penetration and revelation of the holy spirit infinitely more difficult.

Hence the history of Protestantism shows us no more splendid revelations of the heavenly realm. Only its beginning glowed from a passing fire from heaven; but shortly afterwards a withering of the holy sense is apparent. The worldly had now won the upper hand, and the feeling for art suffered in sympathy with religion. . . . With the Reformation Christianity was done for. From hence forth it existed no more. Catholics and Protestants or Reformers stood further apart from one another in their sectarian conflict than from Moslems and pagans. The remaining Catholic states continued to vegetate, not without vaguely feeling the corrupting influence of the neighboring Protestant states. The new politics arose during this time: individual powerful states sought to take possession of the vacant universal see, now transformed into a throne. . . .

The Reformation had been a sign of the times. It was significant for all Europe, even if it had broken out publicly only in free Germany. The better minds of all nations had secretly grown mature,[6] and in the delusive self-confidence of their mission they rebelled all the more boldly against obsolete constraint. In the old order the intellectual was

---

[5]"Pure concept" refers to the ideal of liberty of conscience.

[6]Novalis ironically alludes to Kant's essay "What is Enlightenment?", which defines Enlightenment as humanity's liberation from its self-incurred immaturity.

instinctively an enemy of the clergy. The intellectual and clerical estate, once they were divided, had to fight a war of extermination, for they were fighting for one position. This division became increasingly prominent, and the intellectuals won more ground the more the history of Europe approached the age of triumphant learning, and the more faith and knowledge came into a more decisive opposition. One saw in faith the source of universal stagnation; and through a more penetrating knowledge one hoped to destroy it. Everywhere the sense for the sacred suffered from various persecutions of its past nature, its temporal personality.

The result of the modern manner of thinking one called "philosophy," and regarded it as anything opposed to the old order, especially therefore as any whim contrary to religion. The original personal hatred against the Catholic faith gradually became a hatred of the Bible, of Christian belief, and finally of all religion. Furthermore, the hatred of religion extended very naturally and consistently to all objects of enthusiasm, disparaging fantasy and feeling, morality and the love of art, the future and past. This new philosophy placed man of necessity at the top of the series of natural beings, and made the infinite creative music of the cosmos into the uniform clattering of a gigantic mill—a mill in itself driven by and swimming in the stream of chance, without architect or miller, a genuine *Perpetuum mobile*, a self-grinding mill.[7]

One enthusiasm was generously left to the poor human race, and made indispensable for everyone concerned, as a touchstone of the highest education: the enthusiasm for this splendid, magnificent philosophy, and especially for its priests and mystagogues. France was especially fortunate to be the nursery and home of this new faith, which was stuck together out of pieces of mere knowledge. However disreputable poetry was in this new church, there were still a few poets in it, who for the sake of effect, used the old ornaments and lights; in doing so, however, they were in danger of igniting the new world system with old fire. More clever members knew how to throw cold water on their inspired audience. The members were constantly preoccupied with purging poetry from nature, the earth, the human soul and the sciences. Every trace of the sacred was to be destroyed, all memory of noble events and people was to be spoiled by satire, and the world stripped of colorful ornament. Their favorite theme, on

---

[7]A reference to the deistic materialism of the French *philosophes*. According to deism, God does not interfere with the operations of nature after its creation.

account of its mathematical obedience and impudence, was light. They were pleased that it refracted rather than played with its colors, and so they called their great enterprise "Enlightenment." One was more thorough with this business in Germany: education was reformed, the old religion was given a new, rational and common sense meaning by carefully cleansing it of everything miraculous and mysterious; all scholarship was summoned to cut off taking any refuge in history, which they struggled to ennoble by making it into a domestic and civil portrait of family and morals. God was made into the idle spectator of the great moving drama, performed by intellectuals, whom the poets and actors should entertain and admire at the end.

Rightly, the common people were enlightened with pleasure and educated to an enthusiasm for culture. Hence arose that new European guild: the philanthropists and enlighteners. It is a pity that nature remained so wonderful and incomprehensible, so poetic and infinite, defying all attempts to modernize it. If anywhere there still crept the old superstition of a higher world and the like, alarm was immediately raised from all sides, and wherever possible the dangerous spark would be extinguished by philosophy and wit. Nevertheless, the watchword of the educated was "tolerance," and especially in France it was synonymous with philosophy.

The history of modern unbelief is extremely remarkable, and the key to all the monstrous phenomena of the modern age. Only in this century, and especially in the latter half, has it begun and grown in little time to an immense size and variety. A *second Reformation*,[8] a more comprehensive and proper one, was unavoidable. It would have to affect that country that was most modernized and that had laid in an asthenic state longest because of a lack of freedom. Long ago the supernatural fire would have been released and would have foiled the clever schemes of enlightenment if worldly pressure and influence had not come to their rescue. But at the very moment when a dispute arose between the intellectuals and government, and among the enemies of religion and their whole confederacy, religion had to step forward again as a third leading, mediating party. Every one of its friends should now recognize and proclaim this role, if it is not already clear enough. That the time of the resurrection has come, and that precisely the events that seemed to be directed against its revival and to

---

[8]Novalis makes explicit his association between Protestantism and the French Revolution by calling the latter a "second Reformation."

complete its demise have become the propitious signs of its regenera-tion—this cannot be denied by the historical mind.

True anarchy is the creative element of religion. From the destruc-tion of everything positive it lifts up its glorious head as the creator of a new world.[9] If nothing more binds him, man climbs to heaven by his own powers. The higher faculties, the original germ for the transfor-mation of the earth, free themselves from the uniform mediocre mix-ture, from the complete dissolution of all human talents and powers. The spirit of god hovers over the waters, and a heavenly island becomes visible over the receding waves as the dwelling place of the new man, as the birthplace of eternal life.

Calmly and impartially, the genuine observer considers the new revolutionary times. Does not the revolutionary seem like Sisyphus to him? Now he has reached the summit only for his mighty burden to roll down again. It will never stay on top unless an attraction toward heaven keeps it balanced there. All of your pillars are too weak if your state retains its tendency toward earth. But link it through a higher longing to the heights of heaven and give it a connection to the cos-mos, then you will have a never tiring spring in it and all your efforts will be richly rewarded. I refer you to history. Search in its instruc-tive continuum for similar times and learn to use the magic wand of analogy.

France defends a worldly Protestantism. Should now worldly Jesu-its arise and renew the history of the last centuries? Should the Revo-lution remain French, as the Reformation was Lutheran? Should Protestantism again be established—contrary to nature—as a revolu-tionary government? Should the dead letter be replaced only by another dead letter? Do you seek the seed of corruption also in the old constitution, the old spirit? And do you think you know a better constitution, a better spirit? Oh! that the spirit of spirits fill you and lead you away from this foolish attempt to mold and direct history and humanity. Is history not independent, autonomous, virtually infinitely lovable and prophetic? To study it, to follow it, to learn from it, to keep step with it, faithfully to follow its promises and suggestions—this no one has thought of.

In France much has been done for religion, in not only one of its countless forms, by depriving it of its civil rights and by granting it

---

[9]By "everything positive," Novalis means the destruction of everything established or decreed by authority.

merely the right of asylum. As an insignificant alien orphan it must first win back hearts and be loved everywhere before it is publicly worshipped and combined with worldly things to give friendly advice and heart to the spirit. The attempt of that great iron mask, which went by the name of Robespierre, to make religion the middle point and heart of the republic remains historically remarkable.[10] Equally remarkable is the coldness with which theophilanthropy,[11] the mysticism of the new Enlightenment, has been received, not to mention the conquests of the Jesuits,[12] and the closer relation to the Orient with the new politics.[13]

Concerning the other European countries, except Germany, one can only prophesy that *peace* will bring a new higher religious life and will soon consume all other worldly interests. In Germany, though, one can point out with complete certainty the traces of a new world. In its slow but sure way Germany advances before the other European countries. While the other countries are preoccupied with war, speculation and partisanship, the German diligently educates himself to be the witness of a higher epoch of culture; and such progress must give him a great superiority over other countries in the course of time. In the sciences and arts one perceives a powerful ferment. An infinite amount of spirit is developed. New fresh mines are being tapped. Never were the sciences in better hands, and never have they aroused greater expectations. The most various aspects of things are traced; nothing is left untouched, unjudged or unexamined. No stone is left unturned. Writers become more original and powerful; every monument of history, every art, every science finds new friends and is embraced and made more fruitful. A diversity without parallel, a wonderful depth, a brilliant polish, extensive knowledge and a rich powerful fantasy can be found everywhere and are often boldly joined together. A powerful intuition of creative wilfulness, of boundlessness, of infinite diversity, of sacred originality and the omnipotence of inner humanity appears to stir everywhere. Woken from the morning dream

[10]In May 1794 Robespierre decreed the cult of the Supreme Being.

[11]A deistic, rationalist religious society formed in Paris in 1796 with the purpose of maintaining religion. It was banned in 1802.

[12]This reference to the Jesuits is highly enigmatic. Pope Clement XIV had disbanded the Jesuit Order in 1773, and until their legal reinstatement in 1814, it is difficult to see how their shadowy existence allowed for any "conquests." Novalis may have in mind the 1794 attempt of some ex-Jesuits to resurrect their order as the *Société du Sacré Coeur*, or he may refer more loosely to the successes of the Jesuit missions in Asia, especially China, during the eighteenth century.

[13]Reference to Napoleon's campaign in Egypt in 1798–1799.

of helpless childhood, one part of the human race exercises its powers on the vipers that encircle its cradle and attempt to deprive it of the use of its limbs.[14] These are still intimations, unconnected and crude, but they betray to the historical eye a universal individuality, a new history, a new humanity, the sweetest embrace of a young surprised church and a loving god, not to mention the inner reception of a new messiah in all his thousand forms. Who does not feel hope with sweet shame? The new born will be the image of its father, a new golden age with dark infinite eyes, a prophetic, miraculous, healing, consoling time that generates eternal life. It will be a great age of reconciliation, of a redeemer who, like a true genius, will be at home with men, believed but not seen. He will be visible to the believer in countless forms: consumed as bread and wine, embraced as a lover, breathed as air, heard as word and song, and as death received into the heart of the departing body with heavenly joy and the highest pains of love.

Now we stand high enough to smile back amiably upon those former times and to recognize in those strange follies remarkable crystallizations of historical matter. Thankfully we should shake hands with those intellectuals and philosophers; for this delusion had to be exhausted for the sake of posterity and the scientific view of things had to be legitimated. More charming and colorful, poetry stands like an ornate India in contrast to the cold, dead pointed arches of an academic reason.[15] So that India might be warm and magnificent in the center of our planet, a cold, frozen sea, desolate cliffs and fog, rather than the starry sky and a long night, had to make both poles inhospitable. The deeper meaning of mechanics troubled these hermits in the desert of the understanding. The excitement of their first discovery overwhelmed them, the old order revenged itself on them. With wonderful self-denial they sacrificed the most holy and beautiful things in the world to their first self-awareness. They were the first to recognize and proclaim again the sanctity of nature, the infinitude of art, the necessity of knowledge, the respect for the secular, and the omnipresence of the truly historical. They put an end to a higher, more widespread and horrible reign of phantoms than they themselves believed.

---

[14]Allusion to the Greek myth of Hercules, who as a young child killed snakes in his cradle sent by Hera to strangle him.

[15]The German Romantics considered India the birthplace of poetry. Contributing to this belief was Georg Forster's translation into German of the ancient Indian drama *Sakontala*, which appeared in 1791 with a preface by Johann Gottfried Herder.

Only through a more exact knowledge of religion will one be able to judge the dreadful products of a religious sleep, those dreams and deliria of the sacred organ. Only then will one be able to assess properly the importance of such a gift. Where there are no gods, phantoms rule. The period of the genesis of European phantoms, which also rather completely explains their form, is the period of transition from Greek mythology to Christianity. So come then, you philanthropists and encyclopedists,[16] into the peace making lodge and receive the kiss of brotherhood! Strip off your grey veil and look with young love at the miraculous magnificence of nature, history and humanity. I want to lead you to a brother who shall speak to you,[17] so that your hearts will open again, and so that your dormant intuition,[18] now clothed with a new body, will again embrace and recognize what you feel and what your ponderous earthly intellect cannot grasp.

This brother is the pulse of the new age. Who has felt him does not doubt its coming, and with a sweet pride in his generation steps forward from the mass into the new band of disciples. He has made a new veil for the saints,[19] which betrays their heavenly figure by fitting so close and yet which conceals them more chastely than before. The veil is for the virgin what the spirit is for the body: its indispensable organ, whose folds are the letters of her sweet annunciation. The infinite play of these folds is a secret music, for language is too wooden and impudent for the virgin, whose lips open only for song. To me it is nothing more than the solemn call to a new assembly, the powerful beating of wings of a passing angelic herald. They are the first labor pains; let everyone prepare himself for the birth.

Physics has now reached its heights, and we can now more easily survey the scientific guild. In recent times the poverty of the external sciences has become more apparent the more we have known about them. Nature began to look more barren; and, accustomed to the splendor of our discoveries, we saw more clearly that it was only a borrowed light, and that with our known tools and methods we would

---

[16]Reference to Denis Diderot (1713–1784), Jean D'Alembert (1717–1783), and the other editors of the major work of the French Enlightenment, the *Encyclopedia*, which appeared in twenty-eight volumes between 1751 and 1772.

[17]Novalis means Friedrich Schleiermacher (1768–1834), the Protestant theologian and intimate of the Jena Romantic circle whose *Religion: Speeches to Its Cultured Despisers* (1799) powerfully influenced Novalis during the composition of "Christianity or Europe."

[18]Schleiermacher argued that the divine can be known only through intuition.

[19]"A new veil for the saints" plays on Schleiermacher's name, which means "veil-maker."

not find or construct the essential, or that which we were looking for. Every enquirer must admit that one science is nothing without the other. Hence there arose those attempts at mystification of the sciences,[20] and the wonderful essence of philosophy sprang into being as a pure scientific element for a symmetrical basic norm of the sciences.[21] Others brought the concrete sciences into new relations, promoted their interchange, and sought to clarify their natural historical classification. And so it goes on. It is easy to estimate how promising might be this intimacy with the external and internal world, with the higher development of the understanding, and with the knowledge of the former and stimulation and culture of the latter. It is also easy to estimate how, under these circumstances, the storm will clear and the old heaven and the yearning for it—a living astronomy—must again appear.

Now let us turn to the political drama of our times. The old and new order are locked in struggle. The inadequacy and destitution of the previous political institutions has become apparent in frightful phenomena. If only the historical end of the war were, as in the sciences, a more intimate and varied contact and connection between the European states! If only there were a new stirring of hitherto slumbering Europe! If only Europe wanted to awaken again! And if only a state of states, a new political theory of science, were impending. Should perhaps the hierarchy, the symmetrical basic figure of the sciences, be the principle of the union of states as an intellectual intuition of the political ego? It is impossible that worldly powers come into equilibrium by themselves; only a third element, that is worldly and supernatural at the same time, can achieve this task. No peace can be concluded among the conflicting powers. All peace is only an illusion, only a temporary truce. From the standpoint of the cabinets, and of common opinion, no unity is conceivable.

Both sides have great and necessary claims and must put them forward, driven by the spirit of the world and humanity. Both are indestructible powers within the human breast. On the one hand, there is veneration of the old world, loyalty to the historical constitution, love

---

[20]Novalis intends the word *mystification* positively; he refers to the philosophy of nature of Friedrich Wilhelm Joseph Schelling (1775–1854), which attempts to know the whole of nature through an intellectual intuition.

[21]An allusion to the philosopher Johann Gottlieb Fichte's *Wissenschaftslehre* (Theory of Knowledge, 1794), which Novalis regarded as a "science of sciences." Novalis so admired Fichte that he coined the term *fichteanize* (fichtisieren) as a synonym for *romanticize* (romantisieren).

of the ancestral monuments and of the old glorious royal family, and joy in obedience. On the other hand, there is the rapturous feeling of freedom, the unlimited expectations of a more potent sphere of action, the pleasure in what is new and young, the informal contact with all fellow citizens, the pride in human universality, the joy in personal rights and in the property of the whole community, and the strong civic sense. Neither side should hope to destroy the other. All conquests mean nothing, for the inner capitol of that kingdom lies not behind earthen walls and cannot be stormed.

Who knows whether there has been enough war, whether it will ever cease, unless one seizes the palm branch, which a spiritual power alone can offer. Blood will continue to flow in Europe until the nations recognize their terrible madness. This will continue to drive them into circles until, moved and calmed by sacred music, they step before their past altars in a motley throng. Then they will undertake works of peace, celebrating with hot tears a great banquet of love as a festival of peace on the smoking battlefields. Only religion can reawaken Europe, make the people secure, and install Christianity with new magnificence in its old peace making office, visible to the whole world.

Do not the nations possess everything of man—except his heart—his sacred organ? Do they not become friends, as people do around the coffin of their beloved? Do they not forget all hostility when divine pity speaks to them—and when one misfortune, one lament, one feeling, fills their eyes with tears? Are they not seized by sacrifice and surrender with almighty power, and do they not long to be friends and allies?

Where is that old, dear belief in the government of God on earth, which alone can bring redemption? Where is that sacred trust of men for one another, that sweet devotion in the effusions of an inspired mind, that all-embracing spirit of Christianity?

Christianity has three forms. One is the creative element of religion, the joy in all religion. Another is mediation in general, the belief in the capacity of everything earthly to be the wine and bread of eternal life. Yet a third is the belief in Christ, his mother and the saints. Choose whichever you like. Choose all three. It is indifferent: you are then Christians, members of a single eternal, ineffably happy community.

The old catholic faith, the last of these forms, was applied Christianity come to life. Its omnipresence in life, its love for art, its deep humanity, the sanctity of its marriages, its philanthropic sense of community, its joy in poverty, obedience and loyalty, all make it unmistakable as genuine religion and contain the basic features of its constitution. It is purified through the stream of time; and in indivisible union with the other two forms of Christianity it will bless the earth.

Its accidental form is as good as destroyed. The old papacy lies in the grave, and for a second time Rome has become a ruin.[22] Should not Protestantism finally cease and give way to a new more lasting church? The other parts of the world wait for Europe's reconciliation and resurrection to join with it and become fellow citizens of the kingdom of heaven. Should there not be soon again in Europe a number of truly sacred minds? Should not all kindred religious minds be full of yearning to see heaven on earth? And should they not eagerly meet to sing a holy chorus?

Christianity must again become alive and active, and again form a visible church without regard to national boundaries. Once again it must receive into its bosom all hungry souls and become the mediator of the old and new world.

Christianity must again pour the old cornucopia of blessings over the nations. It will rise again from the bosom of a venerable European council, and the business of religious awakening will be pursued according to a comprehensible divine plan. No one will again protest against Christian and worldly coercion, for the essence of the church will be genuine freedom, and all necessary reforms under its direction will be performed as peaceful and formal processes of state.

When and how soon? That is not to be asked. Have patience. It will and must come, the sacred age of eternal peace, where the new Jerusalem will be the capitol. Until then be calm and brave amid the dangers of the age. Companions of my faith, proclaim by word and deed the divine gospel! Remain loyal to the true, eternal faith until death.

[22]In February 1798, Rome was sacked by French troops under Marshall Louis Alexandre Berthier. Pope Pius VI was taken prisoner and died in French custody on August 29, 1799.

3

WILLIAM WORDSWORTH

Preface to "Lyrical Ballads"

1800

Orphaned at a young age, William Wordsworth (1770–1850) and his siblings came under the care of relatives. He completed his schooling in Cumberland and then studied at Cambridge University. Two trips to France (1790–1791) kindled Wordsworth's enthusiasm for the Revolution, but his ardor cooled in ensuing years as he moved toward a more conservative outlook. In 1799, he and his sister Dorothy, with whom he shared an intense emotional and intellectual bond, rented Dove Cottage in the English Lake District. This rugged, lonely landscape exercised a lifelong hold on Wordsworth's imagination, and many of his greatest poems are set there. In 1813, Wordsworth accepted the position of Stamp Distributor for Westmoreland, giving him a steady income for the first time in his life. When Robert Southey died in 1843, Wordsworth became Poet Laureate, a climactic moment in his journey from young artistic rebel to establishment figure.

Lyrical Ballads, *a collection of poems by Wordsworth and Samuel Taylor Coleridge, was destined to have a revolutionary impact on the ideology, style, and psychology of English poetry, even though it did not stand out immediately among the 150 other books of poetry published in England in 1798. As Coleridge later remembered the collaborative work on* Lyrical Ballads, *"It was agreed that my endeavours should be directed to persons and characters supernatural, or at least romantic. . . . Mr. Wordsworth, on the other hand, was to propose to himself as his object, to give the charm of novelty to things of every day."* [1] *Despite the two friends' many shared convictions, Wordsworth's preface to the second edition of* Lyrical Ballads *describes an artistic program that is his own, as is evident in this excerpt. Much here had already become commonplace by the*

---

[1]Samuel Taylor Coleridge, *Biographia Literaria*, vol. 2, ed. J. Shawcross (Oxford: Oxford University Press, 1965), 6.

William Wordsworth, *The Complete Poetical Works of William Wordsworth* (Boston: Houghton Mifflin and Company, 1911).

late 1790s: Nature as a consoling and moral presence, the authenticity of simple rural folk, anti-urbanism, and the identification of poetry with broad humanitarian sentiment. Yet taken as a whole, this text announces a new direction in English poetics. Wordsworth overturns Neoclassical values, preferring subject matter from common life and rejecting ornate poetic diction in favor of a more idiomatic language. His emphasis on the power of imagination, exaltation of poetic genius, insistence on poetry's high moral mission, and ideal of direct communication between the poet and the reader became touchstones of English Romanticism.

Several of my Friends are anxious for the success of these Poems, from a belief that, if the views with which they were composed were indeed realized, a class of Poetry would be produced, well adapted to interest mankind permanently, and not unimportant in the quality and in the multiplicity of its moral relations: and on this account they have advised me to prefix a systematic defense of the theory upon which the Poems were written. But I was unwilling to undertake the task, knowing that on this occasion the Reader would look coldly upon my arguments, since I might be suspected of having been principally influenced by the selfish and foolish hope of *reasoning* him into an approbation of these particular Poems: and I was still more unwilling to undertake the task, because adequately to display the opinions, and fully to enforce the arguments, would require a space wholly disproportionate to a preface. For, to treat the subject with the clearness and coherence of which it is susceptible, it would be necessary to give a full account of the present state of the public taste in this country, and to determine how far this taste is healthy or depraved; which, again, could not be determined without pointing out in what manner language and the human mind act and re-act on each other, and without retracing the revolutions, not of literature alone, but likewise of society itself. I have therefore altogether declined to enter regularly upon this defense; yet I am sensible that there would be something like impropriety in abruptly obtruding upon the Public, without a few words of introduction, Poems so materially different from those upon which general approbation is at present bestowed.

It is supposed that by the act of writing in verse an Author makes a formal engagement that he will gratify certain known habits of association; that he not only thus apprises the Reader that certain classes of ideas and expressions will be found in his book, but that others will be carefully excluded. This exponent or symbol held forth by metrical language must in different areas of literature have excited very different expectations: for example, in the age of Catullus, Terence, and Lucretius, and that of Statius or Claudian; and in our own country, in the age of Shakespeare and [Francis] Beaumont and [John] Fletcher, and that of [John] Donne and [Abraham] Cowley, or [John] Dryden, or [Alexander] Pope. I will not take upon me to determine the exact import of the promise which, by the act of writing in verse, an Author in the present day makes to his reader; but it will undoubtedly appear to many persons that I have not fulfilled the terms of an engagement thus voluntarily contracted. They who have been accustomed to the gaudiness and inane phraseology of many modern writers, if they persist in reading this book to its conclusion, will, no doubt, frequently have to struggle with feelings of strangeness and awkwardness: they will look round for poetry, and will be induced to inquire by what species of courtesy these attempts can be permitted to assume that title. I hope, therefore, the reader will not censure me for attempting to state what I have proposed to myself to perform; and also (as far as the limits of a preface will permit) to explain some of the chief reasons which have determined me in the choice of my purpose: that at least he may be spared any unpleasant feeling of disappointment, and that I myself may be protected from one of the most dishonorable accusations which can be brought against an Author; namely, that of an indolence which prevents him from endeavoring to ascertain what is his duty, or, when his duty is ascertained, prevents him from performing it.

The principal object, then, proposed in these Poems, was to choose incidents and situations from common life, and to relate or describe them throughout, as far as was possible, in a selection of language really used by men, and, at the same time, to throw over them a certain coloring of imagination, whereby ordinary things should be presented to the mind in an unusual aspect; and further, and above all, to make these incidents and situations interesting by tracing in them, truly though not ostentatiously, the primary laws of our nature: chiefly, as far as regards the manner in which we associate ideas in a state of excitement. Humble and rustic life was generally chosen, because in that condition the essential passions of the heart find a better soil in which they can attain their maturity, are less under restraint, and speak a plainer and more emphatic language; because in that condition of life our elementary feelings co-exist in a state of greater simplicity, and, consequently, may be more accurately contemplated, and more forcibly communicated; because the manners of rural life germinate from those elementary feelings, and, from the necessary character of rural occupations, are more easily comprehended, and are more durable; and, lastly, because in that condition the passions of men are incorporated with the beautiful and permanent forms of nature. The language, too, of these men has been adopted (purified indeed from what appear to be its real defects, from all lasting and rational causes of dislike or disgust), because such men hourly communicate with the best objects from which the best part of language is originally derived; and because, from their rank in society and the sameness and narrow circle of their intercourse, being less under the influence of social vanity, they convey their feelings and notions in simple and unelaborated expressions. Accordingly, such a language, arising out of repeated experience and regular feelings, is a more permanent, and a far more philosophical language, than that which is frequently substituted for it by Poets, who think that they are conferring honor upon themselves and their art in proportion as they separate themselves from the sympathies of men, and indulge in arbitrary and capricious habits of expression, in order to furnish food for fickle tastes and fickle appetites of their own creation.[2]

I cannot, however, be insensible to the present outcry against the triviality and meanness, both of thought and language, which some of my contemporaries have occasionally introduced into their metrical compositions; and I acknowledge that this defect, where it exists, is more dishonorable to the Writer's own character than false refinement or arbitrary innovation, though I should contend at the same time that it is far less pernicious in the sum of its consequences. From such verses the Poems in these volumes will be found distinguished at least by one mark of difference, that each of them has a worthy *purpose*. Not that I always began to write with a distinct purpose formally conceived, but habits of meditation have, I trust, so prompted and regulated my feelings, that my descriptions of such objects as strongly excite those feelings will be found to carry along with them a *purpose*. If this opinion be erroneous, I can have little right to the name of a Poet. For all good poetry is the spontaneous overflow of powerful feelings: and though this be true, Poems to which any value can be attached were never produced on any variety of subjects but by a man

---

[2]It is worthwhile here to observe that the affecting parts of Chaucer are almost always expressed in language pure and universally intelligible even to this day. [Wordsworth's note]

who, being possessed of more than usual organic sensibility, had also thought long and deeply. For our continued influxes of feeling are modified and directed by our thoughts, which are indeed the representatives of all our past feelings; and as, by contemplating the relation of these general representatives to each other, we discover what is really important to men, so, by the repetition and continuance of this act, our feelings will be connected with important subjects, till at length, if we be originally possessed of much sensibility, such habits of mind will be produced that, by obeying blindly and mechanically the impulses of those habits, we shall describe objects, and utter sentiments, of such a nature, and in such connection with each other, that the understanding of the Reader must necessarily be in some degree enlightened, and his affection strengthened and purified.

It has been said that each of these Poems has a purpose. Another circumstance must be mentioned which distinguishes these Poems from the popular Poetry of the day; it is this, that the feeling therein developed gives importance to the action and situation, and not the action and situation to the feeling.

A sense of false modesty shall not prevent me from asserting that the Reader's attention is pointed to this mark of distinction, far less for the sake of these particular Poems than from the general importance of the subject. The subject is indeed important! For the human mind is capable of being excited without the application of gross and violent stimulants; and he must have a very faint perception of its beauty and dignity who does not know this, and who does not further know, that one being is elevated above another in proportion as he possesses this capability. It has therefore appeared to me, that to endeavor to produce or enlarge this capability is one of the best services in which, at any period, a Writer can be engaged; but this service, excellent at all times, is especially so at the present day. For a multitude of causes, unknown to former times, are now acting with a combined force to blunt the discriminating powers of the mind, and, unfitting it for all voluntary exertion, to reduce it to a state of almost savage torpor. The most effective of these causes are the great national events which are daily taking place, and the increasing accumulation of men in cities, where the uniformity of their occupations produces a craving for extraordinary incident which the rapid communication of intelligence hourly gratifies. To this tendency of life and manners the literature and theatrical exhibitions of the country have conformed themselves. The invaluable works of our elder writers, I had almost said the works of Shakespeare and [John] Milton, are driven into neglect by frantic novels, sickly and stupid German Tragedies, and deluges of idle and extravagant stories in verse.—When I think upon this degrading thirst after outrageous stimulation, I am almost ashamed to have spoken of the feeble endeavor made in these volumes to counteract it; and, reflecting upon the magnitude of the general evil, I should be oppressed with no dishonorable melancholy, had I not a deep impression of certain inherent and indestructible qualities of the human mind, and likewise of certain powers in the great and permanent objects that act upon it, which are equally inherent and indestructible; and were there not added to this impression a belief that the time is approaching when the evil will be systematically opposed by men of greater powers, and with far more distinguished success. . . .

Taking up the subject, then, upon general grounds, let me ask, what is meant by the word Poet? What is a Poet? To whom does he address himself? And what language is to be expected from him?— He is a man speaking to men: a man, it is true, endowed with more lively sensibility, more enthusiasm and tenderness, who has a greater knowledge of human nature, and a more comprehensive soul, than are supposed to be common among mankind; a man pleased with his own passions, and volitions, and who rejoices more than other men in the spirit of life that is in him; delighting to contemplate similar volitions and passions as manifested in the goings-on of the Universe, and habitually impelled to create them where he does not find them. To these qualities he has added a disposition to be affected more than any other men by absent things as if they were present; an ability of conjuring up in himself passions, which are indeed far from being the same as those produced by real events, yet (especially in those parts of the general sympathy which are pleasing and delightful) do more nearly resemble the passions produced by real events than anything which, from the motions of their own minds merely, other men are accustomed to feel in themselves:—whence, and from practice, he has acquired a greater readiness and power in expressing what he thinks and feels, and especially those thoughts and feelings which, by his own choice, or from the structure of his own mind, arise in him without the immediate external excitement.

But whatever portion of this faculty we may suppose even the greatest Poet to possess, there cannot be a doubt that the language which it will suggest to him must often, in liveliness and truth, fall short of that which is uttered by men in real life under the actual pressure of those passions, certain shadows of which the Poet thus produces, or feels to be produced, in himself.

However exalted a notion we would wish to cherish of the character of a Poet, it is obvious that, while he describes and imitates passions, his employment is in some degree mechanical compared with the freedom and power of real and substantial action and suffering. So that it will be the wish of the Poet to bring his feelings near to those of the persons whose feelings he describes, nay, for short spaces of time, perhaps, to let himself slip into an entire delusion, and even confound and identify his own feelings with theirs; modifying only the language which is thus suggested to him by a consideration that he describes for a particular purpose, that of giving pleasure. Here, then, he will apply the principle of selection which has been already insisted upon. He will depend upon this for removing what would otherwise be painful or disgusting in the passion; he will feel that there is no necessity to trick out or to elevate nature: and the more industriously he applies this principle the deeper will be his faith that no words, which *his* fancy or imagination can suggest, will be to be compared with those which are the emanations of reality and truth.

But it may be said by those who do not object to the general spirit of these remarks, that, as it is impossible for the Poet to produce upon all occasions language as exquisitely fitted for the passion as that which the real passion itself suggests, it is proper that he should consider himself as in the situation of a translator, who does not scruple to substitute excellences of another kind for those which are unattainable by him; and endeavors occasionally to surpass his original, in order to make some amends for the general inferiority to which he feels he must submit. But this would be to encourage idleness and unmanly despair. Further, it is the language of men who speak of what they do not understand; who talk of Poetry, as of a matter of amusement and idle pleasure; who will converse with us as gravely about a *taste* for Poetry, as they express it, as if it were a thing as indifferent as a taste for rope-dancing, or Frontiniac or Sherry. Aristotle, I have been told, has said, that Poetry is the most philosophic of all writing: it is so: its object is truth, not individual and local, but general and operative; not standing upon external testimony, but carried alive into the heart by passion; truth which is its own testimony, which gives competence and confidence to the tribunal to which it appeals, and receives them from the same tribunal. Poetry is the image of man and nature. The obstacles which stand in the way of the fidelity of the Biographer and Historian, and of their consequent utility, are incalculably greater than those which are to be encountered by the Poet who comprehends the dignity of his art. The Poet writes under one restriction only, namely, the necessity of giving immediate pleasure to a human Being possessed of that information which may be expected from him, not as a lawyer, a physician, a mariner, an astronomer, or a natural philosopher, but as a Man. Except this one restriction, there is no object standing between the Poet and the image of things; between this, and the Biographer and Historian, there are a thousand.

Nor let this necessity of producing immediate pleasure be considered as a degradation of the Poet's art. It is far otherwise. It is an acknowledgment of the beauty of the universe, an acknowledgment the more sincere because not formal, but indirect; it is a task light and easy to him who looks at the world in the spirit of love: further, it is a homage paid to the native and naked dignity of man, to the grand elementary principle of pleasure, by which he knows, and feels, and lives, and moves. We have no sympathy but what is propagated by pleasure: I would not be misunderstood; but wherever we sympathize with pain, it will be found that the sympathy is produced and carried on by subtle combinations with pleasure. We have no knowledge, that is, no general principles drawn from the contemplation of particular facts, but what has been built up by pleasure, and exists in us by pleasure alone. The Man of science, the Chemist and Mathematician, whatever difficulties and disgusts they may have had to struggle with, know and feel this. However painful may be the objects with which the Anatomist's knowledge is connected, he feels that his knowledge is pleasure; and where he has no pleasure he has no knowledge. What then does the Poet? He considers man and the objects that surround him as acting and reacting upon each other, so as to produce an infinite complexity of pain and pleasure; he considers man in his own nature and in his ordinary life as contemplating this with a certain quantity of immediate knowledge, with certain convictions, intuitions, and deductions, which from habit acquire the quality of intuitions; he considers him as looking upon this complex scene of ideas and sensations, and finding everywhere objects that immediately excite in him sympathies, which from the necessities of his nature, are accompanied by an overbalance of enjoyment.

To this knowledge which all men carry about with them, and to these sympathies in which, without any other discipline than that of our daily life, we are fitted to take delight, the Poet principally directs his attention. He considers man and nature as essentially adapted to each other, and the mind of man as naturally the mirror of the fairest and most interesting properties of nature. And thus the Poet, prompted by this feeling of pleasure, which accompanies him through the whole course of his studies, converses with general nature, with affections akin to those which, through labor and length of time, the Man of science has raised up in himself, by conversing with those particular parts of nature which are the objects of his studies. The knowledge both of the Poet and the Man of science is pleasure; but the knowledge of the one cleaves to us as a necessary part of our existence, our natural and unalienable inheritance; the other is a personal and individual acquisition, slow to come to us, and by no habitual and direct sympathy connecting us with our fellow-beings. The Man of science seeks truth as a remote and unknown benefactor; he cherishes and loves it in his solitude: the Poet, singing a song in which all human beings join with him, rejoices in the presence of truth as our visible friend and hourly companion. Poetry is the breath and finer spirit of all knowledge; it is the impassioned expression which is in the countenance of all Science. Emphatically may it be said of the Poet, as Shakespeare hath said of man, "that he looks before and after." He is the rock of defense for human nature; an upholder and preserver, carrying everywhere with him relationship and love. In spite of difference of soil and climate, of language and manners, of laws and customs: in spite of things silently gone out of mind, and things violently destroyed; the Poet binds together by passion and knowledge the vast empire of human society, as it is spread over the whole earth and over all time. The objects of the Poet's thoughts are everywhere; though the eyes and senses of man are, it is true, his favorite guides, yet he will follow wheresoever he can find an atmosphere of sensation in which to move his wings. Poetry is the first and last of all knowledge—it is as immortal as the heart of man. If the labors of Men of science should ever create any material revolution, direct or indirect, in our condition, and in the impressions which we habitually receive, the Poet will sleep then no more than at present; he will be ready to follow the steps of the Man of science, not only in those general indirect effects, but he will be at his side, carrying sensation into the midst of the objects of the science itself. The remotest discoveries of the Chemist, the Botanist, or Mineralogist, will be as proper objects of the Poet's art as any upon which it can be employed, if the time should ever come when these things shall be familiar to us, and the relations under which they are contemplated by the followers of these respective sciences shall be manifestly and palpably material to us as enjoying and suffering beings. If the time should ever come when what is now called science, thus familiarized to men, shall be ready to put on, as it were, a form of flesh and blood, the Poet will lend his divine spirit to aid the transfiguration, and will welcome the Being thus produced as a dear and genuine inmate of the household of man.—It is not, then, to be supposed that any one, who holds that sublime notion of Poetry which I have attempted to convey, will break in upon the sanctity and truth of his pictures by transitory and accidental ornaments, and endeavor to excite admiration of himself by arts, the necessity of which must manifestly depend upon the assumed meanness of his subject.

4

WILLIAM WORDSWORTH

Lines Composed a Few Miles above Tintern Abbey

On Revisiting the Banks of the Wye during a Tour

July 13, 1798

"Tintern Abbey" is the longest and least ballad-like of the poems William Wordsworth included in Lyrical Ballads. *Contemporaries would have recognized it as a "topographical" poem, written while on a walking tour with his sister Dorothy. Addressed to her, the poem goes far beyond merely describing a specific landscape. Wordsworth's return to the river Wye with his younger sister inspires a meditation on human mortality, memory, imagination, and the permanence of nature. The poem chronicles losses, but it also recognizes gains drawn directly from the heart of loss itself.*

Five years have past; five summers, with the length
Of five long winters! and again I hear
These waters, rolling from their mountain-springs
With a soft inland murmur.—Once again
Do I behold these steep and lofty cliffs,

Selected Poetry of William Wordsworth, ed. Mark van Doren (New York: The Modern Library, 2002), 99–103.

That on a wild secluded scene impress
Thoughts of more deep seclusion; and connect
The landscape with the quiet of the sky.
The day is come when I again repose
Here, under this dark sycamore, and view
These plots of cottage-ground, these orchard-tufts,
Which at this season, with their unripe fruits,
Are clad in one green hue, and lose themselves
'Mid groves and copses. Once again I see
These hedge-rows, hardly hedge-rows, little lines
Of sportive wood run wild: these pastoral farms,
Green to the very door; and wreaths of smoke
Sent up, in silence, from among the trees!
With some uncertain notice, as might seem
Of vagrant dwellers in the houseless woods,
Or of some Hermit's cave, where by his fire
The Hermit sits alone.
                              These beauteous forms,
Through a long absence, have not been to me
As is a landscape to blind man's eye:
But oft, in lonely rooms, and 'mid the din
Of towns and cities, I have owed to them
In hours of weariness, sensations sweet,
Felt in the blood, and felt along the heart;
And passing even into my purer mind,
With tranquil restoration:—feelings too
Of unremembered pleasure: such, perhaps,
As have no slight or trivial influence
On that best portion of a good man's life,
His little, nameless, unremembered, acts
Of kindness and of love. Nor less, I trust,
To them I may have owed another gift,
Of aspect more sublime; that blessed mood,
In which the burthen of the mystery,
In which the heavy and the weary weight
Of all this unintelligible world,
Is lightened:—that serene and blessed mood,
In which the affections gently lead us on,—
Until, the breath of this corporeal frame
And even the motion of our human blood
Almost suspended, we are laid asleep

In body, and become a living soul:
While with an eye made quiet by the power
Of harmony, and the deep power of joy,
We see into the life of things.
                                      If this
Be but a vain belief, yet, oh! how oft—
In darkness and amid the many shapes
Of joyless daylight; when the fretful stir
Unprofitable, and the fever of the world,
Have hung upon the beatings of my heart—
How oft, in spirit, have I turned to thee,
O sylvan Wye! thou wanderer thro' the woods,
How often has my spirit turned to thee!
    And now, with gleams of half-extinguished thought,
With many recognitions dim and faint,
And somewhat of a sad perplexity,
The picture of the mind revives again:
While here I stand, not only with the sense
Of present pleasure, but with pleasing thoughts
That in this moment there is life and food
For future years. And so I dare to hope,
Though changed, no doubt, from what I was when first
I came among these hills; when like a roe
I bounded o'er the mountains, by the sides
Of the deep rivers, and the lonely streams,
Wherever nature led: more like a man
Flying from something that he dreads, than one
Who sought the thing he loved. For nature then
(The coarser pleasures of my boyish days,
And their glad animal movements all gone by)
To me was all in all.—I cannot paint
What then I was. The sounding cataract
Haunted me like a passion: the tall rock,
The mountain, and the deep and gloomy wood,
Their colours and their forms, were then to me
An appetite; a feeling and a love,
That had no need of a remoter charm,
By thought supplied, nor any interest
Unborrowed from the eye.—That time is past,
And all its aching joys are now no more,
And all its dizzy raptures. Not for this

Faint I, nor mourn nor murmur; other gifts
Have followed; for such loss, I would believe,
Abundant recompense. For I have learned
To look on nature, not as in the hour
Of thoughtless youth; but hearing oftentimes
The still, sad music of humanity,
Nor harsh nor grating, though of ample power
To chasten and subdue. And I have felt
A presence that disturbs me with the joy
Of elevated thoughts; a sense sublime
Of something far more deeply interfused,
Whose dwelling is the light of setting suns,
And the round ocean and the living air,
And the blue sky, and in the mind of man;
A motion and a spirit, that impels
All thinking things, all objects of all thought,
And rolls through all things. Therefore am I still
A lover of the meadows and the woods,
And mountains; and of all that we behold
From this green earth; of all the mighty world
Of eye, and ear, — both what they half create,
And what perceive; well pleased to recognise
In nature and the language of the sense,
The anchor of my purest thoughts, the nurse,
The guide, the guardian of my heart, and soul
Of all my moral being.
                              Nor perchance,
If I were not thus taught, should I the more
Suffer my genial spirits to decay:
For thou art with me here upon the banks
Of this fair river; thou my dearest Friend,
My dear, dear Friend; and in thy voice I catch
The language of my former heart, and read
My former pleasures in the shooting lights
Of thy wild eyes. Oh! yet a little while
May I behold in thee what I was once,
My dear, dear Sister! and this prayer I make,
Knowing that Nature never did betray
The heart that loved her; 'tis her privilege,
Through all the years of this our life, to lead
From joy to joy: for she can so inform

The mind that is within us, so impress
With quietness and beauty, and so feed
With lofty thoughts, that neither evil tongues,
Rash judgments, nor the sneers of selfish men,
Nor greetings where no kindness is, nor all
The dreary intercourse of daily life,
Shall e'er prevail against us, or disturb
Our cheerful faith, that all which we behold
Is full of blessings. Therefore let the moon
Shine on thee in thy solitary walk;
And let the misty mountain-winds be free
To blow against thee: and, in after years,
When these wild ecstasies shall be matured
Into a sober pleasure; when thy mind
Shall be a mansion for all lovely forms,
Thy memory be as a dwelling-place
For all sweet sounds and harmonies; oh! then,
If solitude, or fear, or pain, or grief,
Should be thy portion, with what healing thoughts
Of tender joy wilt thou remember me,
And these my exhortations! Nor, perchance—
If I should be where I no more can hear
Thy voice, nor catch from thy wild eyes these gleams
Of past existence—wilt thou then forget
That on the banks of this delightful stream
We stood together; and that I, so long
A worshipper of Nature, hither came
Unwearied in that service; rather say
With warmer love—oh! with far deeper zeal
Of holier love. Nor wilt thou then forget,
That after many wanderings, many years
Of absence, these steep woods and lofty cliffs,
And this green pastoral landscape, were to me
More dear, both for themselves and for thy sake!

5

FRIEDRICH SCHLEGEL

Athenaeum Fragment No. 116

1798

After studying philology, art, and literature in Göttingen and Leipzig, Friedrich Schlegel (1772–1829) joined his brother August Wilhelm in the university town Jena in 1796, where they created Athenaeum *(1798), the journal that served as the main literary organ of early German Romanticism. After the breakup of the Jena circle, Friedrich Schlegel drifted steadily toward the political right, but during the Jena years nothing seemed off-limits to his critical intelligence. Animated by the French Revolution, Johann Gottlieb Fichte's philosophy of subjective freedom, and new trends in literature, Schlegel called for an aesthetic revolution based on a new ideal of literature as an endlessly progressive activity. His own writings characteristically took the form of "fragments," literary exercises that in their very form suggested that art is always incomplete, imperfect, and open to the supplement of other works. "Fragment #116" from* Athenaeum *contains Schlegel's most famous definition of "Romantic poetry."*

Romantic poetry is a progressive, universal poetry. Its aim isn't merely to reunite all the separate species of poetry and put poetry in touch with philosophy and rhetoric. It tries to and should mix and fuse poetry and prose, inspiration and criticism, the poetry of art and the poetry of nature; and make poetry lively and sociable, and life and society poetical; poeticize wit and fill and saturate the forms of art with every kind of good, solid matter for instruction, and animate them with the pulsations of humor. It embraces everything that is purely poetic, from the greatest systems of art, containing within themselves still further systems, to the sigh, the kiss that the poetizing child breathes forth in artless song. It can so lose itself in what it describes that one might believe it exists only to characterize poetical individuals of all sorts; and yet there still is no form so fit for expressing the entire spirit of an author: so that many

Friedrich Schlegel, "Athenaeum Fragment #116," *Lucinde and the Fragments*, trans. Peter Firchow (Minneapolis: University of Minnesota Press, 1971), 175–76.

artists who started out to write only a novel ended up by providing us with a portrait of themselves. It alone can become, like the epic, a mirror of the whole circumambient world, an image of the age. And it can also—more than any other form—hover at the midpoint between the portrayed and the portrayer, free of all real and ideal self-interest, on the wings of poetic reflection, and can raise that reflection again and again to a higher power, can multiply it in an endless succession of mirrors. It is capable of the highest and most variegated refinement, not only from within outwards, but also from without inwards; capable in that it organizes—for everything that seeks a wholeness in its effects—the parts along similar lines, so that it opens up a perspective upon an infinitely increasing classicism. Romantic poetry is in the arts what wit is in philosophy, and what society and sociability, friendship and love are in life. Other kinds of poetry are finished and are now capable of being fully analyzed. The romantic kind of poetry is still in the state of becoming; that, in fact, is its real essence: that it should forever be becoming and never be perfected. It can be exhausted by no theory and only a divinatory criticism would dare try to characterize its ideal. It alone is infinite, just as it alone is free; and it recognizes as its first commandment that the will of the poet can tolerate no law above itself. The romantic kind of poetry is the only one that is more than a kind, that is, as it were, poetry itself: for in a certain sense all poetry is or should be romantic.

6

FRIEDRICH SCHLEGEL

On Incomprehensibility

1800

One of Schlegel's key ideas was "irony," which he treated as both a stylistic device and a comprehensive attitude toward art and life. Romantic irony declares the thinker's liberation from any binding code, emphasizing the freedom of the thinker to move between viable but mutually

Friedrich Schlegel, "On Incomprehensibility," *Lucinde and the Fragments*, trans. Peter Firchow (Minneapolis: University of Minnesota Press, 1971), 259–71.

incompatible alternatives. If irony thus expresses Schlegel's consciousness of the relativity of all human knowledge and artistic form, it also strives to overcome all onesidedness by embracing opposites. Irony thus embodies the Romantic dialectic: its sense that wholeness, infinity, and universality are unattainable yet must be striven for nonetheless. Subsequent opponents of Romanticism like Georg Wilhelm Friedrich Hegel or Søren Kierkegaard attacked Schlegel's concept of irony for its apparent lack of commitment; conversely, for Romantic writers like Ludwig Tieck and E. T. A. Hoffmann, irony was an indispensable stylistic and philosophical resource.

As seen in this excerpt, "On Incomprehensibility" offers one of Schlegel's most compelling articulations of what he calls (ironically?) "the system of irony." A contemporary critic had accused Schlegel of incomprehensibility; yet, in Schlegel's hands, this vice becomes a virtue. What is the positive value of incomprehensibility, and what does this say about Schlegel's basic view of the world, his present age, and his hopes for the future?

[T]he complaints of incomprehensibility have been directed so exclusively and so frequently and variously at the *Athenaeum* that my deduction might start off most appropriately right at the spot where the shoe actually hurts.

A penetrating critic in the *Berliner Archiv der Zeit* has already been good enough to defend the *Athenaeum* against these attacks and in so doing has used as an example the notorious fragment about the three tendencies. What a marvelous idea! This is just the way one should attack the problem. I am going to follow the same procedure, and so as to let the reader perceive all the more readily that I really think the fragment good, I shall print it once more in these pages:

> The French Revolution, [Johann Gottlieb] Fichte's philosophy, and [Johann Wolfgang] Goethe's *Meister*[1] are the greatest tendencies of the age. Whoever is offended by this juxtaposition, whoever cannot take any revolution seriously that isn't noisy and materialistic, hasn't yet achieved a lofty, broad perspective on the history of mankind.

---

[1]Goethe's novel *Wilhelm Meisters Lehrjahre* (*Wilhelm Meister's Apprenticeship*) (1795–1796) strongly influenced the Jena Romantics, and it established the model for the *Bildungsroman*, the type of novel concerned with the education and maturing of a young protagonist.

Even in our shabby histories of civilization, which usually resemble a collection of variants accompanied by a running commentary for which the original classical text has been lost; even there many a little book, almost unnoticed by the noisy rabble at the time, plays a greater role than anything they did.

I wrote this fragment with the most honorable intentions and almost without any irony at all. The way that it has been misunderstood has caused me unspeakable surprise because I expected the misunderstanding to come from quite another quarter. That I consider art to be the heart of humanity and the French Revolution a marvelous allegory about the system of transcendental idealism is, to be sure, only one of my most extremely subjective opinions. But I have let this opinion be known so often and in so many different ways that I really might have hoped the reader would have gotten used to it by now. All the rest is mere cryptology. Whoever can't find Goethe's whole spirit in *Wilhelm Meister* won't be able to find it anywhere else. Poetry and idealism are the focal points of German art and culture; everybody knows that. All the greatest truths of every sort are completely trivial and hence nothing is more important than to express them forever in a new way and, wherever possible, forever more paradoxically, so that we won't forget they still exist and that they can never be expressed in their entirety. . . .

To be sure, there is something else in the fragment that might in fact be misunderstood. This lies in the word *tendencies* and this is where the irony begins. For this word can be understood to mean that I consider the *Theory of Knowledge*,[2] for example, to be merely a tendency, a temporary venture like [Immanuel] Kant's *Critique of Pure Reason* which I myself might perhaps have a mind to continue (only rather better) and then bring to completion; or else that I wish to use the jargon that is most usual and appropriate to this kind of conception, to place myself on Fichte's shoulders, just as he placed himself on Reinhold's[3] shoulders, Reinhold on Kant's shoulders, Kant on Leibniz's,[4] and so on infinitely back to the prime shoulder. I was perfectly aware of this, but I thought I would like to try and see if anyone would accuse me of having had so bad an intention. No one seems to have

---

[2] *Wissenschaftslehre* (theory of scientific knowledge) was the name Johann Gottlieb Fichte gave to the philosophical system that he developed during his years as a philosophy professor in Jena.
[3] Karl Leonhard Reinhold (1757–1823), philosopher and follower of Immanuel Kant.
[4] Gottfried Wilhelm Leibniz (1646–1716), philosopher.

noticed it. Why should I provide misunderstandings when no one wants to take them up? And so I now let irony go to the winds and declare point-blank that in the dialect of the *Fragments* the word means that everything now is only a tendency, that the age is the Age of Tendencies. As to whether or not I am of the opinion that all these tendencies are going to be corrected and resolved by me, or maybe by my brother or by [Ludwig] Tieck, or by someone else from our group, or only some son of ours, or grandson, great-grandson, grandson twenty-seven times removed, or only at the last judgment, or never: that I leave to the wisdom of the reader, to whom this question really belongs.

Goethe and Fichte: That is still the easiest and fittest phrase for all the offense the *Athenaeum* has given, and for all the incomprehension it has provoked. Here too probably the best thing would be to aggravate it even more: when this vexation reaches its highest point, then it will burst and disappear, and then the process of understanding can set to work immediately. We haven't gotten far enough in giving offense; but what is not yet may still come to be. Yes, even those names are going to have to be named again—more than once. . . .

A great part of the incomprehensibility of the *Athenaeum* is unquestionably due to the *irony* that to a greater or lesser extent is to be found everywhere in it. Here too I will begin with a text from the *Lyceum [Critical] Fragments*:

> Socratic irony is the only involuntary and yet completely deliberate dissimulation. It is equally impossible to feign it or divulge it. To a person who hasn't got it, it will remain a riddle even after it is openly confessed. It is meant to deceive no one except those who consider it a deception and who either take pleasure in the delightful roguery of making fools of the whole world or else become angry when they get an inkling they themselves might be included. In this sort of irony, everything should be playful and serious, guilelessly open and deeply hidden. It originates in the union of *savoir vivre* and scientific spirit, in the conjunction of a perfectly instinctive and a perfectly conscious philosophy. It contains and arouses a feeling of indissoluble antagonism between the absolute and the relative, between the impossibility and the necessity of complete communication. It is the freest of all licenses, for by its means one transcends oneself; and yet it is also the most lawful, for it is absolutely necessary. It is a very good sign when the harmonious bores are at a loss about how they should react to this continuous self-parody, when they fluctuate endlessly between belief and disbelief until they get dizzy and take what is meant as a joke seriously and what is meant seriously as a

joke. For Lessing irony is instinct; for Hemsterhuis it is classical study; for Hülsen it arises out of the philosophy of philosophy and surpasses these others by far.[5]

Another one of these fragments recommends itself even more by its brevity:

> Irony is the form of paradox. Paradox is everything which is simultaneously good and great.

Won't every reader who is used to the *Athenaeum* fragments find all this simply trifling—yes, even trivial? And yet at the time it seemed incomprehensible to many people because of its relative novelty. For only since then has irony become daily fare, only since the dawn of the new century has such a quantity of great and small ironies of different sorts sprung up. . . . In order to facilitate a survey of the whole system of irony, we would like to mention here a few of the choicest kinds. The first and most distinguished of all is coarse irony. It is to be found in the real nature of things and is one of the most widespread of substances; it is properly at home in the history of mankind. Next there is fine or delicate irony; then extra-fine. Scaramouche[6] employs the last type when he seems to be talking amicably and earnestly with someone when really he is only waiting for the chance to give him— while preserving the social amenities—a kick in the behind. This kind of irony is also to be found in poets, as well as straightforward irony, a type that flourishes most purely and originally in old gardens where wonderfully lovely grottoes lure the sensitive friend of nature into their cool wombs only to be-splash him plentifully from all sides with water and thereby wipe him clean of delicacy. Further, dramatic irony; that is, when an author has written three acts, then unexpectedly turns into another man and now has to write the last two acts. Double irony, when two lines of irony run parallel side-by-side without disturbing each other: one for the gallery, the other for the boxes, though a few little sparks may also manage to get behind the scenes. Finally, there is the irony of irony. Generally speaking, the most fundamental irony of irony probably is that even it becomes tiresome if we

---

[5]Gotthold Ephraim Lessing (1729–1781), one of the great German dramatists of the eighteenth century and a major figure of the German Enlightenment. François Hemsterhuis (1721–1790), Dutch writer on aesthetics, moral philosophy, and theology. August Ludwig Hülsen (1765–1810), writer and occasional contributor to the *Athenaeum*.
[6]Also called *Scaramuccia*, Scaramouche was a roguish stock character in the Italian *commedia dell'arte*, a form of improvisational comic theater that was popular from the sixteenth through the eighteenth centuries.

are always being confronted with it. But what we want this irony to mean in the first place is something that happens in more ways than one. For example, if one speaks of irony without using it, as I have just done; if one speaks of irony ironically without in the process being aware of having fallen into a far more noticeable irony; if one can't disentangle oneself from irony anymore, as seems to be happening in this essay on incomprehensibility; if irony turns into a mannerism and becomes, as it were, ironical about the author; if one has promised to be ironical for some useless book without first having checked one's supply and then having to produce it against one's will, like an actor full of aches and pains; and if irony runs wild and can't be controlled any longer.

What gods will rescue us from all these ironies? The only solution is to find an irony that might be able to swallow up all these big and little ironies and leave no trace of them at all. I must confess that at precisely this moment I feel that mine has a real urge to do just that. But even this would only be a short-term solution. I fear that if I understand correctly what destiny seems to be hinting at, then soon there will arise a new generation of little ironies: for truly the stars augur the fantastic. And even if it should happen that everything were to be peaceful for a long period of time, one still would not be able to put any faith in this seeming calm. Irony is something one simply cannot play games with. It can have incredibly long-lasting aftereffects. I have a suspicion that some of the most conscious artists of earlier times are still carrying on ironically, hundreds of years after their deaths, with their most faithful followers and admirers. Shakespeare has so infinitely many depths, subterfuges, and intentions. Shouldn't he also, then, have had the intention of concealing insidious traps in his works to catch the cleverest artists of posterity, to deceive them and make them believe before they realize what they're doing that they are somewhat like Shakespeare themselves? Surely, he must be in this respect as in so many others much more full of intentions than people usually think.

I've already been forced to admit indirectly that the *Athenaeum* is incomprehensible, and because it happened in the heat of irony, I can hardly take it back without in the process doing violence to that irony.

But is incomprehensibility really something so unmitigatedly contemptible and evil? Methinks the salvation of families and nations rests upon it. If I am not wholly deceived, then states and systems, the most artificial productions of man, are often so artificial that one simply can't admire the wisdom of their creator enough. Only an incredibly minute quantity of it suffices: as long as its truth and purity remain inviolate and no blasphemous rationality dares approach its sacred confines. Yes, even man's most precious possession, his own inner happiness, depends in the last analysis, as anybody can easily verify, on some such point of strength that must be left in the dark, but that nonetheless shores up and supports the whole burden and would crumble the moment one subjected it to rational analysis. Verily, it would fare badly with you if, as you demand, the whole world were ever to become wholly comprehensible in earnest. And isn't this entire, unending world constructed by the understanding out of incomprehensibility or chaos?

Another consolation for the acknowledged incomprehensibility of the *Athenaeum* lies in the very fact of this acknowledgment, because precisely this has taught us that the evil was a passing one. The new age reveals itself as a nimble and quick-footed one. The dawn has donned seven-league boots. For a long time now there has been lightning on the horizon of poetry; the whole thunderous power of the heavens had gathered together in a mighty cloud; at one moment, it thundered loudly, at another the cloud seemed to move away and discharge its lightning bolts in the distance, only to return again in an even more terrible aspect. But soon it won't be simply a matter of one thunderstorm, the whole sky will burn with a single flame and then all your little lightning rods won't help you. Then the nineteenth century will indeed make a beginning of it and then the little riddle of the incomprehensibility of the *Athenaeum* will also be solved. What a catastrophe! Then there will be readers who will know how to read. In the nineteenth century everyone will be able to savor the fragments with much gratification and pleasure in the after-dinner hours and not need a nutcracker for even the hardest and most indigestible ones. In the nineteenth century every human being, every reader will find *Lucinde* innocent, *Genoveva*[7] Protestant, and A. W. Schlegel's didactic *Elegies* almost too simple and transparent. And then too what I prophetically set forth as a maxim in the first fragments will hold true:

> A classical text must never be entirely comprehensible. But those who are cultivated and who cultivate themselves must always want to learn more from it.

---

[7]Friedrich Schlegel's sexually explicit novel *Lucinde* (1799) created a scandal when it appeared. Ludwig Tieck's *Leben und Tod der Heiligen Genoveva* (*Life and Death of St. Genevieve*) (1799) is a play based on medieval Catholic legend.

The great schism between understanding and not understanding will grow more and more widespread, intense, and distinct. Much hidden incomprehension will still erupt. But understanding too will reveal its omnipotence: understanding that ennobles disposition into character, elevates talent into genius, purifies one's feelings and artistic perceptions. Understanding itself will be understood, and people will at last see and admit that everyone can achieve the highest degree and that up to now humanity has been neither malicious nor stupid but simply clumsy and new.

7

FRANÇOIS-RENÉ DE CHATEAUBRIAND

The Genius of Christianity

1802

Born into an old aristocratic family in Bretagne, François-René de Chateaubriand (1768–1848) sought an antidote to his morose childhood by journeying to America (1791–1792). He returned to Europe to fight on the side of the counterrevolution and, after being wounded, went into exile in England. He briefly served in the diplomatic corps under Napoleon but quickly grew disillusioned and left France again. The restoration of the Bourbon monarchy brought Chateaubriand back to France, where he held various diplomatic posts, including that of foreign minister.

A skeptical rationalist in his youth, Chateaubriand had an emotional crisis during his English exile that led him back to the Catholic faith. The Genius of Christianity, *a product of this personal crisis, appeared fortuitously only days after the concordat between Napoleon and Pope Pius VII. Just as that agreement put an end to the anticlerical campaigns of the French Revolution, Chateaubriand's book tries to counter a century of rationalist critique of religion. Significantly, he does not attempt to defend the doctrinal "truth" of Christianity but shifts the argument to sumptuous descriptions of natural sublimity, the power and*

François-René de Chateaubriand, *The Genius of Christianity*, trans. Charles I. White (Baltimore: John Murphy & Co., 1856), 171–73, 296–98, 384–86.

beauty of ritual, and the emotional satisfactions of faith. Madame For-
tunée Hamelin expressed a common response to Chateaubriand's book
when she exclaimed, "What, this is Christianity? But it is delicious!"
Chateaubriand's book played a significant role in the revival of Catholi-
cism in nineteenth-century France, although, like many other works of
early Romanticism, Chateaubriand's intensely aesthetic view of religion
sits uneasily with rigorous Church doctrine. Chateaubriand also con-
tributed to the rise of medievalism in French culture. Indeed, The
Genius of Christianity*, along with Victor Hugo's novel* The Hunchback
of Notre-Dame *(1831), even helped spur the creation of a preservation-*
ist movement in the 1830s that began to salvage the monuments of
France's Gothic period.

Two Views of Nature

The vessel in which we embarked for America having passed the
bearing of any land, space was soon enclosed only by the twofold
azure of the sea and of the sky. The color of the waters resembled that
of liquid glass. A great swell was visible from the west, though the
wind blew from the east, while immense undulations extended from
the north to the south, opening in their valleys long vistas through the
deserts of the deep. The fleeting scenes changed with every minute.
Sometimes a multitude of verdant hillocks appeared to us like a series
of graves in some vast cemetery. Sometimes the curling summits of
the waves resembled white flocks scattered over a heath. Now space
seemed circumscribed for want of an object of comparison; but if a bil-
low reared its mountain crest, if a wave curved like a distant shore, or
a squadron of sea-dogs moved along the horizon, the vastness of space
again suddenly opened before us. We were most powerfully impressed
with an idea of magnitude, when a light fog, creeping along the surface of the deep, [seemed] to increase immensity itself. Oh! how sublime, how awful, at such times, is the aspect of the ocean! Into what
reveries does it plunge you, whether imagination transports you to the
seas of the north, into the midst of frosts and tempests, or wafts you to
southern islands, blessed with happiness and peace!

We often rose at midnight and sat down upon the deck, where we
found only the officer of the watch and a few sailors silently smoking
their pipes. No noise was heard, save the dashing of the prow through
the billows, while sparks of fire ran with a white foam along the sides
of the vessel. God of Christians! it is on the waters of the abyss and on
the vast expanse of the heavens that thou hast particularly engraven

the characters of thy omnipotence! Millions of stars sparkling in the azure of the celestial dome—the moon in the midst of the firmament—a sea unbounded by any shore—infinitude in the skies and on the waves—proclaim with most impressive effect the power of thy arm! Never did thy greatness strike me with profounder awe than in those nights, when, suspended between the stars and the ocean, I beheld immensity over my head and immensity beneath my feet!

I am nothing; I am only a simple, solitary wanderer, and often have I heard men of science disputing on the subject of a Supreme Being, without understanding them; but I have invariably remarked, that it is in the prospect of the sublime scenes of nature that this unknown Being manifests himself to the human heart. One evening, after we had reached the beautiful waters that bathe the shores of Virginia, there was a profound calm, and every sail was furled. I was engaged below, when I heard the bell that summoned the crew to prayers. I hastened to mingle my supplications with those of my travelling companions. The officers of the ship were on the quarter-deck with the passengers, while the chaplain, with a book in his hand, was stationed at a little distance before them; the seamen were scattered at random over the poop; we were all standing, our faces toward the prow of the vessel, which was turned to the west.

The solar orb, about to sink beneath the waves, was seen through the rigging, in the midst of boundless space; and, from the motion of the stern, it appeared as if it changed its horizon every moment. A few clouds wandered confusedly in the east, where the moon was slowly rising. The rest of the sky was serene; and toward the north, a waterspout, forming a glorious triangle with the luminaries of day and night, and glistening with all the colors of the prism, rose from the sea, like a column of crystal supporting the vault of heaven.

He had been well deserving of pity who would not have recognized in this prospect the beauty of God. When my companions, doffing their tarpaulin hats, entoned with hoarse voice their simple hymn to Our Lady of Good Help, the patroness of the seas, the tears flowed from my eyes in spite of myself. How affecting was the prayer of those men, who, from a frail plank in the midst of the ocean, contemplated the sun setting behind the waves! How the appeal of the poor sailor to the Mother of Sorrows went to the heart! The consciousness of our insignificance in the presence of the Infinite,—our hymns, resounding to a distance over the silent waves,—the night approaching with its dangers,—our vessel, itself a wonder among so many wonders,—a religious crew, penetrated with admiration and with awe,—a venerable priest in prayer,—the Almighty bending over the abyss, with one hand staying the sun in the west, with the other raising the moon in the east, and lending, through all immensity, an attentive ear to the feeble voice of his creatures,—all this constituted a scene which no power of art can represent, and which it is scarcely possible for the heart of man to feel. . . .

Of the Unsettled State of the Passions

We have yet to treat of a state of the soul which, as we think, has not been accurately described; we mean that which precedes the development of the strong passions, when all the faculties, fresh, active, and entire, but confined in the breast, act only upon themselves, without object and without end. The more nations advance in civilization, the more this unsettled state of the passions predominates; for then the many examples we have before us, and the multitude of books we possess, give us knowledge without experience; we are undeceived before we have enjoyed; there still remain desires, but no illusions. Our imagination is rich, abundant, and full of wonders; but our existence is poor, insipid, and destitute of charms. With a full heart, we dwell in an empty world, and scarcely have we advanced a few steps when we have nothing more to learn.

It is inconceivable what a shade this state of the soul throws over life; the heart turns a hundred different ways to employ the energies which it feels to be useless to it. The ancients knew but little of this secret inquietude, this irritation of the stifled passions fermenting all together; political affairs, the sports of the Gymnasium and the Campus Martius,[1] the business of the forum and of the popular assemblies, engaged all their time, and left no room for this tedium of the heart.

On the other hand, they were not disposed to exaggerations, to hopes and fears without object, to versatility in ideas and sentiments, and to perpetual inconstancy, which is but a continual disgust,—dispositions which we acquire in the familiar society of the fair sex. Women, independently of the direct passion which they excite among all modern nations, also possess an influence over the other sentiments. They have in their nature a certain ease which they communicate to ours;

---

[1]Campus Martius was a district of ancient Rome, built up by the time of Augustus, but for centuries in the Republic, a grassy meadow in which chariots were raced and athletic games held.

they render the marks of the masculine character less distinct; and our passions, softened by the mixture of theirs, assume, at one and the same time, something uncertain and delicate.

Finally, the Greeks and Romans, looking scarcely any farther than the present life, and having no conception of pleasures more perfect than those which this world affords, were not disposed, like us, by the character of their religion, to meditation and desire. Formed for the relief of our afflictions and our wants, the Christian religion incessantly exhibits to our view the twofold picture of terrestrial griefs and heavenly joys, and thus creates in the heart a source of present evils and distant hopes, whence spring inexhaustible abstractions and meditations. The Christian always looks upon himself as no more than a pilgrim travelling here below through a vale of tears and finding no repose till he reaches the tomb. The world is not the object of his affections, for he knows that the days of man are few, and that this object would speedily escape from his grasp.

The persecutions which the first believers underwent had the effect of strengthening in them this disgust of the things of this life. The invasion of the barbarians raised this feeling to the highest pitch, and the human mind received from it an impression of melancholy, and, perhaps, even a slight tincture of misanthropy, which has never been thoroughly removed. On all sides arose convents; hither retired the unfortunate, smarting under the disappointments of the world, or souls who chose rather to remain strangers to certain sentiments of life than to run the risk of finding themselves cruelly deceived. But, nowadays, when these ardent souls have no monastery to enter, or have not the virtue that would lead them to one, they feel like strangers among men. Disgusted with the age, alarmed by religion, they remain in the world without mingling in its pursuits; and then we behold that culpable sadness which springs up in the midst of the passions, when these passions, without object, burn themselves out in a solitary heart.

Gothic Churches

Every thing *ought to be in its proper place*. This is a truth become trite by repetition; but without its due observance there can be nothing perfect. The Greeks would not have been better pleased with an Egyptian temple at Athens than the Egyptians with a Greek temple at Memphis. These two monuments, by changing places, would have lost their principal beauty; that is to say, their relations with the institutions and habits of the people. This reflection is equally applicable to the ancient monuments of Christianity. It is even curious to remark how readily the poets and novelists of this infidel age, by a natural return toward the manners of our ancestors, introduce dungeons, spectres, castles, and Gothic churches, into their fictions,—so great is the charm of recollections associated with religion and the history of our country. Nations do not throw aside their ancient customs as people do their old clothes. Some part of them may be discarded; but there will remain a portion, which with the new manners will form a very strange mixture.

In vain would you build Grecian temples, ever so elegant and well-lighted, for the purpose of assembling the *good people* of St. Louis and Queen Blanche, and making them adore a *metaphysical God*; they would still regret those *Notre Dames* of Rheims and Paris,—those venerable cathedrals, overgrown with moss, full of generations of the dead and the ashes of their forefathers; they would still regret the tombs of those heroes, the Montmorencys,[2] on which they loved to kneel during mass; to say nothing of the sacred fonts to which they were carried at their birth. The reason is that all these things are essentially interwoven with their manners; that a monument is not venerable, unless a long history of the past be, as it were, inscribed beneath its vaulted canopy, black with age. For this reason, also, there is nothing marvellous in a temple whose erection we have witnessed, whose echoes and whose domes were formed before our eyes. God is the eternal law; his origin, and whatever relates to his worship, ought to be enveloped in the night of time.

You could not enter a Gothic church without feeling a kind of awe and a vague sentiment of the Divinity. You were all at once carried back to those times when a fraternity of cenobites, after having meditated in the woods of their monasteries, met to prostrate themselves before the altar and to chant the praises of the Lord, amid the tranquillity and the silence of night. Ancient France seemed to revive altogether; you beheld all those singular costumes, all that nation so different from what it is at present; you were reminded of its revolutions, its productions, and its arts. The more remote were these times the more magical they appeared, the more they inspired ideas which always end with a reflection on the nothingness of man and the rapidity of life.

---

[2]One of the oldest and most distinguished noble families in France, named for the city of Montmorency near Paris.

The Gothic style, notwithstanding its barbarous proportions, possesses a beauty peculiar to itself.*

The forests were the first temples of the Divinity, and in them men acquired the first idea of architecture. This art must, therefore, have varied according to climates. The Greeks turned the elegant Corinthian column, with its capital of foliage, after the model of the palmtree. The enormous pillars of the ancient Egyptian style represent the massive sycamore, the oriental fig, the banana, and most of the gigantic trees of Africa and Asia.

The forests of Gaul were, in their turn, introduced into the temples of our ancestors, and those celebrated woods of oaks thus maintained their sacred character. Those ceilings sculptured into foliage of different kinds, those buttresses which prop the walls and terminate abruptly like the broken trunks of trees, the coolness of the vaults, the darkness of the sanctuary, the dim twilight of the aisles, the secret passages, the low doorways,—in a word, every thing in a Gothic church reminds you of the labyrinths of a wood; every thing excites a feeling of religious awe, of mystery, and of the Divinity. . . .

Moral Harmonies

POPULAR DEVOTIONS

We now take leave of the physical harmonies of religious monuments and the scenes of nature, and enter upon the moral harmonies of Christianity. The first to be considered are *those popular devotions* which consist in certain opinions and practices of the multitude which are neither enjoined nor absolutely prohibited by the Church. They are, in fact, but harmonies of religion and of nature. When the common people fancy that they hear the voices of the dead in the winds, when they talk of nocturnal apparitions, when they undertake pilgrimages to obtain relief from their afflictions, it is evident that these opinions are only affecting relations between certain scenes of nature, certain sacred doctrines, and the sorrows of our hearts. Hence it follows that the more of these popular devotions a religion embraces, the more poetical it must be; since poetry is founded on the emotions of the soul and the accidents of nature rendered mysterious by the intervention of religious ideas.

---

*Gothic architecture, as well as the sculpture in the same style, is supposed to have been derived from the Arabs. Its affinity to the monuments of Egypt would rather lead us to imagine that it was transmitted to us by the first Christians of the East; but we are more inclined to refer to its origin to nature. [Chateaubriand's note]

We should indeed be deserving of pity, if, subjecting every thing to the rules of reason, we rigorously condemned these notions which assist the common people to endure the woes of life and teach them a morality which the best laws will never give. It is good, and it is something beautiful at the same time, that all our actions should be full of God, and that we should be incessantly surrounded by his miracles.

The vulgar are wiser than philosophers. Every fountain, every cross beside a road, every sigh of the wind at night, brings with it a prodigy. For him who possesses faith, nature is a continual wonder. Is he afflicted? he looks at his little picture or medal, and finds relief. Is he anxious once more to behold a relative, a friend? he makes a vow, seizes the pilgrim's staff, climbs the Alps or the Pyrenees, visits Our Lady of Loretto, or St. James in Galicia; on his knees he implores the saint to restore to him a son (a poor sailor, wandering, perhaps, on the high seas), to prolong the life of a parent or of a virtuous wife. His heart is lightened. He sets out on his return to his cottage: laden with shells, he makes the hamlets resound with his joy, and celebrates, in simple strains, the beneficence of the blessed Virgin, the mother of God. Everybody wishes to have something belonging to the pilgrim. How many ailments have been cured merely by a blessed ribbon! The pilgrim at length reaches home, and the first person that greets him on his arrival is his wife after a happy delivery, a son returned home, or a father restored to health.

Happy, thrice happy they who possess faith! They cannot smile, without thinking that they will rejoice in the eternal smiles of Heaven; they cannot weep, without thinking that the time of their sorrowing will soon be over. Their tears are not lost: religion collects them in her urn, and presents them to the Most High.

The steps of the true believer are never solitary; a good angel watches by his side, counsels him in his dreams, and protects him from the evil spirit. This heavenly friend is so devoted to his interests that he consents for his sake to be an exile upon earth.

Did there exist among the ancients any thing more admirable than the many customs that prevailed among our religious forefathers? If they discovered the body of a murdered man in a forest, they erected a cross on the spot in token of pity. This cross demanded of the Samaritan a tear for the unfortunate traveller, and of the inhabitant of the faithful city a prayer for his brother. And then, this traveller was, perhaps, a poor stranger, who had fallen at a great distance from his native land, like that illustrious Unknown sacrificed by the hands of men far away from his celestial country! What an intercourse between us and God! What prodigious elevation was thus given to human

nature! How astonishing that we should thus discover a resemblance
between our fleeting days and the eternal duration of the Sovereign of
the universe!

We shall say nothing of those jubilees which, substituted for secular
games, plunge all Christendom into the bath of repentance, purify
the conscience, and offer a religious amnesty to repenting sinners.
Neither shall we relate how, in public calamities, both high and low
walked barefoot from church to church, to endeavor to avert the
wrath of God. The pastor headed the solemn procession with a cord
about his neck, the humble victim devoted for the welfare of his flock.
The fear of these evils was not encouraged among the people by an
ebony crucifix, a bit of blessed laurel, or an image of the patron saint.
How often has the Christian knelt before these religious symbols to
ask of God that assistance which could not be obtained from man!

Who has not heard of our Lady of the Woods, who inhabits the
aged thorn or the mossy cavity of a spring, and is so celebrated in the
hamlet for her miracles? Many a matron will tell you, that after having
invoked the good Mary of the Woods she suffered less from the pains
of childbirth. The maiden who had lost her lover would often fancy in
the moonlight that she saw the spirit of her young betrothed in this
solitary spot, or heard his voice in the low murmur of the stream. The
doves that drink from these waters have always the power of generation, and the flowers that grow on their borders never cease to bloom.
It was fitting that the tutelar saint of the forest should accomplish
effects as tender in their nature as the moss amid which she dwells,
and as charming as the fountain that veils her from human sight.

It is particularly in the great events of life that religious customs
impart their consolations to the unfortunate. We once were spectators
of a shipwreck. The mariners, on reaching the shore, stripped off all
their clothes, with the exception of their wet trousers and shirts. They
had made a vow to the Virgin during the storm. They repaired in procession to a little chapel dedicated to St. Thomas, preceded by the
captain, and followed by the people, who joined them in singing the
Ave Maris Stella. The priest said the mass appointed for the ship-
wrecked, and the sailors hung their garments, dripping with sea-water,
as votive offerings, against the walls of the chapel. Philosophy may fill
her pages with high-sounding words, but we question whether the
unfortunate ever go to hang up their garments in her temple.

Death, so poetical because of its bordering upon things immortal,
so mysterious on account of its silence, could not but have a thousand
ways of announcing itself to the vulgar. Sometimes its token was

heard in the ringing of a distant bell; at others, the person whose dis-solution drew nigh heard three knocks upon the floor of his chamber. A nun of St. Benedict, on the point of quitting the world, found a crown of white thorn at the entrance of her cell. Did a mother lose her son abroad, her dreams immediately apprised her of this misfortune. Those who withhold their belief in presentiments will never know the secret channels by which two hearts, bound by the ties of love, hold mutual intercourse from one end of the world to the other. Frequently would some cherished departed one appear to a friend on earth, solic-iting prayers for the rescue of his soul from the purgatorial flame, and its admission to the company of the elect. Thus did religion accord to friendship some share in the sublime prerogative which belongs only to God, of imparting eternal happiness.

Opinions of a different kind, but still of a religious character, in-spired feelings of humanity; and such is their simplicity that they embarrass the writer. To destroy the nest of a swallow, to kill a robin redbreast, a wren, a cricket—the attendant on the rural hearth, a dog grown old in the service of a family, was a deed which never failed, it was said, to be followed by some visitation. From an admirable respect for age, it was thought that persons advanced in years were of propi-tious influence in a house, and that an old servant brought good luck to his master. Here we meet with some traces of the affecting worship of the *Lares*, and are reminded of the daughter of Laban carrying her household gods along with her.

The vulgar were persuaded that no person could commit a wicked action without being haunted all the rest of his life by frightful appari-tions. Antiquity, wiser than we, would have forborne to destroy these useful accordances of religion, of conscience, and of morality. Neither would it have rejected another opinion, according to which it was deemed certain that every man possessing ill-gotten wealth had en-tered into a covenant with the spirit of darkness and made over his soul to hell.

Finally, wind, rain, sunshine, the seasons, agriculture, birth, infancy, marriage, old age, death, had all their respective saints and images, and never were people so surrounded with friendly divinities as were the Christian people.

It is not the question now to enter into a rigid examination of these opinions. So far from laying any injunctions on the subject, religion served, on the contrary, to prevent the abuse of them, and to check their extravagancies. The only question is whether their aim be moral, whether they have a stronger tendency than the laws themselves to keep the multitude in the paths of virtue. What sensible man has any doubt of this? By your incessant declamations against superstition, you will at length open a door for every species of crime. A circumstance that cannot fail to surprise the sophists is, that, amid all the evils which they will have occasioned, they will not even enjoy the satisfaction of seeing the common man more incredulous. If he shakes off the influence of religion, he will supply its place with monstrous opinions. He will be seized with a terror the more strange as he will be ignorant of its object: he will shudder in a churchyard, where he has set up the inscription, *Death is an eternal sleep*; and, while affecting to despise the Divine power, he will go to consult the gypsy, and, trembling, seek his destinies in the motley figures of a card.

The marvellous, a future state, and hope, are required by man, because he feels himself formed to survive this terrestrial existence. *Conjuration, sorcery*, are with the vulgar but the instinct of religion, and one of the most striking proofs of the necessity of a public worship. He who believes nothing is not far from believing every thing; you have conjurors when you cease to have prophets, enchantments when you renounce religious ceremonies, and you open the dens of sorcerers when you shut up the temples of the Lord.

8

KAROLINE VON GÜNDERRODE

Idea of the Earth

ca. 1806

Women played an active role in the tight-knit circles of German Romantic sociability, first in the Jena circle and, somewhat later, in the Berlin salons of the writers Rahel Varnhagen and Bettine von Arnim. Moreover, Romantic women did write, excelling especially in letter-writing as a literary form. Bettine von Arnim took this furthest, gaining some fame with two novels written in an open form that drew upon letters, conver-

Karoline von Günderrode, "Idee der Erde (an Eusebio)," *Gesammelte Werke der Karoline von Günderrode*, ed. Leopold Hirschberg (Berlin: Bibliophiler Verlag Goldschmidt-Gabrielli, 1922), 2: 50–56. Translated by Warren Breckman.

sations, diary entries, and contemporary documents. Goethe's Correspondence with a Child *(1835) was based on von Arnim's own interactions
with Goethe, while* Günderode *(1844) chronicled her friendship with
Karoline von Günderrode (1780–1806). Karoline was the oldest of six
children born to Hector and Louise von Drachstädt von Günderrode. After
her father's death, Karoline was sent in 1797 to Frankfurt to live in a
home for "unmarried gentlewomen." Günderrode suffered intensely from
the tensions between her literary and philosophical ambitions and the
constraints imposed on women. Her suicide in 1806 cut short the career
of one of the most productive and creative of the German women Romantics. Günderrode's poetry, essays, fragmentary writings, dramas, and correspondence reveal a deep engagement with the philosophical and aesthetic
debates of German Romanticism. Inspired by F. W. J. Schelling's philosophy of nature, and blending Neoplatonic and Indian ideas about cosmic
unity, Günderrode's "Idea of the Earth" is an extraordinary expression of
Romantic nature mysticism. How does this vision compare to the Enlightenment view of nature? What do you think of the consolations that Günderrode offers to offset her apparent abandonment of traditional Christian
ideas of immortality? The text is addressed to "Eusebio," Günderrode's
pet name for her lover, the mythologist Friedrich Creuzer. A married man,
Creuzer did everything he could to suppress his scandalous affair after
Günderrode's suicide, including blocking the publication of* Melete, *her
cycle of love poems. A single copy of the poems was discovered nearly a
century later and, in 1906, an edition was finally published.*

One of the greatest periods of my little life is past, Eusebio! I have
stood at the crossroads between life and death. "What is it that people
resist in the face of death?" I said to myself in that moment. I am
pleased every night in that I prefer unconsciousness and dark dreams
to bright life, so why do I dread the long night and the deep slumber?
Which acts, or what better knowledge on earth depend on me that I
must live longer?—A necessity gives birth to personality in us all, a
common night devours us all. Years would give me no better wisdom,
and when learning, activity, and suffering still are demanded down
here, a God would give me what I need. Thus did I comfort myself,
but the thoughts that I love came to me, and the heroes whom I had
worshipped since my youth: "Why do you long for the night in the
high noontime? Tell me that! Why dive into the old sea and therein
melt away with all that is dear to you?" Thus did my thoughts change,
and I thought of you, always of you, and of almost everything else only

in relation to you. And if mortals were permitted to rescue one of their possessions from the shipwreck of earthly life, surely I would have taken your memory with me into the shadows. Yet, the most painful thought was that you could be lost to me. I said that your "I" and mine should be dissolved in the ancient matter of the world. Then I consoled myself further that our befriended elements, obeying the laws of attraction, would seek each other even in infinite space and join each other. So hope and doubt, courage and fear surged up and down in my soul. Destiny willed—I still live.—But what is it, life? this already surrendered, regained possession! So I have often asked myself: what does it mean that from the oneness of Nature a being with such consciousness detaches itself and feels itself torn away from Her? Why does man cling to ideas and opinions with such intensity, as though they were the Eternal? Why can he die for them when these thoughts are lost for him with his death? And why, although these thoughts and concepts die with the individual, why are they always again produced in new individuals and so press themselves through successive generations to an immortality within time? For a long time I had no answer to these questions and they confused me; suddenly everything became clear to me in a revelation and will remain with me forever. Certainly, I know that life is only the product of the deepest contact and attraction of the elements; I know that all its blossoms and leaves, which we call thoughts and feelings, must wither if that contact dissolves; and I know that in this way the individual life is given to the law of mortality; however, as deeply as I know all this, nonetheless I have no doubt about the immortality of life as a whole. This whole is life itself, and the elements surge high and low in its parts. What is more, through dissolution (which we presently name death), the parts go back to the same, where things intermingle according to laws of affinity, that is, the similar with the similar. However, these elements alter after they are pressed into life in the organism. They become livelier, like two who engage in a long struggle are stronger when they end than when they began; so it is with the elements, because they are living and every living power strengthens itself through exercise. Thus, when elements return to earth, they increase the life of the earth. From this returning stuff of life, however, the earth gives birth to other phenomena, until through ever-new transformations all that is capable of life within the earth becomes living. That is how it would be if all substances were organic.

Thus, every dying thing gives back to the earth a heightened, more developed elemental life, which she enhances in ascending forms; and the organism, in that it absorbs ever more developed elements in itself, must thereby become ever more perfect and universal. Thus the totality becomes animated through the individual's decline, and the individual lives on immortally in the totality, the life of which the individual vitally develops while living and elevates and multiplies even after death. And thus through life and death the individual helps to realize the idea of the earth. Whichever way my elements might be scattered, if they join an already living thing, they would raise it. If they unite with something whose life still resembles death, they would animate it. And as I see it, Eusebio! the Indians' idea of the transmigration of souls corresponds with my view; the elements may cease their wandering and searching only when the earth has thoroughly attained the organic existence that is appropriate to her. It must be that all the forms brought forth till now have not satisfied the earth spirit, because she continues to shatter them and seek new ones; she would not be able to destroy forms that truly resembled her precisely because they would be identical and inseparable from her. This perfect identity of the inner essence with the form cannot, it seems to me, be attained in the diversity of forms; the earth-essence is only One, so its form can only be one, not diverse; and the earth would attain her true being only when all of her phenomena dissolve themselves into one common organism; when spirit and body so interpenetrate that all bodies, all form would be equally thoughts and souls and all thought equally form and body, a true transfigured body, immortal, without defects and sickness; this body will be entirely different from what we name body or matter, insofar as we link these to transience, sickness, inertia, and imperfection. That kind of body is, so to speak, only a miscarried attempt to bring forth the immortal, divine body. Whether the earth will succeed in organizing herself so immortally, I do not know. It could be that in her primordial elements there is a misproportion of essence and form that forever hinders it; and perhaps it belongs to the totality of our solar system to bring this balance into being; perhaps even this is not adequate and it is a task for the entire universe.

In this perspective, Eusebio! it has become clear to me what the great thoughts of truth, justice, virtue, love, and beauty intend, [thoughts] that germinate in the soil of personality and, soon overgrowing it, stretch up toward the open heavens, an undying growth that does not come to an end with the soil in which it developed but constantly regenerates itself in new individuals. Thus it is the enduring, the eternal, while the individual is but the frail vessel for the draught of immortality.—Now, let us observe this even closer, Eusebio. Are

not all virtues and excellent things approaches to that highest complete condition, at least insofar as the particular can approach it. The
truth is, after all, only the expression of the self-identical being, and
further, only the eternal, which is subject to no change of time or condition, is perfectly true. Justice is the striving to be equal among each
other within the condition of isolation. Beauty is the external expression of an achieved balance with oneself. Love is the reconciliation of
the personality with the totality, and all the kinds of virtue are only
one, that is, a forgetting of personality and particularity in the totality.
Love and virtue spiritually prepare the condition of the dissolution of
the many in the One. For where love is, only One is meaningful, and
wherever virtue is, there is only striving for actions of justice, good,
and harmony. What is at one with itself, and carries the expression of
this harmonious being both inwardly and externally in itself, what is
one and not torn into plurality, that is precisely that perfect, immortal,
and unchangeable being, that organism, which I regard as the goal of
nature, history, and time, indeed of the universe. Every act of falsity,
injustice, and selfishness drives away that blessed condition, and
throws the god of the earth into new shackles, that god whose longing
for a better life is expressed in every mind's receptivity to excellence,
but who moans in wounded awareness that his blessed, divine life still
remains distant.

9

JOHANN WOLFGANG GOETHE

Faust, Part I

1808

*By the time Romanticism emerged, Johann Wolfgang Goethe (1749–
1832) was the towering figure in German literature. He attained European-wide fame in the 1770s with his novel* The Sorrows of Young
Werther, *the major work of the* Sturm und Drang *(Storm and Stress)*

Johann Wolfgang von Goethe, *Faust: A Tragedy*, trans. Bayard Taylor (Boston:
Houghton Mifflin and Company, 1912), part I: 1064–125.

movement. In the mid-1770s, he accepted an invitation from the Duke of Saxe-Weimar, and he remained at the court of Weimar for much of his life. There, he worked in many official capacities, while also pursuing a staggering range of intellectual projects. His works include many of German literature's most important novels, plays, and poetry. A brilliant polymath, he also pursued scientific interests in the theory of color, optics, morphology, chemistry, and geology.

Goethe provoked ambivalence in the German Romantics. He was a literary hero to be emulated, but he was also a forbidding father figure. In return, Goethe's relationship to the Romantics was complicated. He did not share their enthusiasm for the French Revolution, and he considered himself to be a "classicist," declaring in later life, "Romanticism is disease, Classicism is health." German scholars have long insisted on distinguishing Romanticism from the so-called Weimar Classicism of Goethe and Friedrich Schiller; but Goethe's masterpiece Faust *shows how difficult it is to distinguish sharply between these two tendencies.* Faust *was literally a life-long project. Goethe began writing the play as early as 1772; a version was published in 1775; a complete version of Part One appeared in 1808; he began Part Two in the 1820s and published it in the year of his death. Faust, the medieval scholar who wagers his soul to the devil in exchange for youth, limitless knowledge, and experience provided the Romantic age with one of its greatest archetypes (see Figure 5). Faust's insatiable quest leaves many victims in its wake, and Faust ultimately loses the bet to the devil; but on the brink of damnation, God overturns the wager and redeems Faust precisely because of his ceaseless striving. In the excerpted exchange between Faust and his prosaic, pedestrian assistant Wagner, we encounter some of the master themes of European Romanticism.*

FAUST:

O happy he, who still renews
The hope, from Error's deeps to rise forever!
That which one does not know, one needs to use;
And what one knows, one uses never.
But let us not, by such despondence, so
The fortune of this hour embitter!
Mark how, beneath the evening sunlight's glow,
The green-embosomed houses glitter!
The glow retreats, done is the day of toil;

Figure 5. *Peter von Cornelius,* Faust and Mephistopheles on the Brocken, *1811*

The German artist Peter von Cornelius did a series of woodcuts of scenes from Goethe's *Faust.* This one depicts Faust and Mephistopheles ascending the Brocken mountain to attend the Walpurgisnacht, the witches' Sabbath. The Romantic ideal of the unity of the arts encouraged many major Romantic painters to draw themes from classical and contemporary literature. Cornelius's Faust illustrations may be interestingly compared with the series of Faust illustrations created by Eugène Delacroix.

Plate 10, Bilder zu Goethe's Faust von Peter Cornelius, Frankfurt am Main; F. Wenner, 1816.

It yonder hastes, new fields of life exploring;
Ah, that no wing can lift me from the soil,
Upon its track to follow, follow soaring!
Then would I see eternal Evening gild
The silent world beneath me glowing,
On fire each mountain-peak, with peace each valley filled,
The silver brook to golden rivers flowing.
The mountain-chain, with all its gorges deep,
Would then no more impede my godlike motion;
And now before mine eyes expands the ocean
With all its bays, in shining sleep!
Yet, finally, the weary god is sinking;
The new-born impulse fires my mind, —
I hasten on, his beams eternal drinking,
The Day before me and the Night behind,
Above me heaven unfurled, the floor of waves beneath me, —
A glorious dream! though now the glories fade.
Alas! the wings that lift the mind no aid
Of wings to lift the body can bequeath me.
Yet in each soul is born the pleasure
Of yearning onward, upward and away,
When o'er our heads, lost in the vaulted azure,
The lark sends down his flickering lay, —
When over crags and piny highlands
The poising eagle slowly soars,
And over plains and lakes and islands

The crane sails by to other shores.

WAGNER:

I've had, myself, at times, some odd caprices,
But never yet such impulse felt, as this is.
One soon fatigues, on woods and fields to look,
Nor would I beg the bird his wing to spare us:
How otherwise the mental raptures bear us
From page to page, from book to book!
Then winter nights take loveliness untold,
As warmer life in every limb had crowned you;
And when your hands unroll some parchment rare and old,
All Heaven descends, and opens bright around you!

FAUST:

One impulse art thou conscious of, at best;
O, never seek to know the other!
Two souls, alas! reside within my breast,
And each withdraws from, and repels, its brother.
One with tenacious organs holds in love
And clinging lust the world in its embraces;
The other strongly sweeps, this dust above,
Into the high ancestral spaces.
If there be airy spirits near,
'Twixt Heaven and Earth on potent errands fleeing,
Let them drop down the golden atmosphere,
And bear me forth to new and varied being!
Yea, if a magic mangle once were mine,
To waft me o'er the world at pleasure,
I would not for the costliest stores of treasure—
Not for a monarch's robe—the gift resign.

10

AUGUST WILHELM SCHLEGEL

Lectures on Dramatic Art and Letters

1808

August Wilhelm Schlegel (1767–1845) is often considered less original than his younger brother Friedrich, but his achievements were extraordinary by any measure. His translations of Shakespeare and Dante remain monuments of the German language; he and his wife, Caroline, played the crucial role in forming the Jena circle; his writings established many of the critical and historical categories by which the Romantic age came to judge itself and its place in history; and as a professor of literature and art history in Bonn from 1818 to 1845, he consolidated the study of

August Wilhelm von Schlegel, *A Course of Lectures on Dramatic Art and Letters*, trans. John Black (Philadelphia: Hogan and Thompson, 1833), 1–10, 12–13, 16–17.

Sanskrit and, more broadly, the discipline of philology. Through these achievements, Schlegel may well rank as the central theorist in the international Romantic phenomenon, his impact amplified even further by Madame de Staël, whose understanding of Romanticism rested heavily on Schlegel.

Schlegel, whose marriage to Caroline ended in divorce in 1803, met Staël in 1804 and remained her close companion until her death in 1817, spending many of those years at Staël's Swiss estate. In 1808, Schlegel and Staël journeyed to Vienna, where he delivered a series of lectures on drama that he expanded and published in 1809–1810. Schlegel's book was soon translated into French, English, and Italian. His Vienna lectures synthesize and systematize the aesthetic program of German Romanticism. The historical relativism of Schlegel's aesthetic criteria is fully evident in this excerpt from the Vienna lectures. He does not denigrate the art of the ancients but calls for an end to the slavish imitation of ancient models. He reserves his praise for artists who created styles that spoke to their own culture and age. Above all, he urges the moderns to recognize that they stand on the near side of a great historical, cultural, and spiritual divide between pagan antiquity and the Christian epoch. Indelibly marked by the Christian division between the here and now and the afterlife, Romantic art expresses yearnings, homesickness, and desires that the ancients never knew. Romantic art will always lack the harmoniousness of the ancients; but, for Schlegel, this "imperfection" is the source of Romanticism's greatness.

Lecture I

The object which we propose to ourselves in these Lectures is to investigate the principles of dramatic literature, and to consider whatever is connected with the fable, composition, and representation, of theatrical productions. We have selected the drama in preference to every other department of poetry. It will not be expected of us that we should enter scientifically into the first principles of theory. Poetry is in general closely connected with the other fine arts; and, in some degree, the eldest sister and guide of the rest. The necessity for the fine arts, and the pleasure derivable from them, originate in a principle of our nature, which it is the business of the philosopher to investigate and to classify. This object has given rise to many profound disquisitions, especially in Germany; and the name of *aesthetic* (perceptive)[1] has, with no great degree of propriety, been conferred on this department of philosophy. Aesthetics, or the philosophical theory of beauty and art, is of the utmost importance in its connection with other inquiries into the human mind; but, considered by itself, it is not of sufficient practical instruction; and it can only become so by its union with the history of the arts. We give the appellation of criticism to the intermediate province between general theory and experience or history. The comparing together and judging the existing productions of the human mind must supply us with a knowledge of the means which are requisite for the conception and execution of masterly works of art.

We will therefore endeavor to throw light on the history of the dramatic art by the torch of criticism. In the course of this attempt it will be necessary to adopt many a proposition, without proof, from general theory; but I hope that the manner in which this shall be done will not be considered as objectionable.

Before I proceed farther, I wish to say a few words respecting the spirit of my criticism, a study to which I have devoted a great part of my life. We see numbers of men, and even whole nations, so much fettered by the habits of their education and modes of living, that they cannot shake themselves free from them, even in the enjoyment of the fine arts. Nothing to them appears natural, proper, or beautiful, which is foreign to their language, their manners, or their social relations. In this exclusive mode of seeing and feeling, it is no doubt possible, by means of cultivation, to attain a great nicety of discrimination in the narrow circle within which they are limited and circumscribed. But no man can be a true critic or connoisseur who does not possess a universality of mind, who does not possess the flexibility, which, throwing aside all personal predilections and blind habits, enables him to transport himself into the peculiarities of other ages and nations, to feel them as it were from their proper central point; and, what ennobles human nature, to recognize and respect whatever is beautiful and grand under those external modifications which are necessary to their existence, and which sometimes even seem to disguise them. There is no monopoly of poetry for certain ages and nations; and consequently

---

[1]The etymological base for the word "aesthetic" is the Greek word *aisthetikos* (sensuous perception), but the philosopher Alexander Baumgarten (1714–1762) applied the name to the criticism of taste, what we would recognize as the philosophical discipline of "aesthetics." Immanuel Kant protested this extension of the word, and, in his *Critique of Pure Reason*, the term designates a science of sensuous perception. It is, of course, Baumgarten's, not Kant's usage that has gained widespread acceptance.

that despotism in taste, by which it is attempted to make those rules universal which were at first perhaps arbitrarily established, is a pretension which ought never to be allowed. Poetry, taken in its widest acceptation, as the power of creating what is beautiful, and representing it to the eye or the ear, is a universal gift of Heaven, which is even shared to a certain extent by those whom we call barbarians and savages. Internal excellence is alone decisive, and where this exists we must not allow ourselves to be repelled by external appearances. Everything must be traced up to the root of our existence: if it has sprung from thence, it must possess an undoubted worth; but if, without possessing a living germ, it is merely an external appendage, it can never thrive nor acquire a proper growth. . . .

Let us now think of applying the idea which we have been developing, of the universality of true criticism, to the history of poetry and the fine arts. We generally limit it (although there may be much which deserves to be known beyond this circle) as we limit what we call universal history to whatever has had a nearer or more remote influence on the present cultivation of Europe: consequently to the works of the Greeks and Romans, and of those of the modern European nations, who first and chiefly distinguished themselves in art and literature. It is well known that, three centuries and a half ago, the study of ancient literature, by the diffusion of the Grecian language (for the Latin was never extinct) received a new life: the classical authors were sought after with avidity, and made accessible by means of the press; and the monuments of ancient art were carefully dug up and preserved. All this excited the human mind in a powerful manner, and formed a decided epoch in the history of our cultivation; the fruits have extended to our times, and will extend to a period beyond the power of our calculation. But the study of the ancients was immediately carried to a most pernicious extent. The learned, who were chiefly in the possession of this knowledge, and who were incapable of distinguishing themselves by their own productions, yielded an unlimited deference to the ancients, and with great appearance of reason, as they are models in their kind. They maintained that nothing could be hoped for the human mind but in the imitation of the ancients; and they only esteemed in the works of the moderns whatever resembled, or seemed to bear a resemblance to, those of antiquity. Everything else was rejected by them as barbarous and unnatural. It was quite otherwise with the great poets and artists. However strong their enthusiasm for the ancients, and however determined their purpose of entering into competition with them, they were compelled by the characteristic peculiarity of their minds, to proceed in a track of their own, and to impress upon their productions the stamp of their own genius. Such was the case with Dante among the Italians, the father of modern poetry; he acknowledged Virgil for his instructer, but produced a work which, of all others, differs the most from the Aeneid, and far excels it in our opinion, in strength, truth, depth, and comprehension. It was the same afterwards with [the Italian poet Ludovico] Ariosto, who has most unaccountably been compared to Homer; for nothing can be more unlike. It was the same in the fine arts with Michelangelo and Raphael, who were without doubt well acquainted with the antique. When we ground our judgment of modern painters merely on their resemblance of the ancients, we must necessarily be unjust towards them; and hence Winkelmann[2] has undoubtedly been guilty of injustice to Raphael. As the poets for the most part acquiesced in the doctrines of the learned, we may observe a curious struggle in them between their natural inclination and their imagined duty. When they sacrificed to the latter they were praised by the learned; but by yielding to their own inclinations they became the favorites of the people. What preserves the heroic poems of a [Torquato] Tasso and a [Luis Vaz de] Camoëns to this day alive, in the hearts and on the lips of their countrymen, is by no means their imperfect resemblance to Virgil, or even to Homer, but in Tasso the tender feeling of chivalrous love and honor, and in Camoëns the glowing inspiration of patriotic heroism.

Those very ages, nations, and classes, that were least in want of a poetry of their own, were the most assiduous in their imitation of the ancients. Hence the dull scholastic exercises which could at most excite a cold admiration. But, in the fine arts, mere imitation is always fruitless; what we borrow from others must be again as it were born in us, to produce a poetical effect. Of what avail is all foreign imitation? Art cannot exist without nature, and man can give nothing to his fellow men but himself.

The genuine followers of the ancients, those who attempted to rival them, who from a similarity of disposition and cultivation proceeded in their track, and acted in their spirit, were at all times as few as their mechanical spiritless imitators were numerous. The great body of critics, seduced by external appearance, have been always but too indulgent even to these imitators. They held them up as correct modern

---

[2]Johann Joachim Winkelmann (1717–1768), German art critic, theorist, and art historian, highly influential in the formation of neoclassical norms in the visual arts and in the revival of enthusiasm for ancient Greek, as opposed to Roman, art and culture.

classics, while those animated poets, who had become the favorites of their respective nations, and to whose sublimity it was impossible to be altogether blind, were at most but tolerated by them as rude and wild natural geniuses. But the unqualified separation of genius and taste which they assume is altogether untenable. Genius is the almost unconscious choice of the highest degree of excellence, and consequently it is taste in its greatest perfection.

In this state, nearly, matters continued till a period not far back, when several inquiring minds, chiefly Germans, endeavored to clear up the misconception, and to hold the ancients in proper estimation, without being insensible to the merits of the moderns of a totally different description. The apparent contradiction did not intimidate them.—The groundwork of human nature is no doubt everywhere the same; but in all our investigations we may observe that there is no fundamental power throughout the whole range of nature so simple, but that it is capable of dividing and diverging into opposite directions. The whole play of living motion hinges on harmony and contrast. Why then should not this phenomenon be repeated in the history of man? This idea led, perhaps, to the discovery of the true key to the ancient and modern history of poetry and the fine arts. Those who adopted it gave to the peculiar spirit of *modern* art, as opposed to the *antique* or *classical*, the name of *romantic*. The appellation is certainly not unsuitable: the word is derived from *romance*, the name of the language of the people which was formed from the mixture of Latin and Teutonic, in the same manner as modern cultivation is the fruit of the union of the peculiarities of the northern nations with the fragments of antiquity. Hence the cultivation of the ancients was much more of a piece than ours.

The distinction which we have just stated can hardly fail to appear well founded, if it can be shown that the same contrast in the labors of the ancients and moderns runs symmetrically, I might almost say systematically, throughout every branch of art, as far as our knowledge of antiquity extends; that it is as evident in music and the plastic arts as in poetry. This proposition still remains to be demonstrated in its full extent, though we have many excellent observations on different parts of the subject.

Among the foreign authors who wrote before this school can be said to have been formed in Germany, we may mention [Jean-Jacques] Rousseau, who acknowledged the contrast in music, and demonstrated that rhythmus and melody constituted the prevailing principle of the ancients, and harmony that of the moderns. In his prejudices against harmony, however, we altogether differ from him. On the subject of the plastic arts an ingenious observation was made by Hemsterhuys,[3] that the ancient painters were probably too much sculptors, and that the modern sculptors are too much painters. This is the exact point of difference; for I shall distinctly show, in the sequel, that the spirit of ancient art and poetry is *plastic*, and that of the moderns *picturesque*.[4]

By an example taken from another art, that of architecture, I shall endeavor to illustrate what I mean by this contrast. In the middle ages there prevailed a style of architecture, which, in the last centuries especially, was carried to the utmost degree of perfection; and which, whether justly or unjustly, has been called Gothic architecture. When, on the general revival of classical antiquity, the imitation of Grecian architecture became prevalent, and but too frequently without a due regard to the difference of climate and manners and the destination of the structure, the zealots of this new taste passed a sweeping sentence of condemnation on the Gothic, which they reprobated as tasteless, gloomy, and barbarous. This was in some degree pardonable in the Italians, among whom a love for ancient architecture, from the remains of classical edifices which they inherited, and the similarity of their climate to that of the Greeks, might in some sort be said to be innate. But with us, inhabitants of the North, the first powerful impression on entering a Gothic cathedral is not so easily eradicated. We feel, on the contrary, a strong desire to investigate and to justify the source of this impression. A very slight attention will convince us, that the Gothic architecture not only displays an extraordinary degree of mechanical dexterity, but also an astonishing power of invention; and, on a closer examination, we become impressed with the strongest

---

[3]François Hemsterhuys (1721–1790), Dutch writer on aesthetics, moral philosophy, and theology.
[4]Later in his lectures, Schlegel expanded on the "picturesque spirit of the romantic poetry," likening it to painting, which "delights in exhibiting, in a minute manner, along with the principal figures, the surrounding locality and all the secondary objects, and to open to us in the background a prospect into a boundless distance" (*A Course of Lectures on Dramatic Art and Literature*, I, 348–49). Like many Romantics, Schlegel believed that poetry and painting share a common aspiration for the ideal. Painting's merits stood in contrast to those of sculpture, for even if sculpture could better depict human form, painting seemed to have a greater power to transcend its materiality and express higher symbolic meaning. In linking the spirit of the moderns with the "picturesque," Schlegel thus suggested the typical Romantic desire to unite the particular and the universal, the material and the ideal.

conviction of its profound character, and of its constituting a full and perfect system in itself, as well as the Grecian.

To the application!—The Pantheon is not more different from Westminster Abbey or the church of St. Stephen at Vienna, than the structure of a tragedy of Sophocles from a drama of Shakespeare. The comparison between these wonderful productions of poetry and architecture might be carried still farther. But does our admiration of the one compel us to depreciate the other? May we not admit that each is great and admirable in its kind, although the one is, and ought to be, different from the other? The experiment is worth attempting. We will quarrel with no man for his predilection either for the Grecian or the Gothic. The world is wide, and affords room for a great diversity of objects. Narrow and exclusive prepossessions will never constitute a genuine critic or connoisseur, who ought, on the contrary, to possess the power of elevating himself above all partial views, and of subduing all personal inclinations.

For the justification of our object, namely, the grand division which we lay down in the history of art, and according to which we conceive ourselves equally warranted in establishing the same division in dramatic literature, it might be sufficient merely to have stated this contrast between the ancient, or classical, and the romantic. But as there are exclusive admirers of the ancients, who never cease asserting that all deviation from them is merely the whim of recent critics, who express themselves on the subject in a language full of mystery, but cautiously avoid conveying their sentiments in a tangible shape, I shall endeavor to explain the origin and spirit of the *romantic*, and then leave the world to judge if the use of the word, and of the idea which it is intended to convey, are sufficiently justified.

The formation of the Greeks was a natural education in its utmost perfection. Of a beautiful and noble race, endowed with susceptible senses and a clear understanding, placed beneath a mild heaven, they lived and bloomed in the full health of existence; and, under a singular coincidence of favorable circumstances, performed all of which our circumscribed nature is capable. The whole of their art and their poetry is expressive of the consciousness of this harmony of all their faculties. They have invented the poetry of gladness.

Their religion was the deification of the powers of nature and of the earthly life: but this worship, which, among other nations, clouded the imagination with images of horror, and filled the heart with unrelenting cruelty, assumed, among the Greeks, a mild, a grand, and a dignified form. Superstition, too often the tyrant of the human faculties, seemed to have here contributed to their freest development. It cherished the arts by which it was ornamented, and the idols became models of ideal beauty.

But however far the Greeks may have carried beauty, and even morality, we cannot allow any higher character to their formation than that of a refined and ennobled sensuality. Let it not be understood that I assert this to be true in every instance. The conjectures of a few philosophers, and the irradiations of poetical inspiration, constitute an exception. Man can never altogether turn aside his thoughts from infinity, and some obscure recollections will always remind him of his original home; but we are now speaking of the principal object towards which his endeavors are directed.

Religion is the root of human existence. Were it possible for man to renounce all religion, including that of which he is unconscious, and over which he has no control, he would become a mere surface without any internal substance. When this center is disturbed, the whole system of the mental faculties must receive another direction.

And this is what has actually taken place in modern Europe through the introduction of Christianity. This sublime and beneficent religion has regenerated the ancient world from its state of exhaustion and debasement; it has become the guiding principle in the history of modern nations, and even at this day, when many suppose they have shaken off its authority, they will find themselves in all human affairs much more under its influence than they themselves are aware.

After Christianity, the character of Europe, since the commencement of the middle ages, has been chiefly influenced by the Germanic race of northern conquerors, who infused new life and vigor into a degenerated people. The stern nature of the north drives man back within himself; and what is withdrawn from the free development of the senses, must, in noble dispositions, be added to their earnestness of mind. Hence the honest cordiality with which Christianity was received by all the Teutonic tribes, in whom it penetrated more deeply, displayed more powerful effects, and became more interwoven with all human feelings, than in the case of any other people.

From a union of the rough but honest heroism of the northern conquerors and the sentiments of Christianity, chivalry had its origin, of which the object was, by holy and respected vows, to guard those who bore arms from every rude and ungenerous abuse of strength, into which it was so easy to deviate.

With the virtues of chivalry was associated a new and purer spirit of love, an inspired homage for genuine female worth, which was now revered as the pinnacle of humanity; and, enjoined by religion itself under the image of a virgin mother, infused into all hearts a sentiment of unalloyed goodness.

As Christianity was not, like the heathen worship, satisfied with certain external acts, but claimed a dominion over the whole inward man and the most hidden movements of the heart; the feeling of moral independence was in like manner preserved alive by the laws of honor, a worldly morality, as it were, which was often at variance with the religious, yet in so far resembled it, that it never calculated consequences, but consecrated unconditionally certain principles of action, as truths elevated beyond all the investigation of casuistical reasoning.

Chivalry, love, and honor, with religion itself, are the objects of the natural poetry which poured itself out in the middle ages with incredible fulness, and preceded the more artificial formation of the romantic character. This age had also its mythology, consisting of chivalrous tales and legends; but their wonders and their heroism were the very reverse of those of the ancient mythology.

Several inquirers, who, in other respects, entertain the same conception of the peculiarities of the moderns, and trace them to the same source that we do, have placed the essence of the northern poetry in melancholy; and to this when properly understood, we have nothing to object.

Among the Greeks human nature was in itself all-sufficient; they were conscious of no wants, and aspired at no higher perfection than that which they could actually attain by the exercise of their own faculties. We, however, are taught by superior wisdom that man, through a high offense, forfeited the place for which he was originally destined; and that the whole object of his earthly existence is to strive to regain that situation, which, if left to his own strength, he could never accomplish. The religion of the senses had only in view the possession of outward and perishable blessings; and immortality, in so far as it was believed, appeared in an obscure distance like a shadow, a faint dream of this bright and vivid futurity. The very reverse of all this is the case with the Christian: everything finite and mortal is lost in the contemplation of infinity; life has become a shadow and darkness, and the first dawning of our real existence opens in the world beyond the grave. Such a religion must waken the foreboding, which slumbers in every feeling heart, to the most thorough consciousness, that the happiness after which we strive we can never here attain; that no external object can ever entirely fill our souls; and that every mortal enjoyment is but a fleeting and momentary deception. When the soul, resting as it were under the willows of exile, breathes out its longing for its distant home, the prevailing character of its songs must be melancholy. Hence the poetry of the ancients was the poetry of enjoyment, and ours is that of desire: the former has its foundation in the scene which is present, while the latter hovers betwixt recollection and hope. Let me not be understood to affirm that everything flows in one strain of wailing and complaint, and that the voice of melancholy must always be loudly heard. As the austerity of tragedy was not incompatible with the joyous views of the Greeks, so the romantic poetry can assume every tone, even that of the most lively gladness; but still it will always, in some shape or other, bear traces of the source from which it originated. The feeling of the moderns is, upon the whole, more intense, their fancy more incorporeal, and their thoughts more contemplative. In nature, it is true, the boundaries of objects run more into one another, and things are not so distinctly separated as we must exhibit them for the sake of producing a distinct impression.

The Grecian idea of humanity consisted in a perfect concord and proportion between all the powers, — a natural harmony. The moderns again have arrived at the consciousness of the internal discord which renders such an idea impossible; and hence the endeavor of their poetry is to reconcile these two worlds between which we find ourselves divided, and to melt them indissolubly into one another. The impressions of the senses are consecrated, as it were, from their mysterious connection with higher feelings; and the soul, on the other hand, embodies its forebodings, or nameless visions of infinity, in the phenomena of the senses.

In the Grecian art and poetry we find an original and unconscious unity of form and subject; in the modern, so far as it has remained true to its own spirit, we observe a keen struggle to unite the two, as being naturally in opposition to each other. The Grecian executed what it proposed in the utmost perfection; but the modern can only do justice to its endeavors after what is infinite by approximation; and, from a certain appearance of imperfection, is in greater danger of not being duly appreciated.

11

JOHANN GOTTLIEB FICHTE

What Is a People in the Higher Meaning of the Word, and What Is Love of Fatherland?

1808

As a philosophy professor at the University of Jena (1793–1799), Johann Gottlieb Fichte's (1762–1814) radicalized Kantian philosophy and his support of Jacobinism heavily influenced the first German Romantics. Charges of atheism forced him to leave Jena for Berlin, where he eventually served as rector of the new University of Berlin (1810–1812). Fichte gave lectures on German nationalism in Berlin in the winter of 1807 after France's defeat of Prussia; he published those lectures in 1808 as Addresses to the German Nation. *The* Addresses *played a vital role in stimulating nationalist sentiment and rallying resistance to the French. This excerpt from the "Eighth Address" links the pivotal notion of the people to the "transcendence" and "immortality" of the nation, and from that idea of worldly immortality, Fichte calls for personal sacrifice to the great national cause. This former champion of Jacobinism no longer dreams of creating a republic but summons the fatherland to awaken. The political problem of forming a democratic "General Will" fades before the vision of a primordial bond between the people and the nation. While the* Addresses *may be read as a retreat from the French Revolution's ideals, do revolutionary commitments linger in Fichte's emphasis on freedom and the pursuit of cultural expression and creativity as the highest goals of national life? Like Novalis's "Christianity or Europe," Fichte's* Addresses *powerfully illustrate the ambiguities of Romantic politics and the nationalist project.*

What is a people? This question is similar to another, and when it is answered the other is answered too. The other question, which is often raised and the answers to which are very different, is this: What

Johann Gottlieb Fichte, "Eighth Address: What Is a People in the Higher Meaning of the Word, and What Is Love of Fatherland?" *Addresses to the German Nation*, trans. R. F. Jones and G. H. Turnbull (LaSalle, Ill.: Open Court Publishing Company, 1922), 130–50.

is love of fatherland, or, to express it more correctly, what is the love of the individual for his nation?

If we have hitherto proceeded correctly in the course of our investigation, it must here be obvious at once that only the German—the original man, who has not become dead in an arbitrary organization—really has a people and is entitled to count on one, and that he alone is capable of real and rational love for his nation.

The problem having been thus stated, we prepare the way for its solution by the following observation, which seems at first to have no connection with what has preceded it. . . .

111. Religion, as we have already remarked in our third address, is able to transcend all time and the whole of this present sensuous life, without hereby causing the slightest detriment to the righteousness, morality, and holiness of the life that is permeated by this belief. Even if one is firmly persuaded that all our effort on this earth will not leave the slightest trace behind it nor yield the slightest fruit, nay more, that the divine effort will even be perverted and become an instrument of evil and of still deeper moral corruption, one can nonetheless continue the effort, solely in order to maintain the divine life that has manifested itself in us, and with a view to a higher order of things in a future world, in which no deed that is of divine origin is lost. Thus the apostles, for example, and the primitive Christians in general, because of their belief in heaven had their hearts entirely set on things above the earth even in their lifetime; and earthly affairs—the State, their earthly fatherland, and nation—were abandoned by them so entirely that they no longer deemed them worthy of attention. . . . Although it is true that religion is, for one thing, the consolation of the unjustly oppressed slave, yet this above all is the mark of a religious disposition, viz., to fight against slavery and, as far as possible, to prevent religion from sinking into a mere consolation for captives. . . .

112. The natural impulse of man, which should be abandoned only in case of real necessity, is to find heaven on this earth, and to endow his daily work on earth with permanence and eternity; to plant and to cultivate the eternal in the temporal—not merely in an incomprehensible fashion or in a connection with the eternal that seems to the mortal eye an impenetrable gulf, but in a fashion visible to the moral eye itself.

Let me begin with an example that everyone will understand. What man of noble mind is there who does not earnestly wish to relive his own life in a new and better way in his children and his children's children, and to continue to live on this earth, ennobled and perfected in their lives, long after he is dead? Does he not wish to snatch from the jaws of death the spirit, the mind, and the moral sense by virtue of which, perchance, he was in the days of his life a terror to wrongdoing and corruption, and by which he supported righteousness, aroused men from indolence, and lifted them out of their depression? Does he not wish to deposit these qualities, as his best legacy to posterity, in the souls of those he leaves behind, so that they too, in their turn, may someday hand them on again, increased and made more beautiful? What man of noble mind is there who does not want to scatter, by action or thought, a grain of seed for the unending progress in perfection of his race, to fling something new and unprecedented into time, that it may remain there and become the inexhaustible source of new creations? Does he not wish to pay for his place on this earth and the short span of time allotted to him with something that even here below will endure forever, so that he, the individual, although unnamed in history (for the thirst for posthumous fame is contemptible vanity), may yet in his own consciousness and his faith leave behind him unmistakable memories that he, too, was a dweller on the earth? What man of noble mind is there, I said, who does not want this? But only according to the needs of noble-minded men is the world to be regarded and arranged; as they are, so all men ought to be, and for their sake alone does a world exist. They are its kernel, and those of other mind exist only for their sake, being themselves only a part of the transitory world so long as they are of that mind. Such men must conform to the wishes of the noble-minded until they have become like them.

113. Now, what is it that could warrant this challenge and this faith of the noble-minded man in the permanence and eternity of his work? Obviously nothing but an order of things which he can acknowledge, as in itself eternal and capable of taking up into itself that which is eternal. Such an order of things, however, is the special spiritual nature of human environment which, although indeed it is not to be comprehended in any conception, nevertheless truly exists, and from which he himself, with all his thoughts and deeds and with his belief in their eternity, has proceeded—the people from which he is descended and among which he was educated and grew up to be what he now is. . . . So long as this people exists, every further revelation of the divine will appear and take shape in that people in accordance with the same natural law. But this law itself is further determined by the fact that this man existed and worked as he did, and his influence has become a permanent part of this law. Hence, everything that follows

will be bound to submit itself to, and connect itself with, the law. So he is sure that the improvement achieved by him remains in his people so long as the people itself remains, and that it becomes a permanent determining factor in the evolution of his people.

114. This, then, is a people in the higher meaning of the word, when viewed from the standpoint of a spiritual world: the totality of men continuing to live in society with each other and continually creating themselves naturally and spiritually out of themselves, a totality that arises together out of the divine under a certain special law of divine development. It is the subjection in common to this special law that unites this mass in the eternal world, and therefore in the temporal also, to a natural totality permeated by itself. The significance of this law itself can indeed be comprehended as a whole, as we have comprehended it by the instance of the Germans as an original people; it can even be better understood in many of its further provisions by considering the manifestations of such a people; but it can never be completely grasped by the mind of anyone, for everyone continually remains under its influence unknown to himself, although, in general, it can be clearly seen that such a law exists. . . . That law determines entirely and completes what has been called the national character of a people — that law of the development of the original and divine. From this it is clear that men who, as is the case with what we have described as the foreign spirit, do not believe at all in something original nor in its continuous development, but only in an eternal recurrence of apparent life, and who by their belief become what they believe, are in the higher sense not a people at all. As they in fact, properly speaking, do not exist, they are just as little capable of having a national character.

115. The noble-minded man's belief in the eternal continuance of his influence even on this earth is thus founded on the hope of the eternal continuance of the people from which he has developed, and on the characteristic of the people as indicated in the hidden law of which we have spoken, without admixture of, or corruption by, any alien element which does not belong to the totality of the function of that law. This characteristic is the eternal thing to which he entrusts the eternity of himself and of his continuing influence, the eternal order of things in which he places his portion of eternity; he must will its continuance, for it alone is to him the means by which the short span of his life here below is extended into continuous life here below. His belief and his struggle to plant what is permanent, his conception in which he comprehends his own life as an eternal life, is the bond

which unites first his own nation, and then, through his nation, the whole human race, in a most intimate fashion with himself, and brings all their needs within his widened sympathy until the end of time. This is his love for his people, respecting, trusting, and rejoicing in it, and feeling honored by descent from it. The divine has appeared in it, and that which is original has deemed this people worthy to be made its vesture and its means of directly influencing the world; for this reason there will be further manifestations of the divine in it. Hence, the noble-minded man will be active and effective, and will sacrifice himself for his people. Life merely as such, the mere continuance of changing existence, has in any case never had any value for him; he has wished for it only as the source of what is permanent. But this permanence is promised to him only by the continuous and independent existence of his nation. In order to save his nation he must be ready even to die that it may live, and that he may live in it the only life for which he has ever wished.

116. . . . Man is not able to love even himself unless he conceives himself as eternal; apart from that he cannot even respect, much less approve of himself. Still less can he love anything outside himself without taking it up into the eternity of his faith and of his soul and binding it thereto. He who does not first regard himself as eternal has in him no love of any kind, and, moreover, cannot love a fatherland, a thing which for him does not exist. He who regards his invisible life as eternal, but not his visible life as similarly eternal, may perhaps have a heaven and therein a fatherland, but here below he has no fatherland, for this, too, is regarded only in the image of eternity—eternity visible and made sensuous—and for this reason also he is unable to love his fatherland. If none has been handed down to such a man, he is to be pitied. But he to whom a fatherland has been handed down, and in whose soul heaven and earth, visible and invisible meet and mingle, and thus, and only thus, create a true and enduring heaven—such a man fights to the last drop of his blood to hand on the precious possession unimpaired to his posterity. . . .

117. People and fatherland in this sense, as a support and guarantee of eternity on earth and as that which can be eternal here below, far transcend the State in the ordinary sense of the word, viz., the social order as comprehended by mere intellectual conception and as established and maintained under the guidance of this conception. The aim of the State is positive law, internal peace, and a condition of affairs in which everyone may by diligence earn his daily bread and satisfy the needs of his material existence, so long as God permits him to live. All

this is only a means, a condition, and a framework for what love of fatherland really wants, viz., that the eternal and the divine may blossom in the world and never cease to become more and more pure, perfect, and excellent. That is why this love of fatherland must itself govern the State and be the supreme, final, and absolute authority. Its first exercise of this authority will be to limit the State's choice of means to secure its immediate object—internal peace. To attain this object, the natural freedom of the individual must, of course, be limited in many ways. If the only consideration and intention in regard to individuals were to secure internal peace, it would be well to limit that liberty as much as possible, to bring all their activities under a uniform rule, and to keep them under unceasing supervision. Even supposing such strictness were unnecessary, it could at any rate do no harm, if this were the sole object. It is only the higher view of the human race and of peoples which extends this narrow calculation. Freedom, including freedom in the activities of external life, is the soil in which higher culture germinates; a legislation which keeps the higher culture in view will allow to freedom as wide a field as possible, even at the risk of securing a smaller degree of uniform peace and quietness, and of making the work of government a little harder and more troublesome.

118. . . . If a nation could exist in which there were not even a few men of noble mind to make an exception to the general rule [it] would in fact need no freedom at all, for this is needed only for the higher purposes that transcend the State. . . . Whether this can be said with truth of any nation at all we may leave undecided; this much is clear, that an original people needs freedom, that this is the security for its continuance as an original people, and that, as it goes on, it is able to stand an ever-increasing degree of freedom without the slightest danger. This is the first matter in respect of which love of fatherland must govern the State itself.

119. Then, too, it must be love of fatherland that governs the State by placing before it a higher object than the usual one of maintaining internal peace, property, personal freedom, and the life and well-being of all. For this higher object alone, and with no other intention, does the State assemble an armed force. When the question arises of making use of this, when the call comes to stake everything that the State, in the narrow conception of the word, sets before itself as object, viz., property, personal freedom, life, and well-being, nay, even the continued existence of the State itself; when the call comes to make an original decision with responsibility to God alone, and without a clear and

reasonable idea that what is intended will surely be attained—for this is never possible in such matters—then, and then only, does there live at the helm of the State a truly original and primary life, and at this point, and not before, the true sovereign rights of government enter, like God, to hazard the lower life for the sake of the higher. In the maintenance of the traditional constitution, the laws, and civil prosperity there is absolutely no real true life and no original decision. Conditions and circumstances, and legislators perhaps long since dead, have created these things; succeeding ages go on faithfully in the paths marked out, and so in fact they have no public life of their own; they merely repeat a life that once existed. In such times there is no need of any real government. But, when this regular course is endangered, and it is a question of making decisions in new and unprecedented cases, then there is need of a life that lives of itself. What spirit is it that in such cases may place itself at the helm, that can make its own decisions with sureness and certainty, untroubled by any hesitation? What spirit has an undisputed right to summon and to order everyone concerned, whether he himself be willing or not, and to compel anyone who resists, to risk everything including his life? Not the spirit of the peaceful citizen's love for the constitution and the laws, but the devouring flame of higher patriotism, which embraces the nation as the vesture of the eternal, for which the noble-minded man joyfully sacrifices himself, and the ignoble man, who only exists for the sake of the other, must likewise sacrifice himself. . . . The promise of a life here on earth extending beyond the period of life here on earth—that alone it is which can inspire men even until death for the fatherland. . . .

121. In this belief our earliest common forefathers, the original stock of the new culture, the Germans, as the Romans called them, bravely resisted the on-coming world-dominion of the Romans. . . .

123. From all this it follows that the State, merely as the government of human life in its progress along the ordinary peaceful path, is not something which is primary and which exists for its own sake, but is merely the means to the higher purpose of the eternal, regular, and continuous development of what is purely human in this nation. It follows, too, that the vision and the love of this eternal development, and nothing else, should have the higher supervision of State administration at all times, not excluding periods of peace, and that this alone is able to save the people's independence when it is endangered. In the case of the Germans, among whom as an original people this love of fatherland was possible and, as we firmly believe, did actually exist up

to the present time, it has been able up to now to reckon with great confidence on the security of what was most vital to it. As was the case with the ancient Greeks alone, with the Germans the State and the nation were actually separated from each other, and each was represented for itself, the former in the separate German realms and principalities, the latter represented visibly in the imperial connection[1] and invisibly by virtue of a law, not written, but living and valid in the minds of all, a law whose results struck the eye everywhere—in a mass of customs and institutions. Wherever the German language was spoken, everyone who had first seen the light of day in its domain could consider himself as in a double sense a citizen, on the one hand, of the State where he was born and to whose care he was in the first instance commended, and, on the other hand, of the whole common fatherland of the German nation. To everyone it was permitted to seek out for himself in the whole length and breadth of this fatherland the culture most congenial to him or the sphere of action to which his spirit was best adapted; and talent did not root itself like a tree in the place where it first grew up, but was allowed to seek out its own place. Anyone who, because of the turn taken by his own development, became out of harmony with his immediate environment, easily found a willing reception elsewhere, found new friends in place of those he had lost, found time and leisure to make his meaning plainer and perhaps to win over and to reconcile even those who were offended with him, and so to unite the whole. No German-born prince ever took upon himself to mark out for his subjects as their fatherland, with mountains or rivers as boundaries, the territory over which he ruled, and to regard his subjects as bound to the soil. A truth not permitted to find expression in one place might find expression in another, where it might happen that those truths were forbidden which were permitted in the first. So, in spite of the many instances of one-sidedness and narrowness of heart in the separate States, there was nevertheless in Germany, considered as a whole, the greatest freedom of investigation and publication that any people has ever possessed. Everywhere the higher culture was, and continued to be, the result of the interaction of the citizens of all German States: And then this

---

[1] Ancien régime Germany was a patchwork of independent states and principalities loosely united under the Holy Roman Empire. Napoleon dissolved the Empire in 1806, and from its western regions he created the Confederation of the Rhine, a French protectorate.

higher culture gradually worked its way down in this form to the people at large, which thus never ceased, broadly speaking, to educate itself by itself. This essential security for the continuance of a German nation was, as we have said, not impaired by any man of German spirit seated at the helm of government; and though with respect to other original decisions things may not always have happened as the higher German love of fatherland could not but wish, at any rate there has been no act in direct opposition to its interests; there has been no attempt to undermine that love or to extirpate it and put a love of the opposite kind in its place.

124. But what if the original guidance of that higher culture, as well as the national power which may not be used except to serve that culture and its continuance, the utilization of German property and blood—what if this should pass from the control of the German spirit to that of another? What would then be the inevitable results?

This is the place where there is special need of the disposition which we invoked in our first address—the disposition not to deceive ourselves wilfully about our own affairs, and the courage to be willing to behold the truth and confess it to ourselves. Moreover, it is still permitted to us, so far as I know, to speak to each other in the German language about the fatherland, or at least to sigh over it, and, in my opinion, we should not do well if we anticipated of our own accord such a prohibition, or if we were ready to restrain our courage, which without doubt will already have taken counsel with itself as to the risk to be run, with the chains forged by the timidity of some individuals.

Picture to yourselves, then, the new power, which we are presupposing, as well-disposed and as benevolent as ever you may wish; make it as good as God Himself; will you be able to impart to it divine understanding as well? Even though it wishes in all earnestness the greatest happiness and well-being of everyone, do you suppose that the greatest well-being it is able to conceive will be the same thing as German well-being? In regard to the main point which I have put before you today, I hope I have been thoroughly well understood by you. I hope that several, while they listened to me, thought and felt that I was only expressing in plain words what has always lain in their minds; I hope that the other Germans who will someday read this will have the same feeling—indeed, several Germans have said practically the same thing before I did, and the unconscious basis of the resistance that has been repeatedly manifested to a purely mechanical constitution and policy of the State has been the view of things which I have presented to you.

12

ADAM HEINRICH MÜLLER

Elements of Statecraft

1809

Born in Berlin, Adam Heinrich Müller (1779–1829) studied law and political science at Göttingen. He converted to Catholicism in 1805 and spent part of his career in the diplomatic service of the Austrian crown. His friend Joseph von Eichendorff wrote that Müller "mapped out a domain of his own, the application of Romanticism to the social and political conditions of life." In this excerpt from his major work, Elements of Statecraft, *Müller attacks revolutionary thought for its belief that the individual can voluntarily extricate himself from the community and transform it at will. In presenting society as a living, organic unity, Müller reveals the influence of the leading figures of European conservatism, especially Edmund Burke. Burke's* Reflections on the Revolution in France *(1790) had found a wide audience among German intellectuals, including the Romantics. Indeed, in 1798, Novalis had claimed, "Burke has written a revolutionary book against the Revolution." Influenced in part by Burke, Novalis's "Christianity or Europe" offers the vision of an organic, harmonious society as an antidote to the divisive, fragmented condition of the present day. Johann Gottlieb Fichte's* Addresses to the German Nation *likewise draws on the organic metaphor. Yet if Müller thus bears some resemblance to both Novalis and Fichte, Müller reveals none of Novalis's prophetic tone and none of Fichte's residual commitment to revolutionary ideals. In comparing these three writers, we may thus see the diverse political purposes that Romantic organicism could serve, and we find a measure of how quickly the radical impulses of early German Romanticism could pass into much more conservative forms.*

We must often return to the famous words of Archimedes: "Give me a position outside the earth and I will lift it from its hinges."—It is not

---

Adam Heinrich Müller, *Die Elemente der Staatskunst* (Vienna: Wiener Literarische Anstalt, 1922), 26–31. Translated by Warren Breckman.

easy to think of a false endeavor in life, the state, or science that is not eliminated by the sublime paradox of those great words.

Do not all the unhappy errors of the French Revolution meet (1) in the delusion that the individual can actually step out of the social bond and from outside topple and destroy what is unacceptable to him; that the individual can protest against the work of millennia; that he needs to acknowledge nothing in all the institutions that he encounters; in brief, that there is actually a position outside the state to which he can turn and where he can presage new directions for the great body of the state, make something wholly new from the old body and, instead of the old, imperfect but proven constitution prescribe a new one that is perfect, at least for the next fourteen days?

Is it not the case (2) that most political writers present themselves *either* as if they stand at the *beginning of all time* and as if the states were only now being founded; as if the great works of statecraft which we encounter in history were nothing more than pathetic experiments and history itself nothing other than a course of experimental politics; as if only now are states coming into the world that tackle the problem of governance? *Or* as if they stand at the *end of all time*, and as if the forefathers must acquiesce to what they—the last, wisest grandchildren, fat with the communal reason and experience of all earlier generations—decide concerning the works, the thousandfold statutes and dictums, indeed concerning the graves of the ancestors; in short, as if they really were the last or as if they could guarantee that their successors would accept all that they decided, because they knew in advance all that the future would need and desire? Do not such writers place themselves outside of the state? Do they not wish to lift the town hall from its foundations by means of a wisdom that they have in fact acquired from the town hall?

Finally, (3) where does the entirely false political idea come from, that "the state is a necessary invention, a mere institution of the common good, a human means of information, erected in order to avoid certain discomforts, a mutual security insurance which in an emergency people could live quite well without even if at the expense of some comfort and contentment? That the Legislator is supposed to stand outside his state, like the carpenter stands outside the furniture that he makes, while the customer—the needy nation—should come and select from among all the political furniture the most functional, comfortable, and modern; that he, the statesman, should lay in a stock for every taste?" Where does the general preference for the *concept* of the state come from other than from the fact that one imagines the observer and the actor, the scholar of the state and the politician, always outside the state, grasping and fondling it, and that one has not fathomed the great meaning of Archimedes' words, which apply equally well to physical and political mechanics?

To this triple error that I have depicted, we want to oppose a three-fold truth, and in such a way ground our view of the state on the nature of the thing itself.

(1) Just as every creation of nature is supposed to stand in the *midst* of nature; as every creature, when it wishes to confess the truth, imagines that the whole world moves around it; as no soul believes itself to stand outside nature or at its lowest level; as no worm thinks badly of itself:—so every human being stands in the midst of civic life, interwoven from all sides into the state. As little as he can step outside of himself, even so little can he escape from the state.

(2) Further, just as no one who is not coy and does not want to play a prophet or a Tacitus[1] will in his heart of hearts think badly of his own time and believe himself to be at the beginning or the end of the world, at its dawn or its twilight, but rather in the middle of time, living in the noonday of the world just like everyone else—; just so, every citizen stands in the middle of the state's lifetime, having behind him a past that he respects, before him a future for which he should care stretching equally into the distance. From these temporal bonds no one can escape without contradicting himself. We all complain to each other about the bad times, yearning in unhappy moments for past or coming times, and we would like to be our own ancestors or our own grandchildren. The contradiction is obvious and remains eternal.

(3) Finally, the state is not an artificial organization, not one among the thousands of inventions directed to the benefits and pleasures of civil life. Rather, the state is the whole of this civil life itself, necessary the moment there are people, unavoidable,—rooted in the nature of human beings, I would say, if it were not for the fact that human and civil existence are one and the same, and if with those words I would not simply say something superfluous.

. . .

Permit us to combine these three truths more inwardly and power-fully in a single truth and express it thus: *the human being is unthink-able outside the state.* "How!" I hear asked; "when man gives himself

---

[1] Roman historian (ca. 56–120 CE).

up to the most gentle and tender sensations of life within the family circle, of which the government can know nothing; when he fulfills silent and holy duties, which are attested before no other judge than his own heart; indeed, when he lives in deeper withdrawal, having devoted himself to the sciences—: in each of these cases, does man not stand truly outside the state in a place where the state cannot reach him?—Further: where did those first humans stand, who may have inhabited our earth long before some sort of social contract was even thinkable? What of the savage peoples of today, who have still not left the state of nature? What of a man who goes into exile either willingly or under compulsion? Is it not so, that just as many people and human concerns stand outside the state, as inside it?"—

All of these objections are very well grounded and drawn from daily experiences, from an almost universally disseminated style of thinking; however—what deep corruption of all opinions of the state glares out from this!—According to it, the state is nothing more than a single department of human affairs; man needs a house, courtyard, farm-hand, milk-maid, cow, and some tools, and among these tools are states, that is, great policing agencies, extensive Maréchausséen[2] so that he can safeguard all the large baggage that he must bring along on life's journey. Or: knowledge, the fine arts, friendship, love, domestic bliss—they are the essentials in the life of the cultivated man, and he exists for their sake. The state? All right, it is a necessary evil; an unfortunate makeshift in a world where there are few cultivated people and many good-for-nothing and hungry rabble who must be fended off.—Such depictions of the state were most widespread in Germany until general hardship reminded us that the gods have their seat elsewhere than in the little trivialities of elegant and domestic life; until, under the enormous movements of the age, an inkling came to even the most cowardly and feeble souls that people lack everything when they no longer feel the social bond or the state.—But the idea is still not sufficiently clear that the state is the need of all needs of the heart, the spirit and the body; that without the state, man cannot hear, see, think, feel, love, not only since the last civilized millennium, not only in Europe, but overall and in all times; in brief, *that he is inconceivable except in the state*. All great and deep souls have long recognized this; however, Voltaire's famous saying reveals that even lighter spirits, who were led by unmistakable social tact and brought up more

[2]French mounted police.

to cleverness than to wisdom, ultimately agree with this: "Celui qui n'ose regarder fixement les deux poles de la vie humaine, la religion et le gouvernement, n'est qu'un lâche."[3]

[3]"He who does not dare to look resolutely at the two poles of human life, religion and government, is nothing but a coward."

13

ERNST THEODOR AMADEUS HOFFMANN

Beethoven's Instrumental Music

1813

Of all the German Romantics, Ernst Theodor Amadeus Hoffmann (1776–1822) had perhaps the most varied career, working at different times as a Prussian civil servant, a theatrical music director and producer, and Supreme Court judge in Berlin. Hoffmann is today best remembered for his short stories, but he was also a composer of considerable talent. In addition, he wrote prolifically on music, frequently adopting the fictional persona of a brilliant but tormented musician and composer named Johannes Kreisler to communicate his ideas.

Hoffmann's stories typically mix supernatural and natural elements in such a way that the reader is continually left in ironic suspension between fantasy and reality. In Hoffmann's writings on music, as this excerpt exemplifies, this ironic vacillation is overshadowed by an ideal of pure transcendence attained through instrumental music. Hoffmann's exaltation of instrumental music differs sharply from the eighteenth-century view that such music offers pleasure and emotional arousal but ranks far below vocal music, which better communicates a meaningful "content." In reversing this aesthetic hierarchy, Hoffmann draws on Edmund Burke and Immanuel Kant's idea of the "sublime" to describe instrumental music as a revelation of the infinite. In Hoffmann's pantheon of musical genius, Ludwig van Beethoven (1770–1827) alone ful-

E. T. A. Hoffmann, "Beethoven's Instrumental Music," *E. T. A. Hoffmann's Musical Writings. Kreisleriana, the Poet and the Composer, Musical Criticism*, trans. Martyn Clarke and ed. David Charlton (New York: Cambridge University Press, 1989), 96–103.

fills his criteria for music as the consummate "Romantic" art. Beetho-ven's innovations were so radical that his contemporaries could scarcely find appropriate responses, but Hoffmann's writings mark the beginnings of a veritable Beethoven cult that dominated nineteenth-century musical culture. In "romanticizing" Beethoven, elevating the ideal of "absolute" instrumental music above vocal music and any form of natural imita-tion, and emphasizing the total unity of the artwork, Hoffmann pro-foundly shaped the terms of musical discourse for over a century.

When music is spoken of as an independent art, does not the term properly apply only to instrumental music, which scorns all aid, all admixture of other arts (poetry), and gives pure expression to its own peculiar artistic nature? It is the most romantic of all arts, one might almost say the only one that is genuinely romantic, since its only subject-matter is infinity. Orpheus's lyre opened the gates of Orcus. Music reveals to man an unknown realm, a world quite separate from the outer sensual world surrounding him, a world in which he leaves behind all precise feelings in order to embrace an inexpressible longing. . . .

In singing, where the poetry suggests precise moods through words, the magical power of music acts like the philosopher's miraculous elixir, a few drops of which make any drink so much more wonder-fully delicious. Any passion—love, hate, anger, despair, etc.—pre-sented to us in an opera is clothed by music in the purple shimmer of romanticism, so that even our mundane sensations take us out of the everyday into the realm of the infinite. Such is the power of music's spell that it grows ever stronger and can only burst the fetters of any other art.

It is certainly not merely an improvement in the means of expres-sion (perfection of instruments, greater virtuosity of players), but also a deeper awareness of the peculiar nature of music, that has enabled great composers to raise instrumental music to its present level.

[Wolfgang Amadeus] Mozart and [Joseph] Haydn, the creators of modern instrumental music, first showed us the art in its full glory; but the one who regarded it with total devotion and penetrated to its innermost nature is Beethoven. The instrumental compositions of all three masters breathe the same romantic spirit for the very reason that they all intimately grasp the essential nature of the art; yet the charac-ter of their compositions is markedly different. Haydn's compositions are dominated by a feeling of childlike optimism. His symphonies lead us through endless, green forest-glades, through a motley throng of happy people. Youths and girls sweep past dancing the round; laughing children, lying in wait behind trees and rose-bushes, teasingly throw flowers at each other. A world of love, of bliss, of eternal youth, as though before the Fall; no suffering, no pain; only sweet, melancholy longing for the beloved vision floating far off in the red glow of evening, neither approaching nor receding; and as long as it is there the night will not draw on, for the vision is the evening glow itself illuminating hill and glade.

Mozart leads us deep into the realm of spirits. Dread lies all about us, but withholds its torments and becomes more an intimation of infinity. We hear the gentle spirit-voices of love and melancholy, the night dissolves into a purple shimmer, and with inexpressible yearning we follow the flying figures kindly beckoning to us from the clouds to join their eternal dance of the spheres. (Mozart's Symphony in E flat major, known as the "Swan Song.")

In a similar way Beethoven's instrumental music unveils before us the realm of the mighty and the immeasurable. Here shining rays of light shoot through the darkness of night and we become aware of giant shadows swaying back and forth, moving ever closer around us and destroying *us* but not the pain of infinite yearning, in which every desire, leaping up in sounds of exultation, sinks back and disappears. Only in this pain, in which love, hope, and joy are consumed without being destroyed, which threatens to burst our hearts with a full-chorused cry of all the passions, do we live on as ecstatic visionaries.

Romantic sensibility is rare, and romantic talent even rarer, which is probably why so few are able to strike the lyre whose sound unlocks the wonderful realm of the romantic.

Haydn romantically apprehends the humanity in human life; he is more congenial, more comprehensible to the majority.

Mozart takes more as his province the superhuman, magical quality residing in the inner self.

Beethoven's music sets in motion the machinery of awe, of fear, of terror, of pain, and awakens that infinite yearning which is the essence of romanticism. He is therefore a purely romantic composer. Might this not explain why his vocal music is less successful, since it does not permit a mood of vague yearning but can only depict from the realm of the infinite those feelings capable of being described in words?

Beethoven's mighty genius intimidates the musical rabble; they try in vain to resist it. But wise judges, gazing about them with a superior air, assure us that we can take their word for it as men of great intellect and profound insight: the good Beethoven is by no means lacking in wealth and vigor of imagination, but he does not know how to control it! There is no question of selection and organization of ideas; following the so-called inspired method, he dashes everything down just as the feverish workings of his imagination dictate to him at that moment. But what if it is only *your* inadequate understanding which fails to grasp the inner coherence of every Beethoven composition? What if it is entirely *your* fault that the composer's language is clear to the initiated but not to you, and that the entrance to his innermost mysteries remains closed to you? In truth, he is fully the equal of Haydn and Mozart in rational awareness, his controlling self detached from the inner realm of sounds and ruling it in absolute authority. Our aesthetic overseers have often complained of a total lack of inner unity and inner coherence in Shakespeare, when profounder contemplation shows the splendid tree, leaves, blossom, and fruit as springing from the same seed; in the same way only the most penetrating study of Beethoven's instrumental music can reveal its high level of rational awareness, which is inseparable from true genius and nourished by study of the art.

Which instrumental work by Beethoven confirms all this to a higher degree than the immeasurably magnificent and profound Symphony in C minor? How this wonderful composition irresistibly draws the listener in an ever-rising climax into the spirit-realm of the infinite. . . .

What a deep impression your magnificent piano compositions have made on my mind, sublimest of composers![1] How pale and insignificant everything seems that does not come from you, from the intelligence of Mozart, or from the mighty genius of Sebastian Bach. What pleasure I felt on receiving your two splendid trios, Op. 70, for I knew that after they had been briefly rehearsed I would soon be able to savour their glories. . . .

I have now just repeated from memory some of the striking modulations from both trios on the piano. It is true that the piano remains an instrument more appropriate for harmony than for melody. The most refined expression of which the instrument is capable cannot bring a melody to life with the myriad nuances that the violinist's bow or the wind player's breath is able to call forth. The player struggles in vain with the insuperable difficulty presented to him by the mechanism, which by striking the strings causes them to vibrate and produce the notes. On the other hand there is probably no instrument (with the exception, that is, of the far more limited harp) that is able,

[1]Hoffmann here addresses Beethoven directly.

like the piano, to embrace the realm of harmony with full-voiced chords and unfold its treasures to the connoisseur in the most wonderful forms and shapes. When the composer's imagination has struck upon a complete sound-painting with rich groupings, brilliant highlights and deep shadows, he is able to bring it into being at the piano so that it emerges from his inner world in shining colors. A full score, that true musical book of charms preserving in its symbols all the miracles and mysteries of the most heterogeneous choir of instruments, comes to life at the piano under the hands of a master; and a piece skillfully performed from a score, including all its voices, may be compared to a good copper engraving taken from a great painting. For improvising, then, for playing from a score, for individual sonatas, chords, etc. the piano is excellently suited. Trios, quartets, quintets, and so on, with the usual stringed instruments added, also belong fully in the realm of piano compositions, because if they are composed in the proper manner, that is to say genuinely in four parts, five parts, and so forth, then they depend entirely on harmonic elaboration and automatically exclude brilliant passages for individual instruments. . . .

A composer has truly penetrated the secrets of harmony only if he can use its power to affect the human heart. For him the numerical relationships that remain lifeless formulas for the pedant without genius become magical prescriptions from which he conjures forth an enchanted world.

Despite the geniality that prevails particularly in the first trio, not even excluding its melancholy Largo, Beethoven's spirit remains serious and solemn. The master seems to be implying that the deeper mysteries can never be spoken of in ordinary words, even when the spirit feels itself joyfully uplifted in moments of intimate familiarity with them, but only in expressions of sublime splendor. The dance of the High Priests of Isis can only be a hymn of exultation.

If its effect is to be achieved solely by music in its own right, rather than by serving some specific dramatic purpose, instrumental music must avoid all facetiousness and clowning. The profounder mind seeks intimations of that joy, sublimer than the confines of this world allow, which comes to us from an unknown domain and kindles in the breast an inner bliss, a higher significance than feeble words, confined to the expression of banal earthly pleasures, can communicate. This gravity, which is found in all Beethoven's instrumental and piano music, rules out all the breakneck passages up and down the keyboard with both hands, all the odd leaps, the whimsical flourishes, the towering piles of notes supported by five or six leger lines, with which the most recent piano compositions are replete. In terms of mere dexterity, the piano works of this composer present no great difficulty, since the few runs, triplet figures and the like must be within the powers of any practiced player, and yet they are in many ways extremely difficult to perform. Many so-called virtuosos dismiss Beethoven's works, not only complaining "Very difficult!" but adding "And very ungrateful!" As far as difficulty is concerned, the proper performance of Beethoven's works demands nothing less than that one understands him, that one penetrates to his inner nature, and that in the knowledge of one's own state of grace one ventures boldly into the circle of magical beings that his irresistible spell summons forth. Whoever does not feel this grace within him, whoever regards music solely as amusement, as a pastime for idle hours, as a passing gratification for jaded ears, or as a vehicle for his own ostentation, let him keep away from it. Only such a one could utter the reproach "And very ungrateful!" The true artist lives only in the work that he conceives and then performs as the composer intended it. He disdains to let his own personality intervene in any way; all his endeavors are spent in quickening to vivid life, in a thousand shining colors, all the sublime effects and images the composer's magical authority enclosed within his work, so that they encircle us in bright rings of light, inflaming our imaginings, our innermost soul, and bear us speeding on the wing into the far-off spirit-realm of music.

14

ANNE-LOUISE-GERMAINE DE STAËL

The Spirit of Translation

1816

The Romantic era was a great age of translation. August Wilhelm Schlegel's translations of Shakespeare are just the most famous of the many translations that disseminated the works of world literature throughout Europe. Indeed, the very concept of "world literature" emerged in this period; yet, it was also a period of new and heightened awareness of the

Anne-Louise-Germaine de Staël, "The Spirit of Translation," trans. Joseph Luzzi, *The Romanic Review* 97, no. 3–4 (May–November 2006), 279–84.

uniqueness of each national culture, language, and historical period. Many of the theoretical questions that still concern translators originated in this Romantic search for a universally meaningful literature that nonetheless preserves the uniqueness of the original author's voice and an authentic sense of the cultural and linguistic context in which specific works are born.

Anne-Louise-Germaine de Staël (1766–1817) was active on both sides of this equation. Her studies of literature, especially On Germany *(1813), are pioneering works in literary sociology centered on the close connection between literature and national character. On Germany became an immediate success throughout Europe, and it ensured that German ideas came to dominate the international debate on Romanticism. Indeed, that one can speak of* European *Romanticism owes a great deal to Staël's efforts. "The Spirit of Translation" is a fine example of the great propagandist of Romanticism in action. Published in a Milan journal, the essay attempts to carry the spirit of the northern European Romantics into Italy, the culture that was, in the European imagination, most closely linked to the "classical" tradition because of its Roman and Renaissance past. By 1816, Staël's reputation as one of the most prominent writers in Europe was secure, a fame based not only on her literary scholarship but also on novels like* Corinne, or Italy *(1807). Her international prestige helped make the publication of her essay on translation the "most important event in the drama of Italian Romanticism," as Staël's translator Joseph Luzzi has written. The essay's catalyzing effect on Italian intellectual life can be traced in the many responses that Staël provoked.[1] "The Spirit of Translation" raises interesting questions about the international cultural politics of the early nineteenth century and brilliantly illustrates the Romantic awareness of the complexities of the act of translation.*

Staël's interest in the theoretical issues of translation may also have an autobiographical dimension. She was a consummate cosmopolitan used to navigating between cultures. Her Swiss father had served as Louis XVI's finance minister on the eve of the Revolution; her mother had presided over a Paris salon, where the young Germaine had interacted with some of the great intellectuals of Enlightenment France. She married the Swedish ambassador to Paris in 1785; that loveless marriage was eventually succeeded by relationships with August Wilhelm Schlegel, Benjamin Constant, and Simonde de Sismondi. Her support of

---

[1] For one such response, also translated by Joseph Luzzi, see Alessandro Manzoni, "Letter on Romanticism," *PMLA* 119, no. 2 (March 2004): 299–316.

a moderate constitutional monarchy set her at odds with both revolutionary republicans and Napoleon. From the mid-1790s to Napoleon's final defeat in 1815, Staël's life was marked by exile in England and Switzerland. Her Swiss estate became the meeting place of some of Europe's leading intellectuals and thus played an important role in the international exchange of ideas.

The greatest service we can render literature is to transport the masterpieces of the human intellect from one language to another. So few truly great works exist, and genius of any kind whatsoever is so rare a phenomenon that each modern nation would always remain impoverished if it were reduced to its own treasures. Besides, more than any other form of exchange, the circulation of ideas is the one most likely to prove advantageous.

During the Renaissance, scholars and even poets had thought to write in the same language, Latin, so that they would not need to be translated to be understood. This could have been advantageous for the sciences, whose development does not depend upon the charms of style. But the result was that many of Italy's scientific riches were lost upon the Italians themselves, for the majority of Italian readers understood only their native idiom. It is moreover necessary for authors to invent words that do not exist in ancient literature when they write about science and philosophy. The learned who wrote in Latin availed themselves of a language that was at once dead and artificial, while the poets stuck to purely classical expressions. Renaissance Italy, where Latin still echoed on the banks of the Tiber, possessed writers—including Fracastoro, Poliziano, and Sannazaro—who were close to Horace and Virgil in style. But if their reputations endure, their works find no readers today outside of erudite circles. The literary glory based on imitation is, after all, a sad one. These Latin poets of the Middle Ages were translated into Italian by their countrymen, for it is much more natural to prefer a language that refers to the emotions of real life rather than one that can only be recreated through study!

I admit that the best way to avoid translation would be to know all those languages in which the works of the great poets were composed: Greek, Latin, Italian, French, English, Spanish, Portuguese,

---

The notes in this selection are partly adapted from Joseph Luzzi's notes in *The Romanic Review*'s edition of "The Spirit of Translation."

and German. But such work would require a great deal of time and assistance, and we can never flatter ourselves into believing that erudition this difficult to attain can be universal. If we wish to benefit humankind, however, it is toward the universal that we must aspire. I would add that even if one were to understand the foreign languages, one might still experience a more familiar and intimate pleasure thanks to a fine translation done in one's own language. These naturalized beauties imbue a national literary style with new turns of phrase and original expressions. More efficiently than anything else, translations of foreign poets can protect a nation's literature from those banal modes of expression that are the most obvious signs of its decline.

In order to gain the most from this practice, however, we must not follow the French and impose our national style upon all that we translate. Even if, in so doing, we were to change all that we touch into gold, the ensuing results would provide little nourishment. Translating in the French manner would not produce new food for thought; it would only allow us to see the same face decorated with slightly different adornment. This rebuke, justly merited by the French, has its origins in all the manner of obstacles in their language in the art of writing verse. The rarity of rhyme, the uniformity of the verse, and the difficulty of the inversions trap the poet in a kind of circle, which necessarily brings back—if not with the same thoughts—at least the same hemistiches[2] and all kinds of poetic monotony that genius escapes when it reaches high, but that it cannot avoid in the transition, developments, and in sum all that prepares and reunites the great effects.

With the exception of the Abbé Delille's translation of the *Georgics*, one would be hard pressed to find a good verse translation in French literature.[3] The literary works of France contain some beautiful imitations and conquests that will always be confused with the nation's treasures. But it would be impossible to list a verse work that bears a trace of foreignness, and I also do not believe that such a work could ever be successful. If Abbé Delille's *Georgics* have been justly admired, it is because the French language can assimilate to Latin more easily than it can to any other language. French derives from Latin and has preserved its pomp and majesty, but the modern languages are so dif-

---

[2]In French versification, a "hemistiche" is half a line of verse, usually marked by a caesura or pause.

[3]Jacques Delille (1738–1813), French writer whose translation of Virgil's *Georgics* (1769) won widespread acclaim.

ferent that French poetry does not know how to accommodate them with any grace.

The English, whose language allows inversions and whose versification observes rules much less severe than those of the French, could have enriched their literature with both accurate and natural translations. Their great authors, however, did not undertake such an endeavor. The only one who did devote himself to this task, Alexander Pope, made two beautiful poems from the *Iliad* and the *Odyssey*. Yet he did not preserve that ancient simplicity that makes us feel the secret of Homer's superiority.[4]

In fact, it is unlikely that the genius of a single man, Homer, has surpassed for three thousand years the genius of all the other poets. Yet there was something primitive in the traditions, mores, opinions, and atmosphere of that ancient epoch, whose charm is inexhaustible. When we read Homer, it is this birth of humankind and childhood of time that renew in our soul the same sort of emotions we feel when we remember our infancy. Such emotions, indistinguishable from dreams of the golden age, compel us to prefer the most ancient of poets to all his successors. If you remove the simplicity of the first days of the world from his work, all that is unique in it disappears.

In Germany, many learned men have alleged that a single man did not compose the works of Homer, and that we should consider the *Iliad* and *Odyssey* to be a collection of the heroic chants sung in Greece to celebrate the conquest of Troy and the return of the victors.[5] It seems easy to me to combat this opinion, which above all the unity of the *Iliad* does not permit us to accept. For example, why would the *Iliad* have limited itself to the story of the wrath of Achilles? The subsequent events and the conquest of Troy that concludes them would naturally have been part of a collection of rhapsodies that, one imagines, belonged to various authors. The concept of the unity of one event, the wrath of Achilles, could only be the plan of a single man. I do not wish, however, to discuss a theory that, to prove or disprove,

---

[4]Alexander Pope's translations of the *Iliad* (1715–1720) and *Odyssey* (1723–1725) reflect the ornate diction and syntax of his Augustan literary circles. Staël's comment expresses the Romantic association of Homer's poetry with a primitive and robust age. The unruliness, spontaneity, and passion of the Homeric epics were quite to the liking of the Romantics, particularly in distinction to the more polished works of later Latin antiquity.

[5]Near the end of the eighteenth century, a heated debate broke out among German literary scholars over whether Homer ever actually existed and whether the *Iliad* and the *Odyssey* were composed by a single author or by different authors over a long period of time.

would require a frightening arsenal of erudition. We might at least admit, however, that Homer derives his principal greatness from his epoch, since it was believed that the ancient poets, or at least a great number of them, had worked upon the *Iliad*. This is further proof that the *Iliad* is the image of human society at a certain point in civilization, and that this work continues to bear more the mark of its age than of a single man.

The Germans did not limit themselves to this sort of erudite inquiry into the existence of Homer: they tried to bring him to life in their own culture, and [Johann Heinrich] Voss's version of Homer is acknowledged to be the most accurate in any language.[6] He employs the rhythm of the ancients, and people concur that his German hexameter follows nearly verbatim the Greek hexameter. A translation of this nature serves as a helpful guide to an accurate understanding of the ancient poem—but is it certain that the poem's charm, which neither rules nor study can ensure, has been entirely transported into the German language? The syllabic quantities of the *Iliad* have been preserved, but the aural harmony could not be the same. German poetry loses some of its natural sound when it follows the Greek model, and it is incapable of acquiring the beauty of musical language that was sung with the accompaniment of the lyre.

Of all the modern languages, Italian is the one that best lends itself to providing us with the sensations produced by the Homeric Greek. It is true that the Italian language lacks the same rhythm as the original; the hexameter can hardly be introduced into our modern idioms. The long and short syllables of the modern languages are not clearly delineated enough for us to be able to rival the Greeks in this regard. Italian words, however, exhibit a harmony that does not need the symmetry of dactyls and spondees, and grammatical construction in Italian is suited perfectly for the imitation of Greek inversions. Liberated from rhyme, *versi sciolti* [Italian blank verse] does not pose an obstacle to thought any more than prose does, as it completely maintains the grace and balance of poetry.

Of all the translations of Homer in Europe, Monti's is certainly the one that most closely approximates the pleasure that the original itself could have elicited.[7] [Vincenzo] Monti's work combines both pomp and simplicity: the most common everyday sayings, clothing, and ban-

---

[6]Voss's German translations of the *Odyssey* and *Iliad* appeared, respectively, in 1781 and 1793.
[7]Monti's Italian translation of the *Iliad* appeared in 1810.

quets are all elevated by the natural dignity of the expressions, and the greatest of circumstances are made accessible to us by the accuracy of the descriptions and facility of the style. Henceforth, nobody in Italy will translate the *Iliad*. In this work Homer has donned the mantle of Monti. And it seems to me that, even in the other countries of Europe, Monti's translation will give an idea of the pleasure that Homer can bring to the person who cannot elevate himself to the point of reading him in the original. Translating a poet does not mean picking up a compass and copying the dimensions of a building. It means filling a different instrument with the same breath of life. One demands even more the same kind of pleasure instead of perfectly similar traits.

It would be highly desirable, I believe, for the Italians to busy themselves with carefully translating the new poetry of the Germans and the English. Doing so would allow them to introduce a new literary genre to their countrymen, who for the most part are concerned with images taken from ancient mythology. Yet these mythological images are beginning to lose their appeal: paganism in poetry barely exists in the rest of Europe. For thought to progress in beautiful Italy, it must begin to look beyond the Alps, not to borrow but to learn, and not to imitate but to rid itself of certain commonplace forms that literature maintains as the official parlance of society—commonplace forms that banish also all natural truth.

If poetic translations can enrich *belles lettres*, theatrical translations can exercise an even greater influence, for the theater is truly the executive power of literature. A. W. Schlegel has produced a translation of Shakespeare that, by joining accuracy with inspiration, has something typically German in it. Transformed in such a way, the English text is performed in German theaters, where now Shakespeare and Friedrich Schiller have become fellow countrymen.[8] The same result could occur in Italy; the French dramatic authors are as close to the Italian taste as Shakespeare is to the German. And perhaps the Italians could successfully perform [Jean] Racine's *Athalie* at that beautiful theater in Milan, by adding the accompaniment of the admirable Italian music to the choruses. Even if one says that Italians do not go to the theater to listen but rather to gossip and meet their inner circles in the loges, it is nonetheless certain that listening every

---

[8]Friedrich Schiller (1759–1805) was one of the German language's greatest playwrights. His theatrical works include *The Robbers* (1781), *Don Carlos* (1787), the *Wallenstein* trilogy (1796–1799), *Maria Stuart* (1801), and *Wilhelm Tell* (1804).

day for five or so hours to the so-called lyrics of most Italian operas is, in the long term, a sure way to undermine the intellectual abilities of a nation. As long as [Giovanni Battista] Casti was producing comic operas and [Pietro] Metastasio was adapting such fine music to thoughts full of charm and elevation, no pleasure was lost [at the theater], and reason gained a great deal there.[9] If one can manage to elicit ideas and emotions through pleasure, one can shape the intellect with something serious and of lasting value, even in the midst of the habitual frivolity of social life, where people look to escape from themselves through the help of others.

Italian literature is now divided between the learned who sift and re-sift the ashes of the past to find some specks of gold in there, and the writers who trust in the harmony of their language to produce agreement without ideas and to put together exclamations, declarations, and invocations in which there is not a single word that either issues from the heart or arrives there. Would it not be then possible, through active emulation such as we find in successful theatrical works, to regain slowly originality of intellect and truthfulness of style, without which there can be neither literature nor any of the qualities necessary in order to have one.

The taste for sentimental drama has taken possession of the Italian theater. Instead of that cutting gaiety that used to reign on the Italian stage—and instead of those comic characters now considered classics throughout Europe—we now see performed from the first scene onward, pardon me for saying, the miserable spectacle of the most insipid assassinations imaginable. Are not these oft-repeated pleasures a poor form of education for a considerable number of people? The Italian taste in the fine arts is as simple as it is noble. But language is also a fine art, and we must imbue it with a suitable character. Language most intimately belongs to everything that constitutes humankind. And it would be easier to be deprived of paintings and monuments than of the feelings to which they should be dedicated.

Italians are extremely enthusiastic about their language. Great men have brought distinction to it; and these intellectual distinctions have been the sole pleasure, and often the sole consolation, of the Italian nation. In order for each reflective individual to believe that he is capable of self-improvement, all nations must take an active interest.

---

[9]Casti (1724–1803) authored numerous comic opera librettos and bawdy poems, including the satirical *The Talking Animals* (1802). The popular writer and librettist Metastasio (1698–1782) spent most of his career in the Viennese Habsburg court.

Some nations are military, others are political. The Italians need to assert their prominence through literature and fine arts. If not, their nation could fall into a kind of torpor, from which the sun itself might not be able to wake it.

15

MARY WOLLSTONECRAFT SHELLEY

Frankenstein: Or, the Modern Prometheus

1818

Mary Wollstonecraft Shelley (1797–1851) was the daughter of William Godwin and Mary Wollstonecraft, who died of an infection shortly after Mary's birth. Mary was seventeen when she met Percy Bysshe Shelley and eloped with him to postwar France, and she was nineteen when she wrote Frankenstein. *In the frequently reprinted preface that Mary Shelley wrote for the second edition, she recounts the novel's birth during the Shelleys' stay at Lord Byron's Swiss home in the summer of 1816. Day after day, bad weather kept the party indoors, so as a diversion, Byron proposed a competition to see who could write the best ghost story. Mary Shelley recalls how intimidated she was to be in contest with the two great poets, yet her efforts ultimately yielded the most enduringly popular of all English Romantic novels.*

The tale of Victor Frankenstein and the unhappy creature he so rashly brings to life is a gripping story, sharing many elements with the "gothic" thriller that was then such a popular genre. Yet its enduring power lies in the rich ambiguities of its allegorical meaning. Is Frankenstein *a cautionary tale about the excesses of rationalism and science or a parable about the egocentrism of Romanticism and its fantasy of the artist as a god-like creator? This excerpt comes from volume II, chapter X. Frankenstein, despairing over the path of destruction wrought by his creature, wanders high into the Alps, where he will eventually encounter the creature itself on a glacier. The passage offers a wonderful example of*

Mary Shelley, *Frankenstein*, Second Edition, ed. Johanna M. Smith (Boston and New York: Bedford/St. Martin's, 2000), 90–92.

a "sublime" landscape—a keystone of Romantic sensibility—and its effects on the human spirit. Set in the shadows of Mont Blanc, Mary Shelley's description warrants comparison with her husband's poem "Mont Blanc"; and with its strongly visual effects, this prose passage invites parallels with the alpine paintings of Romantic artists like J. M. W. Turner, Caspar David Friedrich, and Joseph Anton Koch.

Chapter X

I spent the following day roaming through the valley. I stood beside the sources of the Arveiron, which take their rise in a glacier, that with slow pace is advancing down from the summit of the hills, to barricade the valley. The abrupt sides of vast mountains were before me; the icy wall of the glacier overhung me; a few shattered pines were scattered around; and the solemn silence of this glorious presence-chamber of imperial Nature was broken only by the brawling waves, or the fall of some vast fragment, the thunder sound of the avalanche, or the cracking, reverberated along the mountains, of the accumulated ice, which, through the silent working of immutable laws, was ever and anon rent and torn, as if it had been but a plaything in their hands. These sublime and magnificent scenes afforded me the greatest consolation that I was capable of receiving. They elevated me from all littleness of feeling; and although they did not remove my grief, they subdued and tranquillized it. In some degree, also, they diverted my mind from the thoughts over which it had brooded for the last month. I retired to rest at night; my slumbers, as it were, waited on and ministered to by the assemblance of grand shapes which I had contemplated during the day. They congregated round me; the unstained snowy mountaintop, the glittering pinnacle, the pine woods, and ragged bare ravine; the eagle, soaring amidst the clouds—they all gathered round me, and bade me be at peace.

Where had they fled when the next morning I awoke? All of soul-inspiriting fled with sleep, and dark melancholy clouded every thought. The rain was pouring in torrents, and thick mists hid the summits of the mountains, so that I even saw not the faces of those mighty friends. Still I would penetrate their misty veil, and seek them in their cloudy retreats. What were rain and storm to me? My mule was brought to the door, and I resolved to ascend to the summit of Montanvert. I remembered the effect that the view of the tremendous and ever-moving glacier had produced upon my mind when I first saw it. It had then filled me with a sublime ecstasy, that gave wings to the soul, and allowed it to soar from the obscure world to light and joy. The sight of the awful and majestic in nature had indeed always the effect of solemnizing my mind, and causing me to forget the passing cares of life. I determined to go without a guide, for I was well acquainted with the path, and the presence of another would destroy the solitary grandeur of the scene.

The ascent is precipitous, but the path is cut into continual and short windings, which enable you to surmount the perpendicularity of the mountain. It is a scene terrifically desolate. In a thousand spots the traces of the winter avalanche may be perceived, where trees lie broken and strewed on the ground; some entirely destroyed, others bent, leaning upon the jutting rocks of the mountain, or transversely upon other trees. The path, as you ascend higher, is intersected by ravines of snow, down which stones continually roll from above; one of them is particularly dangerous, as the slightest sound, such as even speaking in a loud voice, produces a concussion of air sufficient to draw destruction upon the head of the speaker. The pines are not tall or luxuriant, but they are sombre, and add an air of severity to the scene. I looked on the valley beneath; vast mists were rising from the rivers which ran through it, and curling in thick wreaths around the opposite mountains, whose summits were hid in the uniform clouds, while rain poured from the dark sky, and added to the melancholy impression I received from the objects around me. Alas! why does man boast of sensibilities superior to those apparent in the brute; it only renders them more necessary beings. If our impulses were confined to hunger, thirst, and desire, we might be nearly free; but now we are moved by every wind that blows, and a chance word or scene that that word may convey to us.

> We rest; a dream has power to poison sleep.
>   We rise; one wand'ring thought pollutes the day.
> We feel, conceive, or reason; laugh or weep,
>   Embrace fond woe, or cast our cares away;
> It is the same: for, be it joy or sorrow,
>   The path of its departure still is free.
> Man's yesterday may ne'er be like his morrow;
>   Nought may endure but mutability![1]

[1]The final section of Percy Bysshe Shelley's "Mutability" (1816).

It was nearly noon when I arrived at the top of the ascent. For some time I sat upon the rock that overlooks the sea of ice. A mist covered both that and the surrounding mountains. Presently a breeze dissipated the cloud, and I descended upon the glacier. The surface is very uneven, rising like the waves of a troubled sea, descending low, and interspersed by rifts that sink deep. The field of ice is almost a league in width, but I spent nearly two hours in crossing it. The opposite mountain is a bare perpendicular rock. From the side where I now stood Montanvert was exactly opposite, at the distance of a league; and above it rose Mont Blanc, in awful majesty. I remained in a recess of the rock, gazing on this wonderful and stupendous scene. The sea, or rather the vast river of ice, wound among its dependent mountains, whose aerial summits hung over its recesses. Their icy and glittering peaks shone in the sunlight over the clouds. My heart, which was before sorrowful, now swelled with something like joy; I exclaimed — "Wandering spirits, if indeed ye wander, and do not rest in your narrow beds, allow me this faint happiness, or take me, as your companion, away from the joys of life."

16

PERCY BYSSHE SHELLEY

A Defence of Poetry

1821

Percy Bysshe Shelley (1792–1822) was the son of a Whig Member of Parliament and heir to a baronetcy. He was educated at Eton and then sent to Oxford, which expelled him after six months for his pamphlet The Necessity of Atheism *(1811). Constantly fighting with his father over money, political and religious matters, and personal behavior, his strained family relations broke entirely when Shelley eloped with Harriet Westbrook in 1811. He left her in 1814 for Mary Wollstonecraft and*

Percy Bysshe Shelley, "A Defence of Poetry," *Shelley's Literary and Philosophic Criticism* (London: H. Frowde, 1909), 120–59.

William Godwin's daughter Mary, whom Shelley married after Harriet committed suicide. Shelley's political and religious views, scandalous love life, and constant money troubles made self-imposed exile on the continent preferable to life in England. Turbulent as those years were, Shelley was remarkably productive, composing lyrical poetry, dramas, prose essays, and radical political tracts. He died in 1822 in a boating accident in Italy.

"A Defence of Poetry" replies to "The Four Ages of Poetry" (1820), by Shelley's acquaintance, the satirist Thomas Love Peacock. Peacock, whose novel Nightmare Abbey *(1818) includes humorous lampoons of Samuel Taylor Coleridge and Shelley, argued that poetry belongs properly to primitive stages of humankind but loses its utility in more advanced societies. Peacock's half-serious diatribe provoked Shelley into a ringing defense of poetry's moral and social function. In this excerpt, Shelley's views on the imagination, the sources of inspiration, the origins of poetry, and the status of poets share much in common with the older generation of English Romantics; but Shelley had long before dismissed the older poets as reactionaries. In contrast to William Wordsworth's "Preface to* Lyrical Ballads,*" Shelley's "Defence of Poetry" is much more explicit in criticizing present-day politics, commercial society, and the utilitarian spirit; and, in insisting on the power of poetry to transform social and political relations, Shelley expresses a utopian hope that is absent from his older contemporaries.*

According to one mode of regarding those two classes of mental action, which are called reason and imagination, the former may be considered as mind contemplating the relations borne by one thought to another, however produced; and the latter, as mind acting upon those thoughts so as to color them with its own light, and composing from them, as from elements, other thoughts, each containing within itself the principle of its own integrity. The one is τὸ ποιεῖν, or the principle of synthesis, and has for its objects those forms which are common to universal nature and existence itself; the other is the τὸ λογίζειν, or the principle of analysis, and its action regards the relations of things, simply as relations; considering thoughts, not in their integral unity, but as the algebraical representations which conduct to certain general results. Reason is the enumeration of quantities already known; imagination is the perception of the value of those quantities, both separately and as a whole. Reason respects the differences, and imagination the similitudes of things. Reason is to the imagination as the instrument to the agent, as the body to the spirit, as the shadow to the substance.

Poetry, in a general sense, may be defined to be "the expression of the imagination": and poetry is connate with the origin of man. Man is an instrument over which a series of external and internal impressions are driven, like the alternations of an ever-changing wind over an Aeolian lyre, which move it by their motion to ever-changing melody. But there is a principle within the human being, and perhaps within all sentient beings, which acts otherwise than in the lyre, and produces not melody alone, but harmony, by an internal adjustment of the sounds or motions thus excited to the impressions which excite them. It is as if the lyre could accommodate its chords to the motions of that which strikes them, in a determined proportion of sound; even as the musician can accommodate his voice to the sound of the lyre. A child at play by itself will express its delight by its voice and motions; and every inflection of tone and every gesture will bear exact relation to a corresponding antitype in the pleasurable impressions which awakened it; it will be the reflected image of that impression; and as the lyre trembles and sounds after the wind has died away, so the child seeks, by prolonging in its voice and motions the duration of the effect, to prolong also a consciousness of the cause. In relation to the objects which delight a child, these expressions are, what poetry is to higher objects. The savage (for the savage is to ages what the child is to years) expresses the emotions produced in him by surrounding objects in a similar manner; and language and gesture, together with plastic or pictorial imitation, become the image of the combined effect of those objects, and of his apprehension of them. Man in society, with all his passions and his pleasures, next becomes the object of the passions and pleasures of man; an additional class of emotions produces an augmented treasure of expressions; and language, gesture, and the imitative arts, become at once the representation and the medium, the pencil and the picture, the chisel and the statue, the chord and the harmony. The social sympathies, or those laws from which, as from its elements, society results, begin to develop themselves from the moment that two human beings coexist; the future is contained within the present, as the plant within the seed; and equality, diversity, unity, contrast, mutual dependence, become the principles alone capable of affording the motives according to which the will of a social being is determined to action, inasmuch as he is social; and constitute pleasure in sensation, virtue in sentiment, beauty in art, truth in reasoning, and love in the intercourse of kind. Hence men, even in the infancy of society, observe a certain order in their words and actions, distinct from that of the objects and the impressions represented by them, all expression being subject to the laws of that from which it proceeds. . . .

[The poet's] language is vitally metaphorical; that is, it marks the before unapprehended relations of things and perpetuates their apprehension, until the words which represent them become, through time, signs for portions or classes of thoughts instead of pictures of integral thoughts; and then if no new poets should arise to create afresh the associations which have been thus disorganized, language will be dead to all the nobler purposes of human intercourse. These similitudes or relations are finely said by Lord Bacon to be "the same footsteps of nature impressed upon the various subjects of the world";[1] and he considers the faculty which perceives them as the storehouse of axioms common to all knowledge. In the infancy of society every author is necessarily a poet, because language itself is poetry; and to be a poet is to apprehend the true and the beautiful, in a word, the good which exists in the relation, subsisting, first between existence and perception, and secondly between perception and expression. Every original language near to its source is in itself the chaos of a cyclic poem: the copiousness of lexicography and the distinctions of grammar are the works of a later age, and are merely the catalogue and the form of the creations of poetry.

But poets, or those who imagine and express this indestructible order, are not only the authors of language and of music, of the dance, and architecture, and statuary, and painting; they are the institutors of laws, and the founders of civil society, and the inventors of the arts of life, and the teachers, who draw into a certain propinquity with the beautiful and the true, that partial apprehension of the agencies of the invisible world which is called religion. Hence all original religions are allegorical, or susceptible of allegory, and, like Janus, have a double face of false and true. Poets, according to the circumstances of the age and nation in which they appeared, were called, in the earlier epochs of the world, legislators, or prophets: a poet essentially comprises and unites both these characters. For he not only beholds intensely the present as it is, and discovers those laws according to which present things ought to be ordered, but he beholds the future in the present, and his thoughts are the germs of the flower and the fruit of latest time. Not that I assert poets to be prophets in the gross sense of the

---

[1] *De Augment. Scient.*, cap. i, lib. iii. [Shelley's note]

word, or that they can foretell the form as surely as they foreknow the spirit of events: such is the pretense of superstition, which would make poetry an attribute of prophecy, rather than prophecy an attribute of poetry. A poet participates in the eternal, the infinite, and the one; as far as relates to his conceptions, time and place and numbers are not. . . .

Language, color, form, and religious and civil habits of action, are all the instruments and materials of poetry; they may be called poetry by that figure of speech which considers the effect as a synonym of the cause. But poetry in a more restricted sense expresses those arrangements of language, and especially metrical language, which are created by that imperial faculty, whose throne is curtained within the invisible nature of man. And this springs from the nature itself of language, which is a more direct representation of the actions and passions of our internal being, and is susceptible of more various and delicate combinations, than color, form, or motion, and is more plastic and obedient to the control of that faculty of which it is the creation. For language is arbitrarily produced by the imagination, and has relation to thoughts alone; but all other materials, instruments, and conditions of art, have relations among each other, which limit and interpose between conception and expression. . . .

The whole objection, however, of the immorality of poetry rests upon a misconception of the manner in which poetry acts to produce the moral improvement of man. Ethical science arranges the elements which poetry has created, and propounds schemes and proposes examples of civil and domestic life: nor is it for want of admirable doctrines that men hate, and despise, and censure, and deceive, and subjugate one another. But poetry acts in another and diviner manner. It awakens and enlarges the mind itself by rendering it the receptacle of a thousand unapprehended combinations of thought. Poetry lifts the veil from the hidden beauty of the world, and makes familiar objects be as if they were not familiar; it reproduces all that it represents, and the impersonations clothed in its Elysian light stand thenceforward in the minds of those who have once contemplated them, as memorials of that gentle and exalted content which extends itself over all thoughts and actions with which it coexists. The great secret of morals is love; or a going out of our own nature, and an identification of ourselves with the beautiful which exists in thought, action, or person, not our own. A man, to be greatly good, must imagine intensely and comprehensively; he must put himself in the place of another and of many others; the pains and pleasures of his species must become his own.

The great instrument of moral good is the imagination; and poetry administers to the effect by acting upon the cause. Poetry enlarges the circumference of the imagination by replenishing it with thoughts of ever new delight, which have the power of attracting and assimilating to their own nature all other thoughts, and which form new intervals and interstices whose void for ever craves fresh food. Poetry strengthens the faculty which is the organ of the moral nature of man, in the same manner as exercise strengthens a limb. . . . Poetry ever communicates all the pleasure which men are capable of receiving: it is ever still the light of life; the source of whatever of beautiful or generous or true can have place in an evil time. It will readily be confessed that those among the luxurious citizens of Syracuse and Alexandria, who were delighted with the poems of Theocritus, were less cold, cruel, and sensual than the remnant of their tribe. But corruption must utterly have destroyed the fabric of human society before poetry can ever cease. The sacred links of that chain have never been entirely disjoined, which descending through the minds of many men is attached to those great minds, whence as from a magnet the invisible effluence is sent forth, which at once connects, animates, and sustains the life of all. It is the faculty which contains within itself the seeds at once of its own and of social renovation. . . .

But poets have been challenged to resign the civic crown to reasoners and mechanists. . . . It is admitted that the exercise of the imagination is most delightful, but it is alleged that that of reason is more useful. Let us examine as the grounds of this distinction, what is here meant by utility. Pleasure or good, in a general sense, is that which the consciousness of a sensitive and intelligent being seeks, and in which, when found, it acquiesces. There are two kinds of pleasure, one durable, universal and permanent; the other transitory and particular. Utility may either express the means of producing the former or the latter. In the former sense, whatever strengthens and purifies the affections, enlarges the imagination, and adds spirit to sense, is useful. But a narrower meaning may be assigned to the word utility, confining it to express that which banishes the importunity of the wants of our animal nature, the surrounding [of] men with security of life, the dispersing [of] the grosser delusions of superstition, and the conciliating [of] such a degree of mutual forbearance among men as may consist with the motives of personal advantage.

Undoubtedly the promoters of utility, in this limited sense, have their appointed office in society. They follow the footsteps of poets, and copy the sketches of their creations into the book of common life.

They make space, and give time. Their exertions are of the highest value, so long as they confine their administration of the concerns of the inferior powers of our nature within the limits due to the superior ones. But whilst the skeptic destroys gross superstitions, let him spare to deface, as some of the French writers have defaced, the eternal truths charactered upon the imaginations of men. Whilst the mechanist abridges, and the political economist combines labor, let them beware that their speculations, for want of correspondence with those first principles which belong to the imagination, do not tend, as they have in modern England, to exasperate at once the extremes of luxury and want. They have exemplified the saying, "To him that hath, more shall be given; and from him that hath not, the little that he hath shall be taken away." The rich have become richer, and the poor have become poorer; and the vessel of the state is driven between the Scylla and Charybdis of anarchy and despotism. Such are the effects which must ever flow from an unmitigated exercise of the calculating faculty.

It is difficult to define pleasure in its highest sense; the definition involving a number of apparent paradoxes. For, from an inexplicable defect of harmony in the constitution of human nature, the pain of the inferior is frequently connected with the pleasures of the superior portions of our being. Sorrow, terror, anguish, despair itself, are often the chosen expressions of an approximation of the highest good. Our sympathy in tragic fiction depends on this principle; tragedy delights by affording a shadow of the pleasure which exists in pain. This is the source also of the melancholy which is inseparable from the sweetest melody. The pleasure that is in sorrow is sweeter than the pleasure of pleasure itself. And hence the saying, "It is better to go to the house of mourning, than to the house of mirth." Not that this highest species of pleasure is necessarily linked with pain. The delight of love and friendship, the ecstasy of the admiration of nature, the joy of the perception and still more of the creation of poetry, is often wholly unalloyed.

The production and assurance of pleasure in this highest sense is true utility. Those who produce and preserve this pleasure are poets or poetical philosophers.

The exertions of [John] Locke, [David] Hume, [Edward] Gibbon, Voltaire, [Jean-Jacques] Rousseau,[2] and their disciples, in favor of

---

[2]Although Rousseau has been thus classed, he was essentially a poet. The others, even Voltaire, were mere reasoners. [Shelley's note]

oppressed and deluded humanity, are entitled to the gratitude of mankind. Yet it is easy to calculate the degree of moral and intellectual improvement which the world would have exhibited, had they never lived. A little more nonsense would have been talked for a century or two; and perhaps a few more men, women, and children, burnt as heretics. We might not at this moment have been congratulating each other on the abolition of the Inquisition in Spain. But it exceeds all imagination to conceive what would have been the moral condition of the world if neither Dante, Petrarch, Boccaccio, Chaucer, Shakespeare, Calderon, Lord Bacon, nor Milton, had ever existed; if Raphael and Michael Angelo had never been born; if the Hebrew poetry had never been translated; if a revival of the study of Greek literature had never taken place; if no monuments of ancient sculpture had been handed down to us; and if the poetry of the religion of the ancient world had been extinguished together with its belief. The human mind could never, except by the intervention of these excitements, have been awakened to the invention of the grosser sciences, and that application of analytical reasoning to the aberrations of society, which it is now attempted to exalt over the direct expression of the inventive and creative faculty itself.

We have more moral, political and historical wisdom, than we know how to reduce into practice; we have more scientific and economical knowledge than can be accommodated to the just distribution of the produce which it multiplies. The poetry in these systems of thought, is concealed by the accumulation of facts and calculating processes. There is no want of knowledge respecting what is wisest and best in morals, government, and political economy, or at least, what is wiser and better than what men now practice and endure. But we let "*I dare not* wait upon *I would,* like the poor cat in the adage." We want the creative faculty to imagine that which we know; we want the generous impulse to act that which we imagine; we want the poetry of life: our calculations have outrun conception; we have eaten more than we can digest. The cultivation of those sciences which have enlarged the limits of the empire of man over the external world, has, for want of the poetical faculty, proportionally circumscribed those of the internal world; and man, having enslaved the elements, remains himself a slave. To what but a cultivation of the mechanical arts in a degree disproportioned to the presence of the creative faculty, which is the basis of all knowledge, is to be attributed the abuse of all invention for abridging and combining labor, to the exasperation of the inequality of mankind? From what other cause has it arisen that the discoveries which should have lightened, have added a weight to the curse imposed on Adam? Poetry, and the principle of Self, of which money is the visible incarnation, are the God and Mammon of the world.

The functions of the poetical faculty are two-fold; by one it creates new materials of knowledge and power and pleasure; by the other it engenders in the mind a desire to reproduce and arrange them according to a certain rhythm and order which may be called the beautiful and the good. The cultivation of poetry is never more to be desired than at periods when, from an excess of the selfish and calculating principle, the accumulation of the materials of external life exceed the quantity of the power of assimilating them to the internal laws of human nature. The body has then become too unwieldy for that which animates it.

Poetry is indeed something divine. It is at once the center and circumference of knowledge; it is that which comprehends all science, and that to which all science must be referred. It is at the same time the root and blossom of all other systems of thought; it is that from which all spring, and that which adorns all; and that which, if blighted, denies the fruit and the seed, and withholds from the barren world the nourishment and the succession of the scions of the tree of life. It is the perfect and consummate surface and bloom of all things; it is as the odor and the color of the rose to the texture of the elements which compose it, as the form and splendor of unfaded beauty to the secrets of anatomy and corruption. What were virtue, love, patriotism, friendship—what were the scenery of this beautiful universe which we inhabit; what were our consolations on this side of the grave—and what were our aspirations beyond it, if poetry did not ascend to bring light and fire from those eternal regions where the owl-winged faculty of calculation dare not ever soar? Poetry is not like reasoning, a power to be exerted according to the determination of the will. A man cannot say, "I will compose poetry." The greatest poet even cannot say it; for the mind in creation is as a fading coal, which some invisible influence, like an inconstant wind, awakens to transitory brightness; this power arises from within, like the color of a flower which fades and changes as it is developed, and the conscious portions of our natures are unprophetic either of its approach or its departure. Could this influence be durable in its original purity and force, it is impossible to predict the greatness of the results; but when composition begins, inspiration is already on the decline, and the most glorious poetry that has ever been communicated to the world is probably a feeble shadow of the original conceptions of the poet. I appeal to the greatest poets of the present day, whether it is not an error to assert that the finest passages of poetry are produced by labor and study. . . .

Poetry is the record of the best and happiest moments of the happiest and best minds. We are aware of evanescent visitations of thought and feeling sometimes associated with place or person, sometimes regarding our own mind alone, and always arising unforeseen and departing unbidden, but elevating and delightful beyond all expression: so that even in the desire and regret they leave, there cannot but be pleasure, participating as it does in the nature of its object. It is as it were the interpenetration of a diviner nature through our own; but its footsteps are like those of a wind over the sea, which the coming calm erases, and whose traces remain only, as on the wrinkled sand which paves it. . . . Poetry thus makes immortal all that is best and most beautiful in the world; it arrests the vanishing apparitions which haunt the interlunations of life, and veiling them, or in language or in form, sends them forth among mankind, bearing sweet news of kindred joy to those with whom their sisters abide—abide, because there is no portal of expression from the caverns of the spirit which they inhabit into the universe of things. Poetry redeems from decay the visitations of the divinity in man.

Poetry turns all things to loveliness; it exalts the beauty of that which is most beautiful, and it adds beauty to that which is most deformed; it marries exultation and horror, grief and pleasure, eternity and change; it subdues to union under its light yoke, all irreconcilable things. It transmutes all that it touches, and every form moving within the radiance of its presence is changed by wondrous sympathy to an incarnation of the spirit which it breathes: its secret alchemy turns to potable gold the poisonous waters which flow from death through life; it strips the veil of familiarity from the world, and lays bare the naked and sleeping beauty, which is the spirit of its forms.

All things exist as they are perceived; at least in relation to the percipient. "The mind is its own place, and of itself can make a heaven of hell, a hell of heaven." But poetry defeats the curse which binds us to be subjected to the accident of surrounding impressions. And whether it spreads its own figured curtain, or withdraws life's dark veil from before the scene of things, it equally creates for us a being within our being. It makes us the inhabitants of a world to which the familiar world is a chaos. It reproduces the common universe of which we are portions and percipients, and it purges from our inward sight the film of familiarity which obscures from us the wonder of our being. It compels us to feel that which we perceive, and to imagine that which we know. It creates anew the universe, after it has been annihilated in our minds by the recurrence of impressions blunted by reiteration. . . .

Poets are the hierophants of an unapprehended inspiration; the mirrors of the gigantic shadows which futurity casts upon the present; the words which express what they understand not; the trumpets which sing to battle, and feel not what they inspire; the influence which is moved not, but moves. Poets are the unacknowledged legislators of the world.

17

PERCY BYSSHE SHELLEY

Mont Blanc: Lines Written in the Vale of Chamouni

1816

Percy Bysshe Shelley's optimism, exemplified in "A Defence of Poetry," was complicated by a certain skepticism expressed in his work. As his poem "Mont Blanc" shows, Shelley's soaring idealism competes with the threat of despair, just as the image of an empowering correspondence between nature and mind contends with the possibility of an unbridgeable gap between the human mind's imaginings and a colossal vastness that does not in fact speak to humans.

I.

The everlasting universe of things
Flows through the mind, and rolls its rapid waves,
Now dark—now glittering—now reflecting gloom—
Now lending splendour, where from secret springs
The source of human thought its tribute brings
Of waters,—with a sound but half its own,

Percy Bysshe Shelley, "Mont Blanc," *Shelley's Poetry and Prose*, 2nd ed., ed. Donald H. Reiman and Neil Fraistat (New York: W. W. Norton, 2002), 97–101.

Such as a feeble brook will oft assume
In the wild woods, among the mountains lone,
Where waterfalls around it leap for ever,
Where woods and winds contend, and a vast river
Over its rocks ceaselessly bursts and raves.

II.

Thus thou, Ravine of Arve — dark, deep Ravine —
Thou many-coloured, many-voiced vale,
Over whose pines, and crags, and caverns sail
Fast cloud shadows and sunbeams: awful scene,
Where Power in likeness of the Arve comes down
From the ice gulphs that gird his secret throne,
Bursting through these dark mountains like the flame
Of lightning through the tempest; — thou dost lie,
Thy giant brood of pines around thee clinging,
Children of elder time, in whose devotion
The chainless winds still come and ever came
To drink their odours, and their mighty swinging
To hear — an old and solemn harmony;
Thine earthly rainbows stretched across the sweep
Of the ethereal waterfall, whose veil
Robes some unsculptured image; the strange sleep
Which when the voices of the desert fail
Wraps all in its own deep eternity; —
Thy caverns echoing to the Arve's commotion,
A loud, lone sound no other sound can tame;
Thou art pervaded with that ceaseless motion,
Thou art the path of that unresting sound —
Dizzy Ravine! and when I gaze on thee
I seem as in a trance sublime and strange
To muse on my own separate phantasy,
My own, my human mind, which passively
Now renders and receives fast influencings,
Holding an unremitting interchange
With the clear universe of things around;
One legion of wild thoughts, whose wandering wings
Now float above thy darkness, and now rest
Where that or thou art no unbidden guest,
In the still cave of the witch Poesy,
Seeking among the shadows that pass by

Ghosts of all things that are, some shade of thee,
Some phantom, some faint image; till the breast
From which they fled recalls them, thou art there!

III.

Some say that gleams of a remoter world
Visit the soul in sleep,—that death is slumber,
And that its shapes the busy thoughts outnumber
Of those who wake and live.—I look on high;
Has some unknown omnipotence unfurled
The veil of life and death? or do I lie
In dream, and does the mightier world of sleep
Spread far around and inaccessibly
Its circles? For the very spirit fails,
Driven like a homeless cloud from steep to steep
That vanishes among the viewless gales!
Far, far above, piercing the infinite sky,
Mont Blanc appears,—still, snowy, and serene—
Its subject mountains their unearthly forms
Pile around it, ice and rock; broad vales between
Of frozen floods, unfathomable deeps,
Blue as the overhanging heaven, that spread
And wind among the accumulated steeps;
A desert peopled by the storms alone,
Save when the eagle brings some hunter's bone,
And the wolf tracks her there—how hideously
Its shapes are heaped around! rude, bare, and high,
Ghastly, and scarred, and riven.—Is this the scene
Where the old Earthquake-daemon taught her young
Ruin? Were these their toys? or did a sea
Of fire envelop once this silent snow?
None can reply—all seems eternal now.
The wilderness has a mysterious tongue

(Opposite) **Figure 6.** *J. M. W. Turner,* Bonneville, Savoy, with Mont Blanc, *1803*

The Alps were a favorite destination for Romantic artists, and Mont Blanc was the very incarnation of the Romantic idea of the sublime.

Oil on canvas. Overall: 36¼ × 48½ in. (92.07 × 123.19 cm.) Dallas Museum of Art, Foundation for the Arts Collection, gift of Nancy Hamon in memory of Jake L. Hamon with additional donations from Mrs. Eugene D. McDermott, Mrs. James H. Clark, Mrs. Edward Marcus, and the Leland Fikes Foundation, Inc.

Which teaches awful doubt, or faith so mild,
So solemn, so serene, that man may be
But for such faith with nature reconciled;
Thou hast a voice, great Mountain, to repeal
Large codes of fraud and woe; not understood
By all, but which the wise, and great, and good
Interpret, or make felt, or deeply feel.

IV.

The fields, the lakes, the forests, and the streams,
Ocean, and all the living things that dwell
Within the daedal[1] earth; lightning, and rain,
Earthquake, and fiery flood, and hurricane,
The torpor of the year when feeble dreams
Visit the hidden buds, or dreamless sleep
Holds every future leaf and flower; — the bound
With which from that detested trance they leap;
The works and ways of man, their death and birth,
And that of him and all that his may be;
All things that move and breathe with toil and sound
Are born and die; revolve, subside and swell.
Power dwells apart in its tranquillity
Remote, serene, and inaccessible:
And *this*, the naked countenance of earth,
On which I gaze, even these primeval mountains
Teach the adverting mind. The glaciers creep
Like snakes that watch their prey, from their far fountains,
Slow rolling on; there, many a precipice,
Frost and the Sun in scorn of mortal power
Have piled: dome, pyramid, and pinnacle,
A city of death, distinct with many a tower
And wall impregnable of beaming ice.
Yet not a city, but a flood of ruin
Is there, that from the boundaries of the sky
Rolls its perpetual stream; vast pines are strewing
Its destined path, or in the mangled soil

---

[1]Complex, varied, or intricate in form and invention. Shelley used "daedal" frequently. Here it strongly echoes Edmund Spenser, *The Faerie Queene* (1590), Book IV, Canto X, 45.

Branchless and shattered stand: the rocks, drawn down
From yon remotest waste, have overthrown
The limits of the dead and living world,
Never to be reclaimed. The dwelling-place
Of insects, beasts, and birds, becomes its spoil;
Their food and their retreat for ever gone,
So much of life and joy is lost. The race
Of man, flies far in dread; his work and dwelling
Vanish, like smoke before the tempest's stream,
And their place is not known. Below, vast caves
Shine in the rushing torrents' restless gleam,
Which from those secret chasms in tumult welling
Meet in the vale, and one majestic River,
The breath and blood of distant lands,[2] for ever
Rolls its loud waters to the ocean waves,
Breathes its swift vapours to the circling air.

V.

Mont Blanc yet gleams on high: — the power is there,
The still and solemn power of many sights,
And many sounds, and much of life and death.
In the calm darkness of the moonless nights,
In the lone glare of day, the snows descend
Upon that Mountain; none beholds them there,
Nor when the flakes burn in the sinking sun,
Or the star-beams dart through them: — Winds contend
Silently there, and heap the snow with breath
Rapid and strong, but silently! Its home
The voiceless lightning in these solitudes
Keeps innocently, and like vapour broods
Over the snow. The secret strength of things
Which governs thought, and to the infinite dome
Of heaven is as a law, inhabits thee!
And what were thou, and earth, and stars, and sea,
If to the human mind's imaginings
Silence and solitude were vacancy?

---

[2]The River Arve begins in the Valley of Chamonix at the foot of Mont Blanc and flows into Lake Geneva. Lake Geneva empties into the Rhone River, which wends its way south through France to the Mediterranean Sea.

18

STENDHAL

The Salon of 1824

1824

The French writer Stendhal, the pen name adopted by Marie-Henri Beyle (1783–1842) in 1814, is celebrated for his novels The Red and the Black *(1830) and* The Charterhouse of Parma *(1839). In the 1820s, Stendhal's literary and art criticism played an important role in moving French Romanticism toward political liberalism. His understanding of Romanticism was forged in Italy, where he lived from 1814 to 1821 in close contact with liberal Milan circles. When he returned to France, he found himself at odds with the conservative Romanticism of François-René de Chateaubriand and the young poets clustered around Victor Hugo. Indeed, the excitement of modernity is central to the Romanticism that Stendhal articulated in his book* Racine and Shakespeare *(1823). There, he gave August Wilhelm Schlegel's categories an irreverent twist, claiming, "Romanticism is the art of offering people the literary works which, in the present state of their customs and beliefs, can give them the greatest pleasure. Classicism, by contrast, offers them the literature which gave the greatest possible pleasure to their great-grandfathers." Stendhal wryly sidestepped the vexing question of what is Classic and what is Romantic, for by his own definition Sophocles, Euripides, Racine, and Shakespeare could all be "Romantic," because, within their context, they were able to speak most powerfully to their contemporaries.*

This resolute commitment to modernism guides Stendhal's assessment of the Salon of 1824. Held under the auspices of the French state, the great annual exhibitions of contemporary art defined the officially sanctioned tastes of French society. The Salon of 1824 is often remembered as the "Romantic Salon" because of the number of paintings perceived as belonging to the new school, including Eugène Delacroix's Scenes from the Massacres at Chios. *This was the first painting to which French critics applied the term "Romantic," to distinguish its vivid and free-flowing composition and intense expression of suffering from the high fin-*

Stendhal, *Salons*, ed. Stéphane Guégan and Martine Reid (Paris: Gallimard, 2002), 58–59, 65–67, 68–69, 78–81, 140–41. Translated by Warren Breckman.

ish, harmony, and emotional restraint of the Classicist style. Though Delacroix is considered by many as the greatest of French Romantic painters, he was in fact skeptical of the Romantic label, accepting it, as he wrote in his journal, only "if by Romanticism one understands the free manifestation of my personal impressions, my aversion to the models copied in the schools, and my loathing for academic formulas." Stendhal shared this hostility toward the academic system of art training and the patronage system that accompanied it. In this excerpt, much of Stendhal's vehemence focuses on Jacques-Louis David, the consummate academic painter who had dominated French art for decades (see Document 19). Though David, a fervent supporter of the French Republic and Napoleonic Empire, had fallen from grace with the restoration of the Bourbon monarchy, his powerful influence persisted in the official art system that Stendhal attacks. Surveying the Salon of 1824, Stendhal clearly believed that Romanticism had not yet won the battle against Classicism, but he judged France to be on the eve of a "revolution" in the fine arts (see Figure 7).

Musée Royal: Exhibition of 1824

. . .

It appears this year that the people engaged in criticism of the Salon are divided into two violently opposed camps. War has already commenced. The *Débats*[1] are going to stand for Classicism, that is, to swear by nobody but David[2] and to proclaim: "Every painted figure must be the copy of a statue," which the spectator must admire even if it bores him to tears. The *Constitutionnel*, for its part, makes fine-sounding, rather vague phrases—that is the vice of our century—but finally it does defend new ideas. It has the courage to maintain that art must be allowed to progress, even after M. David; that it is not the sole merit of a picture to portray a quantity of fine, correctly drawn muscles; and that it is a strange pretension to want the French school to remain as *static* as Government shares, simply because it was fortunate enough to produce the greatest painter of the eighteenth century, M. David. . . .

[1] *Journal des Débats* and *Le Constitutionnel* were two influential Parisian journals.
[2] Jacques-Louis David, the most important neoclassical painter in France. (See Document 19.)

Salon de 1827

Entreront-ils n'entreront-ils pas

Grand Combat entre le Romantique
et le Classique.
à la porte du Musé

First Article

. . .

"But," people will say, "who are you to dare discuss the arts with so little modesty and in such a sharp tone? Are you an artist? Has your mettle been tested at the Salon by two or three ridiculed pictures? If so, I would listen to you with some respect." The reply of the author of this article is that I was born about thirty years ago on the famous banks of the Rhine, not far from Coblenz. I was trained for a profession closely connected with drawing, and at an early age I set out for Rome. I was to have stayed for fifteen months, but I forgot myself there for ten years. Once I had attained my independence, I resolved to see Paris, for the delights of her literature and inhabitants have won this city such a high place in the European esteem that it has become the only capital of Europe.[3] I had scarcely been there a few months when I was asked to review the Exhibition of 1824 in a newspaper. I am only interested in the number of the paper's readers and not at all in its political doctrines, because I have strong views on everything: I owe this honest confession to my reader. This is the main fault that makes me unacceptable in society, and I have no desire to change. Content with my modest fortune, full of pride, and asking for nothing, I spare only what I like; and I like only genius. "Don't you like anyone, then?" people exclaim from all sides. "Certainly. I like young painters with fire in their souls and candor in their spirits, who aren't secretly hoping to win their fortune and future promotion by going to spend dreary evenings with Madame So-and-so or playing whist with Monsieur Someone Else. . . ."

We are on the eve of a revolution in the fine arts. Large pictures composed of thirty naked figures copied from classical statues, and heavy five-act tragedies in verse are doubtless very respectable works.

---

[3]These autobiographical details are pure fabrication.

(Opposite) **Figure 7.** The Great Battle between the Romantic and the Classic at the Door to the Museum, *1827*

This anonymous lithograph condenses the overlapping stylistic, cultural, and political issues that made the clash between Romanticism and Classicism so polemically charged in France. Created three years after Stendhal's attack against the school of Jacques-Louis David, the image attests to the public's continuing preoccupation with the question of Romanticism. Yet it also suggests that at least some French people were capable of viewing this cultural battle with humorous detachment.
Paris, Bibliothèque Nationale, Département des Estampes et de la Photographie.

But, whatever people say, they are beginning to bore us, and if the painting of the *Sabines*[4] were to appear today, the figures would be found passionless, and people would find it ridiculous to march into battle without any clothes on. "But this is normal in classical bas-relief!" protest the classicists, those people who swear by nothing but David and never pronounce three words without speaking of *style*. And what do I care about classical bas-relief? We must try to do good modern painting. The Greeks liked the naked body, but we, for our part, never see it. I would even say it disgusts us.

Ignoring the clamors of my opponents, I shall tell the public, honestly and simply, what I think about each of the pictures to which it devotes some attention. I shall state the reasons for my own particular viewpoint. My aim is to make each spectator question his own heart, articulate his own manner of feeling, and thus form a personal judgment and a vision based on his own character, tastes, and dominating passions—providing, that is, he *has* emotions, because unfortunately they are essential for the appreciation of art. My second aim is to cure young painters from imitating the school of David and Horace Vernet.[5] It is the love of art that inspires me.

The eminently reasonable man of sound judgment has all my esteem in society. He will make an excellent magistrate, good citizen, good husband, in fact admirable in every way, and I shall honor him everywhere except in the exhibition rooms. The conversation I like to follow in the Louvre is that of the young man—with wild eyes, sudden movements and rather disheveled dress. Just this morning I have overheard twenty judgments on the same number of prominent pictures, and if I had not been afraid of being taken for an eavesdropper, I should have hurriedly copied them down in my notebook. The same ideas may come back into my mind, but I shall never find the secret of saying them so well and with such passion.

Second Article

. . .

In Paris, the more a painter works, the poorer he is. A young artist endowed with the least of the social graces—and generally speaking young artists are amiable, they love fame so openly and confess to it

---

[4]"The Sabine Women" (1796–1799), painted by Jacques-Louis David. See Document 19.

[5]Émile Jean-Horace Vernet (1789–1863), French painter, best known for his panoramic battle scenes and orientalist themes.

so delightfully—can easily manage between one exhibition and the next to form some connection with newspaper editors. When he exhibits, he looks so polished himself that it would make him miserable to be told the truth; so that, however devoid of merit his pictures, and however awkward his heroes, he can always rely on some well-disposed newspaper to praise them and delude him. And so he sees his pictures described in grandiloquent style as minor masterpieces; but they are never sold. Now, to paint a picture, you need models, and this is more expensive than people think; then you need colors and canvas, and finally you have to live. A young painter of the modern school can only meet these basic conditions of his art by incurring debts—always paid off honorably (I do those young men this justice with pleasure). But in the end the young painter, reduced to taking his pictures home with him after the exhibition, lives only from illusions, deprivation, and disappointed hopes. Then one day he discovers a sure way of having some money to spare—*by no longer working.*

This is certainly an extraordinary fact in the history of art, which one would hardly suspect from the pompous tone of the usual feuilletons[6] on the exhibition. Here, as in everything else, hypocrisy in ideas leads to misfortune in real life. For the young painter who has just made himself better off by throwing his brushes out the window is already thirty. The best part of his life was wasted or at best devoted to acquiring a talent that he now abandons. What can he do? What can he become? My quill refuses to list the sad responses to those questions.

Voilà, the grievous result of the excessive encouragement given to painting by the budget of the Ministry of the Interior; *voilà*, the result in part of academic competitions and journeys to Rome, contrary even to the intentions of the sponsors. In all these competitions I can see elderly artists gravely occupied in judging how well the young have copied their own style of painting. Twenty pupils of David congregate to examine a young man's pictures. If, like Prud'hon,[7] the young artist has genius and refuses to copy David because this style *does not satisfy his own spiritual needs*, all David's pupils stand up and, with the full weight of their authority, declare in a unanimous vote (which to the general public seems most impressive) that Prud'hon has no talent. Or, in another genre, just look at the fuss the public makes of the speeches and poems that the French Academy never fails to consecrate every year. Who reads them or bothers about them? What place do the speeches for which prizes were awarded fifty years ago have in

---

[6]Newspaper articles dedicated to light literature, opinion, and cultural criticism.
[7]Pierre Paul Prud'hon (1758–1823), French neoclassical painter.

our libraries today? And yet I think the gentlemen of the French Academy are quite as good as the members of the Academy of Fine Arts. The only difference is that in literature the public is not so easily deceived. And also a sharp, knowing public like the French will never take seriously judges who are asked to pronounce on their own cause. Academicians always look at a young candidate's work to see if he is working in line with their own method and style. But genius imitates nobody, least of all academicians. . . .

Fourth Article

THE CASE AGAINST DAVID'S SCHOOL

Throw into prison the most ordinary man, one the least familiar with art or literature, in short, one of the countless ignorant loafers of which all capital cities are full, and once he's gotten over the shock, tell him he will gain his liberty if he is capable of exhibiting at the Salon a nude figure perfectly drawn according to David's system. You would be astonished to see the prisoner put to this test reappear in the world after two or three years. That's because correct, learned draftsmanship copied from the Antique, as understood by the school of David, is an exact science like arithmetic, geometry, trigonometry, etc.; in other words, with infinite patience and the shining genius of Barême,[8] one can arrive in two or three years at a knowledge of the shape and precise position of the hundred muscles that cover the human body and be able to reproduce them with a brush. During the thirty years of David's tyrannical government, the public was obligated, under penalty of being accused of bad taste, to believe that to have the necessary patience to acquire the *exact science* of drawing was to have genius. Do you still remember those handsome pictures of naked bodies by Madame *******? The last excess of this system was M. Girodet's *Scenes from a Deluge*, which can be seen at the Luxembourg Palace.[9]

But I return to the prisoner we have thrown into a tower of Mont-

---

[8]François Barême (1640–1703), French mathematician.

[9]Anne-Louis Girodet de Roucy (1767–1824), French artist who initially painted in the style of his teacher, Jacques-Louis David, but developed an increasingly dreamlike and evocative manner that has led many to identify him as a pioneer of French Romantic painting. *Scenes from a Deluge*, painted in 1806, reflects the influence of proto-Romantic painters like Henry Fuseli and belongs to the period of Girodet's rebellion against David, so one could certainly contest Stendhal's treatment of the painting as an example of the David school.

Saint-Michel. Tell him: "You will be free when you are able to depict in a manner recognizable by the public the despair of a lover who has just lost his mistress, or the joy of a good father who sees his son return whom he believed dead"; and the miserable man will find himself condemned to perpetual imprisonment. This is because, unfortunately, for many artists, the passions are not an *exact science* that the most ignorant man can master. To be able to paint the passions, you must have seen them and felt their devouring flames. Note well, I do not say that all passionate people are good painters; I do say that all great artists have been men of passion. This is equally true of all the arts, from Giorgione[10] dying of love at thirty-three because his pupil, Morto da Feltre, had run away with his mistress, to Mozart, who died because he imagined that an angel appeared to him disguised as a venerable old man and called him to heaven. And Tasso! And Pascal![11]

The school of David *can only paint bodies; it is decidedly inept at painting souls.*

It is this quality, or rather the lack of it, in so many pictures praised to the skies in the last twenty years that will prevent them from reaching posterity. They are well-painted, cleverly drawn, this I admit; but they *bore* us. And as soon as boredom rears its head among the fine arts, we might as well give up. . . .

People will protest at this injustice, this denigration. Well, try to find at this year's Salon a picture expressing some passion of the human heart or spiritual impulse in a vivid manner intelligible to the general public. I tried out this disastrous experiment on Saturday with three friends. As soon as you look at the exhibition from this angle, doesn't one feel abandoned amidst more than two thousand pictures? I expect painting to have a soul; but this multitude of figures of so many different nations and styles, whose creators have ransacked history, mythology, Ossian's poems, M. de Forbin's travels,[12] etc.—as soon as I look for a soul, all this looks like nothing better than a *vast human desert.*

---

[10]Giorgione (1477–1510), Italian painter, leading figure in the Venetian school.

[11]Torquato Tasso (1544–1595), Italian poet best known for *Jerusalem Delivered*, his epic poem chronicling the combat between Christians and Muslims during the First Crusade. Blaise Pascal (1623–1662), French mathematician and physicist, best known for his deeply religious reflections, published posthumously under the title *Pensées* (*Thoughts*).

[12]Claude de Forbin-Gardanne (1656–1733), French naval commander whose memoirs (1730) established his fame as one of the most dashing and adventurous sailors of the age.

At a distance, I can make out figures taking part in some action that ought to arouse all the passionate feelings that in the course of habitual life lie dormant in men's hearts. But when I come closer, I find only impassive characters like the Romulus in M. David's *Sabine Women*. (See Document 19.) This man is supposed to be fighting for his throne and for his life; there he is, face to face in armed combat with the rival determined to usurp and kill him, and yet all he can do is strike an attitude, show off his fine muscles, and throw his javelin gracefully. There is not one of our common soldiers who is not twenty times more expressive in his obscure battle to win the respect of his company, without the least personal hatred of the enemy. Romulus ought to offer us the ideal of a man inflamed by power, fighting for everything he holds most dear. But far from this spiritual rapport, he is below even the most commonplace reality, and he is ideal only in the form of his beautiful muscles, correctly imitated from the antique. . . .

Sixteenth Article

. . .

A critic, a great enemy of Romanticism,[13] has foisted the strange epithet of *Shakespearean* upon Monsieur H. Vernet's picture, while he calls the pictures of Raphael[14] and David *Homeric*. He might as well say: *"I shall call Romantic everything which is not excellent."* By this simple trick, the word *Romanticism* would gradually become synonymous with bad art in the eyes of the public.

Romanticism in painting is that masterpiece of Monsieur H. Vernet, the *Battle of Montmirail*, which contains everything, even chiaroscuro. *Classicism* is a battle by Salvator Rosa,[15] almost of the same size, which can be seen at the far end of the long gallery on the side of the Seine. *Romanticism* in all the arts is what represents the men of today

---

[13]Stendhal refers to Étienne Jean Delécluze (1781–1863), art critic and outspoken opponent of Romanticism.

[14]Raphael (1483–1520), Italian painter, one of the greatest masters of the Renaissance. Although Delécluze claimed Raphael for the Classicists, he was, in fact, revered by the Romantics.

[15]Salvator Rosa (1615–1673), Italian baroque painter. Rosa's depictions of wild mountainous landscapes, tempests, and macabre subjects led many in the early nineteenth century to see him as a prototypical Romantic, so Stendhal's association of him with Classicism must be considered idiosyncratic.

and not the men of those heroic times so distant from us, and which probably never existed anyway. If you want to take the trouble to compare these two battles I have just pointed out, and above all, to judge the amount of pleasure they give to the spectator, you will form a clear idea of what constitutes Romanticism in painting. Classicism, on the contrary, is those completely naked men who fill up the picture of the *Sabines*. Granted equality of talent, Monsieur H. Vernet's battle would be better than Monsieur David's. What sympathy can a Frenchman, who has struck a few saber blows in his lifetime, feel for people fighting *totally nude?* The most ordinary common sense tells us that the legs of those soldiers would soon be covered in blood and that it was absurd to go naked into battle at any time in history. What can console Romanticism for the attacks of the *Journal des Débats* is the fact that *common sense applied to the arts* has made great progress these last four years, especially among the highest ranks of society.

I must leave this digression on Romanticism, which was not provoked by me. The *Débats* have often returned to the debate, but, whatever the outcome, Heaven preserve us from the great word *Shakespearian!*"

19

JACQUES-LOUIS DAVID

The Sabine Women

1796–1799

The history of Neoclassicism in the visual arts followed a rather different trajectory from literary Neoclassicism. Whereas neoclassical literary taste emerged in the very early eighteenth century, Neoclassical painting and sculpture emerged in the century's second half. Its turn to an austere and anti-sensualist ideal based on antique models was a reaction to the extravagance of Baroque and Rococo art. Through the powerful figure of Jacques-Louis David (1748–1825), Neoclassicism was the dominant

style in the visual arts right through the years of the French Revolution, having become ensconced in the most influential of Europe's art schools, the French Academy. David was a supporter of Robespierre, and he was imprisoned after the fall of the Jacobins. Upon his release, he painted the monumental picture The Sabine Women, *based on a legendary episode in the early history of Rome. The Romans have abducted the daughters of their neighbors, the Sabines. After some years, the Sabines attack Rome; however, the abducted women are now the wives and mothers of Romans, including Hersilia, the daughter of the Sabine leader Tatius, who is married to the Roman leader, Romulus. In choosing to depict Hersilia interposing herself between her father and her husband, David offered an image of reconciliation to a French nation traumatized by the excesses of the Terror. The painting immediately became an icon of French Neoclassicism. Note the frieze-like style, reminiscent of classical bas-reliefs, with the action halted, the figures statuesque. Stendhal objects strenuously to the nudity of these warriors, but one might reply that David's aim was not to create a realistic representation of combat; he has stripped the painting of inessentials until what remains is a severe ideal of heroism and sacrifice.*

20

VICTOR HUGO

Preface to "Cromwell"

1827

The leader of French Romanticism and the dominant figure in nineteenth-century French literature, Victor Hugo (1802–1885) was born in Besançon to Sophie and Joseph-Léopold-Sigisbert Hugo, a military man who rose to the rank of general under Napoleon. In the early 1820s, Hugo's ini-

Victor Hugo, "Preface to *Cromwell*," *The Dramatic Works of Victor Hugo*, trans. George Burnham Ives (New York: Little, Brown and Company, 1909), 3, 5–8, 11–12, 17–18, 21–31, 33–35, 40–41, 47–48, 50–51.

tial commitment to Romantic aesthetics intersected with a conservative outlook, supporting the restored Bourbon monarchy and the reconstructive role of the Church in a France traumatized by the Revolution. By the mid-1820s, Hugo was already beginning to identify the new aesthetics with political and social freedom. The preface that Hugo wrote for his play Cromwell *(1827) consummates this move toward the political Left. Like Stendhal, Hugo vigorously defends the liberty of art against the despotism of codes and rules; but, as this excerpt shows, in contrast to Stendhal's definition of Romanticism as that which is contemporary, Hugo's Romanticism is deeply rooted in a historical sensibility. August Wilhelm Schlegel's influence is evident in Hugo's equation of Romanticism with the Christian era, a concept capacious enough to embrace the Middle Ages and the Renaissance, Dante and Shakespeare, while sidelining the epoch of Louis XIV, when classical values had reigned supreme. Building on Schlegel's account of the divided consciousness of the Christian (see Document 10), Hugo breaks with Classicism's ideal of formal beauty and insists that art, if it is to be complete, must embrace the grotesque and the sublime, the absurd and the terrible, comedy and tragedy. The modern drama exemplified by Shakespeare emerges for Hugo as the genre best suited to the task of accommodating these extremes. Ironically, very few Romantic era dramas have become part of the theatrical canon, except through the medium of opera, which in the nineteenth century found a motherlode of story lines in Romantic drama. So, for example, although Hugo's play* Hernani *caused fisticuffs between Romantics and Classicists when it premiered in 1830, Hugo's plot really lives on in the form of Giuseppe Verdi's opera* Ernani *(1840); likewise with Verdi's* Rigoletto *(1851), based on Hugo's play* Le roi s'amuse *(1832). As for Hugo's own talents, his enduring fame rests not on his plays, but on his poetry and fictional work, particularly the epic novels* Notre-Dame de Paris *(*The Hunchback of Notre Dame, *1831) and* Les Misérables *(1862).*

Let us set out from a fact. The same type of civilization, or to use a more exact, although more extended expression, the same society, has not always inhabited the earth. The human race as a whole has grown, has developed, has matured, like one of ourselves. It was once a child, it was once a man: we are now looking on at its impressive old age. Before the epoch which modern society has dubbed "ancient," there was another epoch which the ancients called "fabulous," but which it would be more accurate to call "primitive." Now, as poetry is always superposed upon society, we propose to try to demonstrate, from the form of its society, what the character of the poetry must have been in those three great ages of the world—primitive times, ancient times, modern times.

In primitive times, when man awakes in a world that is newly created, poetry awakes with him. In the face of the marvellous things that dazzle and intoxicate him, his first speech is a hymn simply. He is still so close to God that all his meditations are ecstatic, all his dreams are visions. His bosom swells, he sings as he breathes. His lyre has but three strings—God, the soul, creation; but this threefold mystery envelops everything, this threefold idea embraces everything. The earth is still almost deserted. There are families, but no nations; patriarchs, but no kings. Each race exists at its own pleasure; no property, no laws, no contentions, no wars. Everything belongs to each and to all. Society is a community. Man is restrained in nought. He leads that nomadic pastoral life with which all civilizations begin, and which is so well adapted to solitary contemplation, to fanciful reverie. He follows every suggestion, he goes hither and thither, at random. His thought, like his life, resembles a cloud that changes its shape and its direction according to the wind that drives it. Such is the first man, such is the first poet. He is young, he is cynical. Prayer is his sole religion, the ode is his only form of poetry. . . .

By slow degrees, however, this youth of the world passes away. All the spheres progress; the family becomes a tribe, the tribe becomes a nation. Each of these groups of men camps about a common center, and kingdoms appear. The social instinct succeeds the nomadic instinct. The camp gives place to the city, the tent to the palace, the ark to the temple. The chiefs of these nascent states are still shepherds, it is true, but shepherds of nations; the pastoral staff has already assumed the shape of a scepter. Everything tends to become stationary and fixed. Religion takes on a definite shape; prayer is governed by rites; dogma sets bounds to worship. Thus the priest and king share the paternity of the people; thus theocratic society succeeds the patriarchal community.

Meanwhile the nations are beginning to be packed too closely on the earth's surface. They annoy and jostle one another; hence the clash of empires—war. They overflow upon another; hence, the migrations of nations—voyages. Poetry reflects these momentous events; from ideas it proceeds to things. It sings of ages, of nations, of empires. It becomes epic, it gives birth to Homer. . . .

But it is in the ancient tragedy, above all, that the epic breaks out at every turn. It mounts the Greek stage without losing aught, so to speak, of its immeasurable, gigantic proportions. Its characters are still heroes, demi-gods, gods; its themes are visions, oracles, fatality; its scenes are battles, funeral rites, catalogues. That which the rhapsodists formerly sang, the actors declaim—that is the whole difference. . . .

But the age of the epic draws near its end. Like the society that it represents, this form of poetry wears itself out revolving upon itself. Rome reproduces Greece, Virgil copies Homer, and, as if to make a becoming end, epic poetry expires in the last parturition.

It was time. Another era is about to begin, for the world and for poetry.

A spiritual religion, supplanting the material and external paganism, makes its way to the heart of the ancient society, kills it, and deposits, in that corpse of a decrepit civilization, the germ of modern civilization. This religion is complete, because it is true; between its dogma and its cult, it embraces a deep-rooted moral. And first of all, as a fundamental truth, it teaches man that he has two lives to live, one ephemeral, the other immortal; one on earth, the other in heaven. It shows him that he, like his destiny, is twofold; that there is in him an animal and an intellect, a body and a soul; in a word, that he is the point of intersection, the common link of the two chains of beings which embrace all creation—of the chain of material beings and the chain of incorporeal beings; the first starting from the rock to arrive at man, the second starting from man to end at God. . . .

Behold, then, a new religion, a new society; upon this twofold foundation there must inevitably spring up a new poetry. Previously—we beg pardon for setting forth a result which the reader has probably already foreseen from what has been said above—previously, following therein the course pursued by the ancient polytheism and philosophy, the purely epic muse of the ancients had studied nature in only a single aspect, casting aside without pity almost everything in art which, in the world subjected to its imitation, had not relation to a certain type of beauty. A type which was magnificent at first, but, as always happens with everything systematic, became in later times false, trivial and conventional. Christianity leads poetry to the truth. Like it, the modern muse will see things in a higher and broader light. It will realize that everything in creation is not humanly *beautiful*, that the ugly exists beside the beautiful, the unshapely beside the graceful, the grotesque on the reverse of the sublime, evil with good, darkness with light. It will ask itself if the narrow and relative sense of the artist should prevail over the infinite, absolute sense of the Creator; if it is for man to correct God; if a mutilated nature will be the more beautiful for the mutilation, if art has the right to duplicate, so to speak, man, life, creation; if things will progress better when their muscles and their vigor have been taken from them; if, in short, to be incomplete is the best way to be harmonious. Then it is that, with its eyes fixed upon events that are both laughable and redoubtable, poetry will take a great step, a decisive step, a step which, like the upheaval of an earthquake, will change the whole face of the intellectual world. It will set about doing as nature does, mingling in its creations—but without confounding them—darkness and light, the grotesque and the sublime; in other words, the body and the soul, the beast and the intellect; for the starting-point of religion is always the starting-point of poetry. All things are connected.

Thus, then, we see a principle unknown to the ancients, a new type, introduced in poetry; and as an additional element in anything modifies the whole of the thing, a new form of the art is developed. This type is the grotesque; its new form is comedy.

And we beg leave to dwell upon this point; for we have now indicated the significant feature, the fundamental difference which, in our opinion, separates modern from ancient art, the present form from the defunct form; or, to use less definite but more popular terms, *romantic* literature from *classical* literature. . . .

We have now reached the poetic culmination of modern times. Shakespeare is the drama; and the drama, which with the same breath molds the grotesque and the sublime, the terrible and the absurd, tragedy and comedy—the drama is the distinguishing characteristic of the third epoch of poetry, of the literature of the present day. . . .

The poetry born of Christianity, the poetry of our time, is, therefore, the drama; the real results from the wholly natural combination of two types, the sublime and the grotesque, which meet in the drama, as they meet in life and in creation. For true poetry, complete poetry, consists in the harmony of contraries. Hence, it is time to say aloud— and it is here above all that exceptions prove the rule—that everything that exists in nature exists in art.

On taking one's stand at this point of view, to pass judgment on our petty conventional rules, to disentangle all those trivial problems which the critics of the last two centuries have laboriously built up about the art, one is struck by the promptitude with which the question of the modern stage is made clear and distinct. The drama has but to take a step to break all the spider's webs with which the militia of Lilliput have attempted to fetter its sleep.

And so, let addle-pated pedants (one does not exclude the other) claim that the deformed, the ugly, the grotesque should never be imitated in art; one replies that the grotesque is comedy, and that comedy apparently makes a part of art. Tartuffe is not handsome, Pourceaugnac is not noble, but Pourceaugnac and Tartuffe are admirable flashes of art.[1]

If, driven back from this entrenchment to their second line of custom-houses, they renew their prohibition of the grotesque coupled with the sublime, of comedy melted into tragedy, we prove to them that, in the poetry of Christian nations, the first of these two types represents the human beast, the second the soul. These two stalks of art, if we prevent their branches from mingling, if we persistently separate them, will produce by way of fruit, on the one hand abstract vices and absurdities, on the other, abstract crime, heroism and virtue. The two types, thus isolated and left to themselves, will go each its own way, leaving the real between them, at the left hand of one, at the right hand of the other. Whence it follows that after all these abstractions there will remain something to represent—man; after these tragedies and comedies, something to create—the drama.

In the drama, as it may be conceived at least, if not executed, all things are connected and follow one another as in real life. The body plays its part no less than the mind; and men and events, set in motion by this twofold agent, pass across the stage, burlesque and terrible in turn, and sometimes both at once. Thus the judge will say: "Off with his head and let us go to dinner!" Thus the Roman Senate will deliberate over Domitian's turbot. Thus Socrates, drinking the hemlock and discoursing on the immortal soul and the only God, will interrupt himself to suggest that a cock be sacrificed at Aesculapius. Thus Elizabeth will swear and talk Latin. Thus Richelieu will submit to Joseph the Capuchin, and Louis XI to his barber, Maitre Olivier le Diable. Thus Cromwell will say: "I have Parliament in my bag and the King in my pocket"; or, with the hand that signed the death sentence of Charles the First, smear with ink the face of a regicide who smilingly returns

---

[1] The main characters of Molière's comic plays *Le Tartuffe ou L'imposteur* (1669) and *Monsieur de Pourceaugnac* (1669).

the compliment. Thus Caesar, in his triumphal car, will be afraid of overturning. For men of genius, however great they be, have always within them a touch of the beast which mocks at their intelligence. Therein they are akin to mankind in general, for therein they are dramatic. "It is but a step from the sublime to the ridiculous," said Napoleon, when he was convinced that he was mere man; and that outburst of a soul on fire illumines art and history at once; that cry of anguish is the résumé of the drama and of life. . . .

We see how quickly the arbitrary distinction between the species of poetry vanishes before common sense and taste. No less easily one might demolish the alleged rule of the two unities.[2] We say *two* and not *three* unities, because unity of plot or of *ensemble*, the only true and well-founded one, was long ago removed from the sphere of discussion.

Distinguished contemporaries, foreigners and Frenchmen, have already attacked, both in theory and in practice, that fundamental law of the pseudo-Aristotelian code. Indeed, the combat was not likely to be a long one. At the first blow it cracked, so worm-eaten was that timber of the old scholastic hovel! . . .

"But," someone will say, "this rule that you discard is borrowed from the Greek drama." Wherein, pray, do the Greek stage and drama resemble our stage and drama? Moreover, we have already shown that the vast extent of the ancient stage enabled it to include a whole locality, so that the poet could, according to the exigencies of the plot, transport it at his pleasure from one part of the stage to another, which is practically equivalent to a change of stage-setting. Curious contradiction! the Greek theatre, restricted as it was to a national and religious object, was much more free than ours, whose only object is the enjoyment, and, if you please, the instruction, of the spectator. The reason is that the one obeys only the laws that are suited to it, while the other takes upon itself conditions of existence which are absolutely foreign to its essence. One is artistic, the other artificial. . . .

Unity of time rests on no firmer foundation than unity of place. A plot forcibly confined within twenty-four hours is as absurd as one confined within a peristyle. Every plot has its proper duration as well

[2]Obedience to the dramatic unities of time, action, and place described by Aristotle was a fundamental rule of neoclassical drama in the seventeenth and eighteenth centuries.

as its appropriate place. Think of administering the same dose of time to all events! of applying the same measure to everything! You would laugh at a cobbler who should attempt to put the same shoe on every foot. To cross unity of time and unity of place like the bars of a cage, and pedantically to introduce therein, in the name of Aristotle, all the deeds, all the nations, all the figures which Providence sets before us in such vast numbers in real life,—to proceed thus is to mutilate men and things, to cause history to make wry faces. Let us say, rather, that everything will die in the operation, and so the dogmatic mutilaters reach their ordinary result: what was alive in the chronicles is dead in tragedy. That is why the cage of the unities often contains only a skeleton. . . .

But still the same refrain is repeated, and will be, no doubt, for a long while to come: "Follow the rules! Copy the models! It was the rules that shaped the models." . . .

Whom shall we copy, then? The moderns? What! Copy copies! God forbid! . . .

Let us then speak boldly. The time for it has come, and it would be strange if, in this age, liberty, like the light, should penetrate everywhere except to the one place where freedom is most natural—the domain of thought. Let us take the hammer to theories and poetic systems. Let us throw down the old plastering that conceals the facade of art. There are neither rules nor models; or, rather, there are no other rules than the general laws of nature, which soar above the whole field of art, and the special rules which result from the conditions appropriate to the subject of each composition. The former are of the essence, eternal, and do not change; the latter are variable, external, and are used but once. The former are the framework that supports the house; the latter the scaffolding which is used in building it, and which is made anew for each building. In a word, the former are the flesh and bones, the latter the clothing, of the drama. But these rules are not written in the treatises on poetry. Richelet[3] has no idea of their existence. Genius, which divines rather than learns, devises for each work the general rules from the general plan of things, the special rules from the separate *ensemble* of the subject treated; not after the manner of the chemist, who lights the fire under his furnace, heats his crucible, analyzes and destroys; but after the manner of the bee,

[3]Pierre Richelet (1626–1698), French author of an influential dictionary of the French language as well as works on poetics.

which flies on its golden wings, lights on each flower and extracts its honey, leaving it as brilliant and fragrant as before.

The poet—let us insist on this point—should take counsel therefore only of nature, truth, and inspiration which is itself both truth and nature. . . .

There is to-day the old literary régime as well as the old political régime. The last century still weighs upon the present one at almost every point. It is notably oppressive in the matter of criticism. For instance, you find living men who repeat to you this definition of taste let fall by Voltaire: "Taste in poetry is no different from what it is in women's clothes." Taste, then, is coquetry. Remarkable words, which depict marvellously the painted, *moucheté*, powdered poetry of the eighteenth century—that literature in paniers, pompons and falbalas. They give an admirable résumé of an age with which the loftiest geniuses could not come in contact without becoming petty, in one respect or another; of an age when Montesquieu was able and apt to produce *Le Temple de Gnide*, Voltaire *Le Temple du Goût*, Jean-Jacques [Rousseau] *Le Devin du Village*.

Taste is the common sense of genius. This is what will soon be demonstrated by another school of criticism, powerful, outspoken, well-formed,—a school of the century which is beginning to put forth vigorous shoots under the dead and withered branches of the old school. This youthful criticism, as serious as the other is frivolous, as learned as the other is ignorant, has already established organs that are listened to, and one is sometimes surprised to find, even in the least important sheets, excellent articles emanating from it. Joining hands with all that is fearless and superior in letters, it will deliver us from two scourges: tottering *classicism*, and false *romanticism*, which has the presumption to show itself at the feet of the true. For modern genius already has its shadow, its copy, its parasite, its *classic*, which forms itself upon it, smears itself with its colors, assumes its livery, picks up its crumbs, and *like the sorcerer's pupil*, puts in play, with words retained by the memory, elements of theatrical action of which it has not the secret. Thus it does idiotic things which its master many a time has much difficulty in making good. But the thing that must be destroyed first of all is the old false taste. Present-day literature must be cleansed of its rust. In vain does the rust eat into it and tarnish it. It is addressing a young, stern, vigorous generation, which does not understand it. The train of the eighteenth century is still dragging in the nineteenth; but we, we young men who have seen Bonaparte, are not the ones who will carry it.

21

GIUSEPPE MAZZINI

The Duties of Man

1844

A physician by training, Giuseppe Mazzini (1805–1872) early on dedicated his life to the nationalist cause in Italy. Throughout his life, he never wavered from the goals of ending Austrian hegemony in Italy, neutralizing the temporal power of the pope, and creating a unified Italy governed by a democratic republic. Driven into exile in France in the early 1830s because of his involvement in the Carbonari, a conspiratorial secret society, Mazzini founded the nationalist movement "Young Italy." Although it was ultimately more pragmatic politicians like Count Camillo Benso di Cavour who eventually dominated the creation of the Kingdom of Italy in the 1860s, Mazzini's idealism played a vital role in inspiring the national Risorgimento (Resurgence). The excerpt from Mazzini's "The Duties of Man" neatly expresses two features of nationalism in the years before 1848. On the one hand, Mazzini mixes a "liberal" concern for national self-determination with a strong desire for the betterment of working-class people. He thus links the "national question" to the "social question"; however, he rejects what he considers the "materialism" of socialism in favor of the "spiritual" goal of creating a national community, within which bonds of solidarity would serve as springs to social action. On the other hand, Mazzini professes that liberty of the fatherland is inseparable from a universal struggle for human liberty, avowing that national brotherhood is the precondition for a brotherhood of all nations. Potent as this belief in the harmony of nationalism and cosmopolitanism was in the years leading to the revolutions of 1848, it proved ephemeral in the face of the revolutions' hard lessons.

I: To the Italian Working-Men

For the last fifty years whatever has been done for the cause of progress and of good against absolute governments and hereditary

Giuseppe Mazzini, "The Duties of Man," *The Duties of Man and Other Essays*, trans. Ella Noyes (London: J. M. Dent and Co., 1907), 8–19, 51–59.

aristocracies has been done in the name of the Rights of Man; in the name of liberty as the means, and of *well-being* as the object of existence. All the acts of the French Revolution and of the revolutions which followed and imitated it were consequences of a Declaration of the Rights of Man. All the works of the philosophers who prepared it were based upon a theory of liberty, and upon the need of making known to every individual his own rights. All the revolutionary schools preached that man is born for happiness, that he has the right to seek it by all the means in his power, that no one has the right to impede him in this search, and that he has the right of overthrowing all the obstacles which he may encounter on his path. And the obstacles were overthrown; liberty was conquered. It endured for years in many countries; in some it still endures. Has the condition of the people improved? Have the millions who live by the daily labor of their hands gained the least fraction of the well-being hoped for and promised to them?

No; the condition of the people has not improved; rather it has grown and grows worse in nearly every country, and especially here where I write the price of the necessaries of life has gone on continually rising, the wages of the working-man in many branches of industry falling, and the population multiplying. In nearly every country the lot of workers has become more uncertain, more precarious, and the labor crises which condemn thousands of working-men to idleness for a time have become more frequent. The yearly increase of emigration from one country to another, and from Europe to other parts of the world, and the ever-growing number of beneficent institutions, the increase of poor rates and provisions for the destitute, are enough to prove this. The latter prove also that public attention is waking more and more to the ills of the people; but their inability to lessen those ills to any visible extent points to a no less continual increase of poverty among the classes which they endeavor to help.

And nevertheless, in these last fifty years, the sources of social wealth and the sum of material blessings have steadily increased. Production has doubled. Commerce, amid continual crises, inevitable in the utter absence of organization, has acquired a greater force of activity and a wider sphere for its operations. Communication has almost everywhere been made secure and rapid, and the price of commodities has fallen in consequence of the diminished cost of transport. And, on the other hand, the idea of rights inherent in human nature is today generally accepted; accepted in word and, hypocritically, even by those who seek to evade it in deed. Why, then, has the condition of the people not improved? Why is the consumption of products, instead of being divided equally among all the members of the social body in Europe, concentrated in the hands of a small number of men forming a new aristocracy? Why has the new impulse given to industry and commerce produced, not the well-being of the many, but the luxury of the few?

The answer is clear to those who will look a little more closely into things. Men are creatures of education, and act only according to the principle of education given to them. The men who have promoted revolutions hitherto have based them upon the idea of the rights belonging to the individual: The revolutions conquered liberty—individual liberty, liberty of teaching, liberty of belief, liberty of trade, liberty in everything and for everybody. But of what use was the recognition of their rights to those who had no means of exercising them? What did liberty of teaching mean to those who had neither time nor means to profit by it, or liberty of trade to those who had nothing to trade with, neither capital nor credit? In all the countries where these principles were proclaimed society was composed of a small number of individuals who possessed the land, the credit, the capital, and of vast multitudes of men who had nothing but their own hands and were forced to give the labor of them to the former class, on any terms, in order to live, and forced to spend the whole day in material and monotonous toil. For these, constrained to battle with hunger, what was liberty but an illusion and a bitter irony? To make it anything else it would have been necessary for the men of the well-to-do classes to consent to reduce the hours of labor, to increase the remuneration, to institute free and uniform education for the masses, to make the instruments of labor accessible to all, and to provide a bonus fund for the working-man endowed with capacity and good intentions. But why should they do it? Was not *well-being* the supreme object in life? Were not material blessings desirable before all other things? Why should they lessen their own enjoyment for the advantage of others? Let those who could, help themselves. When society has secured to everybody who can use them the free exercise of the rights belonging to human nature, it does all that is required of it. If there be anyone who is unable from the fatality of his own circumstances to exercise any of these rights, he must resign himself and not blame others.

It was natural that they should say thus, and thus, in fact, they did say. And this attitude of mind towards the poor in the classes privileged by fortune soon became the attitude of every individual towards every other. Each man looked after his own rights and the improvement of his own condition without seeking to provide for others; and when his rights clashed with those of others, there was war; not a war of blood, but of gold and of cunning; a war less manly than the other, but equally destructive; cruel war, in which those who had the means and were strong relentlessly crushed the weak or the unskilled. In this continual warfare, men were educated in egoism and in greed for material welfare exclusively. Liberty of belief destroyed all community of faith. Liberty of education produced more anarchy. Men without a common tie, without unity of religious belief and of aim, and whose sole vocation was enjoyment, sought every one his own road, not heeding if in pursuing it they were trampling upon the heads of their brothers—brothers in name and enemies in fact. To this we are come today, thanks to the theory of *rights*.

Certainly rights exist; but where the rights of an individual come into conflict with those of another, how can we hope to reconcile and harmonize them, without appealing to something superior to all rights? And where the rights of an individual, or of many individuals, clash with the rights of the Country, to what tribunal are we to appeal? If the right to *well-being*, to the greatest possible well-being, belongs to every living person, who will solve the difficulty between the working-man and the manufacturer? If the right to existence is the first and inviolable right of every man, who shall demand the sacrifice of that existence for the benefit of other men? Will you demand it in the name of Country, of Society, of the multitude of your brothers? What is Country, in the opinion of those of whom I speak, but the place in which our individual rights are most secure? What is Society but a collection of men who have agreed to bring the strength of the many in support of the rights of each? And after having taught the individual for fifty years that Society is established for the purpose of *assuring to him the exercise of his rights*, would you ask him to sacrifice them all to Society, to submit himself, if need be, to continuous toil, to prison, to exile, for the sake of improving it? After having preached to him everywhere that the object of life is *well-being*, would you all at once bid him give up well-being and life itself to free his country from the foreigner, or to procure better conditions for a class which is not his own? After having talked to him for years of *material* interests, how can you maintain that, finding wealth and power in his reach, he ought not to stretch out his hand to grasp them even to the injury of his brothers? . . .

The vital question agitating our century is a question of education. What we have to do is not to establish a new order of things by violence. An order of things so established is always tyrannical even when it is better than the old. *We have to overthrow by force the brute force which opposes itself today to every attempt at improvement,* and then propose for the approval of the nation, free to express its will, what we believe to be the best order of things and by every possible means educate men to develop it and act in conformity with it. The theory of *rights* enables us to rise and overthrow obstacles, but not to found a strong and lasting accord between all the elements which compose the nation. With the theory of happiness, of *well-being,* as the primary aim of existence we shall only form egoistic men, worshipers of the material, who will carry the old passions into the new order of things and corrupt it in a few months. We have therefore to find a principle of education superior to any such theory, which shall guide men to better things, teach them constancy in self-sacrifice, and link them with their fellow men without making them dependent on the ideas of a single man or on the strength of all. And this principle is Duty. We must convince men that they, sons of one only God, must obey one only law, here on earth; that each one of them must live, not for himself, but for others; that the object of their life is not to be more or less happy, but to make themselves and others better; that to fight against injustice and error for the benefit of their brothers is not only a *right,* but a *duty;* a duty not to be neglected without sin, — the duty of their whole life.

Italian Working-men, my Brothers! understand me fully. When I say that the knowledge of their *rights* is not enough to enable men to effect any appreciable or lasting improvement, I do not ask you to renounce these rights; I only say that they cannot exist except as a consequence of duties fulfilled, and that one must begin with the latter in order to arrive at the former. And when I say that by proposing *happiness, well-being,* or *material* interest as the aim of existence, we run the risk of producing egoists, I do not mean that you should never strive after these things. I say that material interests pursued alone, and not as a means, but as an end, lead always to this most disastrous result. . . . Material improvement is essential, and we shall strive to win it for ourselves; but not because the one thing necessary for man is to be well fed and housed, but rather because you cannot have a sense of your own dignity or any moral development while you are engaged, as at the present day, in a continual duel with want. . . .

Italian Working-men, my Brothers! When Christ came and changed the face of the world, He did not speak of rights to the rich, who had no need to conquer them; nor to the poor, who would perhaps have abused them, in imitation of the rich. He did not speak of utility or of self-interest to a people whom utility and self-interest had corrupted. He spoke of Duty, He spoke of Love, of Sacrifice, of Faith: He said that *they only should be first among all who had done good to all by their work*. And these thoughts, breathed into the ear of a society which had no longer any spark of life, reanimated it, conquered the millions, conquered the world, and caused the education of the human race to progress a degree. Italian Working-men! we live in an epoch like Christ's. We live in the midst of a society rotten as that of the Roman Empire, and feel in our souls the need of reviving and transforming it, of associating all its members and its workers in one single faith, under one single law, and for one purpose; the free and progressive development of all the faculties which God has planted in His creatures. We seek the reign of God upon earth as in heaven, or better, that the earth shall be a preparation for heaven, and society an endeavor towards a progressive approach to the Divine Idea. . . .

V. Duties to Country

Your first Duties—first, at least, in importance—are, as I have told you, to Humanity. You are *men* before you are *citizens* or *fathers*. If you do not embrace the whole human family in your love, if you do not confess your faith in its unity—consequent on the unity of God—and in the brotherhood of the Peoples who are appointed to reduce that unity to fact—if wherever one of your fellow men groans, wherever the dignity of human nature is violated by falsehood or tyranny, you are not prompt, being able, to succor that wretched one, or do not feel yourself called, being able, to fight for the purpose of relieving the deceived or oppressed—you disobey your law of life, or do not comprehend the religion which will bless the future.

But what can *each* of you, with his isolated powers, *do* for the moral improvement, for the progress of Humanity? You can, from time to time, give sterile expression to your belief; you may, on some rare occasion, perform an act of *charity* to a brother not belonging to your own land, no more. Now, *charity* is not the watchword of the future faith. The watchword of the future faith is *association*, fraternal cooperation towards a common aim, and this is as much superior to *charity* as the work of many uniting to raise with one accord a building for the habitation of all together would be superior to that which you would accomplish by raising a separate hut each for himself, and only helping one another by exchanging stones and bricks and mortar. But divided as you are in language, tendencies, habits, and capacities, you cannot attempt this common work. The *individual* is too weak, and Humanity too vast. *My God*, prays the Breton mariner as he puts out to sea, *protect me, my ship is so little, and Thy ocean so great!* And this prayer sums up the condition of each of you, if no means is found of multiplying your forces and your powers of action indefinitely. But God gave you this means when he gave you a Country, when, like a wise overseer of labor, who distributes the different parts of the work according to the capacity of the workmen, he divided Humanity into distinct groups upon the face of our globe, and thus planted the seeds of nations. Bad governments have disfigured the design of God, which you may see clearly marked out, as far, at least, as regards Europe, by the courses of the great rivers, by the lines of the lofty mountains, and by other geographical conditions; they have disfigured it by conquest, by greed, by jealousy of the just sovereignty of others; disfigured it so much that today there is perhaps no nation except England and France whose confines correspond to this design. They did not, and they do not, recognize any country except their own families and dynasties, the egoism of caste. But the divine design will infallibly be fulfilled. Natural divisions, the innate spontaneous tendencies of the peoples will replace the arbitrary divisions sanctioned by bad governments. The map of Europe will be remade. The Countries of the People will rise, defined by the voice of the free, upon the ruins of the Countries of Kings and privileged castes. Between these Countries there will be harmony and brotherhood. And then the work of Humanity for the general amelioration, for the discovery and application of the real law of life, carried on in association and distributed according to local capacities, will be accomplished by peaceful and progressive development; then each of you, strong in the affections and in the aid of many millions of men speaking the same language, endowed with the same tendencies, and educated by the same historic tradition, may hope by your personal effort to benefit the whole of Humanity.

To you, who have been born in Italy, God has allotted, as if favoring you specially, the best-defined country in Europe. In other lands, marked by more uncertain or more interrupted limits, questions may arise which the pacific vote of all will one day solve, but which have cost, and will yet perhaps cost, tears and blood; in yours, no. God has stretched round you sublime and indisputable boundaries; on one side the highest mountains of Europe, the Alps; on the other the sea, the immeasurable sea. Take a map of Europe and place one point of a pair of compasses in the north of Italy on Parma; point the other to the mouth of the Var, and describe a semicircle with it in the direction of the Alps; this point, which will fall, when the semicircle is completed, upon the mouth of the Isonzo, will have marked the frontier which God has given you. As far as this frontier your language is spoken and understood; beyond this you have no rights. Sicily, Sardinia, Corsica, and the smaller islands between them and the mainland of Italy belong undeniably to you. Brute force may for a little while contest these frontiers with you, but they have been recognized from of old by the tacit general consent of the peoples; and the day when, rising with one accord for the final trial, you plant your tricolored flag upon that frontier, the whole of Europe will acclaim re-risen Italy, and receive her into the community of the nations. To this final trial all your efforts must be directed.

Without Country you have neither name, token, voice, nor rights, no admission as brothers into the fellowship of the Peoples. You are the bastards of Humanity. Soldiers without a banner, Israelites among the nations, you will find neither faith nor protection; none will be sureties for you. Do not beguile yourselves with the hope of emancipation from unjust social conditions if you do not first conquer a Country for yourselves; where there is no Country there is no common agreement to which you can appeal; the egoism of self-interest rules alone, and he who has the upper hand keeps it, since there is no common safeguard for the interests of all. Do not be led away by the idea of improving your material conditions without first solving the national question. You cannot do it. Your industrial associations and mutual aid societies are useful as a means of educating and disciplining yourselves; as an economic fact they will remain barren until you have an Italy. . . .

Our Country is our field of labor; the products of our activity must go forth from it for the benefit of the whole earth; but the instruments of labor which we can use best and most effectively exist in it, and we may not reject them without being unfaithful to God's purpose and diminishing our own strength. In laboring according to true principles for our Country we are laboring for Humanity; our Country is the fulcrum of the lever which we have to wield for the common good. If we give up this fulcrum we run the risk of becoming useless to our Country and to Humanity. Before *associating* ourselves with the Nations which compose Humanity we must exist as a Nation. There can be no association except among equals; and you have no recognized collective existence.

Humanity is a great army moving to the conquest of unknown
lands, against powerful and wary enemies. The Peoples are the different corps and divisions of that army. Each has a post entrusted to it;
each a special operation to perform; and the common victory depends
on the exactness with which the different operations are carried out.
Do not disturb the order of the battle. Do not abandon the banner
which God has given you. Wherever you may be, into the midst of
whatever people circumstances may have driven you, fight for the liberty of that people if the moment calls for it; but fight as Italians, so
that the blood which you shed may win honor and love, not for you
only, but for your Country. And may the constant thought of your soul
be for Italy, may all the acts of your life be worthy of her, and may the
standard beneath which you range yourselves to work for Humanity
be Italy's. Do not say *I*; say *we*. Be every one of you an incarnation of
your Country, and feel himself and make himself responsible for his
fellow-countrymen; let each one of you learn to act in such a way that
in him men shall respect and love his Country. . . .

A Country is a fellowship of free and equal men bound together in
a brotherly concord of labor towards a single end. You must make it
and maintain it such. A Country is not an aggregation, it is an *associa-*
tion. There is no true Country without a uniform right. There is no
true Country where the uniformity of that right is violated by the existence of caste, privilege, and inequality—where the powers and
faculties of a large number of individuals are suppressed or dormant—where there is no common principle accepted, recognized,
and developed by all. In such a state of things there can be no Nation,
no People, but only a multitude, a fortuitous agglomeration of men
whom circumstances have brought together and different circumstances will separate. In the name of your love for your Country you
must combat without truce the existence of every privilege, every
inequality, upon the soul which has given you birth. One privilege only
is lawful—the privilege of Genius when Genius reveals itself in brotherhood with Virtue; but it is a privilege conceded by God and not by
men, and when you acknowledge it and follow its inspirations, you
acknowledge it freely by the exercise of your own reason and your
own choice. Whatever privilege claims your submission in virtue of
force or heredity, or any right which is not a common right, is a
usurpation and a tyranny, and you ought to combat it and annihilate it.
Your Country should be your Temple. God at the summit, a People of
equals at the base. Do not accept any other formula, any other moral

law, if you do not want to dishonor your Country and yourselves. Let the secondary laws for the gradual regulation of your existence be the progressive application of this supreme law.

And in order that they should be so, it is necessary that *all* should contribute to the making of them. The laws made by one fraction of the citizens only can never by the nature of things and men do otherwise than reflect the thoughts and aspirations and desires of that fraction; they represent, not the whole country, but a third, a fourth part, a class, a zone of the country. The law must express the general aspiration, promote the good of all, respond to a beat of the nation's heart. The whole nation therefore should be, directly or indirectly, the legislator. By yielding this mission to a few men, you put the egoism of one class in the place of the Country, which is the union of *all* the classes.

A Country is not a mere territory; the particular territory is only its foundation. The Country is the idea which rises upon that foundation; it is the sentiment of love, the sense of fellowship which binds together all the sons of that territory. So long as a single one of your brothers is not represented by his own vote in the development of the national life — so long as a single one vegetates uneducated among the educated — so long as a single one able and willing to work languishes in poverty for want of work — you have not got a Country such as it ought to be, the Country of all and for all. *Votes, education, work* are the three main pillars of the nation; do not rest until your hands have solidly erected them.

And when they have been erected — when you have secured for every one of you food for both body and soul — when freely united, entwining your right hands like brothers round a beloved mother, you advance in beautiful and holy concord towards the development of your faculties and the fulfilment of the Italian mission — remember that that mission is the moral unity of Europe; remember the immense duties which it imposes upon you. Italy is the only land that has twice uttered the great word of unification to the disjoined nations. Twice Rome has been the metropolis, the temple, of the European world; the first time when our conquering eagles traversed the known world from end to end and prepared it for union by introducing civilized institutions; the second time when, after the Northern conquerors had themselves been subdued by the potency of Nature, of great memories and of religious inspiration, the genius of Italy incarnated itself in the Papacy and undertook the solemn mission — abandoned four centuries ago — of preaching the union of souls to the peoples of the

Christian world. Today a third mission is dawning for our Italy; as much vaster than those of old as the Italian People, the free and united Country which you are going to found, will be greater and more powerful than Caesars or Popes. The presentiment of this mission agitates Europe and keeps the eye and the thought of the nations chained to Italy.

Your duties to your Country are proportioned to the loftiness of this mission. You have to keep it pure from egoism, uncontaminated by falsehood and by the arts of the political Jesuitism which they call diplomacy.

The government of the country will be based through your labors upon the worship of principles, not upon the idolatrous worship of interests and of opportunity. There are countries in Europe where Liberty is sacred within, but is systematically violated without; peoples who say, *Truth is one thing, utility another: Theory is one thing, practice another.* Those countries will have inevitably to expiate their guilt in long isolation, oppression, and anarchy. But you know the mission of our Country, and will pursue another path. Through you Italy will have, with one only God in the heavens, one only truth, one only faith, one only rule of political life upon earth. Upon the edifice, sublimer than Capitol or Vatican, which the people of Italy will raise, you will plant the banner of Liberty and of Association, so that it shines in the sight of all the nations, nor will you lower it ever for terror of despots or lust for the gains of a day. You will have boldness as you have faith. You will speak out aloud to the world, and to those who call themselves the lords of the world, the thought which thrills in the heart of Italy. You will never deny the sister nations. The life of the Country shall grow through you in beauty and in strength, free from servile fears and the hesitations of doubt, keeping as its *foundation* the people, as its *rule* the consequences of its principles logically deduced and energetically applied, as its *strength* the strength of all, as its *outcome* the amelioration of all, as its *end* the fulfilment of the mission which God has given it. And because you will be ready to die for Humanity, the life of your Country will be immortal.

22

JULES MICHELET

Our Native Land:
Are Nationalities About to Disappear?

1846

Jules Michelet (1798–1874) was perhaps the greatest French historian during the nineteenth century. His monumental masterpiece, the multi-volume History of France, *is characterized by a lively narrative style, a search for symbolic meaning in history, and imaginative empathy with the lives and thoughts of people in the past. Michelet's eminently Romantic aspiration to recreate the past in all its richness culminated in his sense of historical writing's power to overcome the oblivion of the grave: "I have given to many dead that assistance of which I myself shall be in need," he wrote. "I have exhumed them for a second life. . . . Thus a family is formed, a common city between the living and the dead." Born the son of a modest printer, Michelet strongly identified with the common folk. He saw the people as the true engine of history; of the French Revolution, he claimed, "This was the first model of a revolution without heroes, without proper names. Society did everything." This theme reaches a crescendo in* The People, *Michelet's 1846 paean to the power of the masses to shape history. This excerpt considers the question whether national feeling is declining. Michelet concedes that national animosities seem to be dissipating, while commerce and the circulation of ideas seem to have eroded national differences. Though he endorses this apparent trend toward peaceful coexistence, Michelet argues that one would have to be ignorant of both history and human nature to believe that nationalities are about to disappear. Michelet shares much of Mazzini's utopian belief that nationalism is the pathway to universal brotherhood; yet in ending by elevating France over all other nations, we see how thin the line was between cosmopolitanism and parochial national pride. Given our own current concerns with the effects of globalization on the sovereignty of national governments, Michelet's questions gain further, surprising relevance for today.*

Jules Michelet, "Our Native Land: Are Nationalities About to Disappear?" *The People,* trans. G. H. Smith (New York: D. Appleton and Company, 1846), 160–64.

National antipathies have decreased, the law of nations been ameliorated, and, in comparison with the hates of the middle age, we have entered upon a new era of goodwill and brotherhood. Nations are already in some degree amalgamated by interests, and have borrowed from each other fashions and literature. Are we hence to infer that nationalities are dying away? Let us examine. It is certain that internal distinctions are leaving fewer traces in every nation. Our French provincialities are rapidly disappearing. Scotland and Wales have joined the unity of Britain. Germany is laboring at her own unity; and believes herself ready to sacrifice to it a host of conflicting interests, which have hitherto kept her divided. There can be no doubt that this sacrifice of different internal nationalities to the great nationality which embraces them all, contributes to strengthen the latter. It may perchance efface the salient, picturesque minutiae which characterized a people in the eyes of the superficial observer, but it strengthens the peculiar genius of a nation, and helps its manifestation. It was at the moment France suppressed within her bosom all divergent Frances, that she revealed herself in her loftiness and originality. She made the discovery of herself; and whilst she proclaimed the future common rights of the world, separated herself more distinctly from the world than she had ever done before.

We may say the same of England. With her machines, ships, and her fifteen millions of workmen, she differs at this very moment from all other nations much more than in Elizabeth's day. Germany, which was blindly groping for herself in the seventeenth and eighteenth centuries, at last discovered herself in [Johann Wolfgang von] Goethe, [F. W. J.] Schelling, and [Ludwig van] Beethoven; and it is only from that moment that she was enabled with any purpose to aspire to unity. So far from nationalities disappearing, I see them daily assuming a deeper moral character, and from collections of men growing into persons. This is the natural progress of life. Each man, at the outset, feels his genius confusedly, and in his early years appears to be like any other man. It is only as time goes over his head that he learns to understand himself, and that his character acquires outward expression in his works and acts. He gradually assumes personality, quits class, and deserves a name.

I know but two ways of inferring that nationalities are about to disappear;—first, to be ignorant of history, and to know it only in shallow formulas, like philosophers, who never study it, or in literary commonplaces, like women, in order to talk about it. To those whose knowledge is of either kind, history appears in the past like a small, obscure point, which may be blotted out at will:—secondly, one must be as ignorant of nature as of history, and forget that national characteristics do not take their rise in our caprices, but are profoundly based on the influences of climate, of food, of natural productions, and may be modified in degree, but never effaced. They who are not fettered by their acquaintance either with physiology or history, and who construct humanity without ever inquiring into man or nature, may be allowed to efface frontiers, fill up rivers, and level mountains. But I warn them that nations will still last, unless they take care to sweep away the towns, those grand centers of civilization, where nationalities have concentrated their genius.

Towards the close of the Second Part I observed, that if God has set anywhere the type of the political City, it was in all probability in the moral City, that is, in the soul of man. Now, what are the first movements of this soul? It fixes itself in one spot, meditates there, and organizes for itself a body, a residence, a train of ideas. Then it can act. In the same manner, the soul of the people ought to construct for itself a central point of organism, seat itself in one spot, collect itself, meditate, and harmoniously identify itself with the aspect of nature; as infant Rome with the seven hills, or our France with the sea, the Rhine, the Alps, and the Pyrenees—our seven hills.

To circumscribe oneself, to carve something for oneself out of space and time, to bite a piece which shall be one's own out of the bosom of indifferent and all-dissolving nature, who seeks ever to confound, is power for every life. This is to exist; this is to live. A mind fixed on one point will go on acquiring profundity. A mind, floating in space, dissipates itself and disappears. The man who goes on bestowing his love on all things, passes away without ever having known love. Let him love once and long, he finds in one passion the infinitude of nature, and the whole progress of the world. The Native Land, the City, far from being opposed to nature, are the sole and the all-powerful means which the soul of the people resident there possesses for realizing her nature, affording her at once the point from which to start into life, and the liberty of development. Fancy the Athenian genius *minus* Athens; it wavers, wanders, is lost, and dies unknown. Enclosed within the narrow but pregnant precincts of such a city, fixed on that glorious soil where the bee gathers honey from Sophocles and Plato, the powerful genius of Athens, of a city hardly perceptible on the earth's broad surface, has done as much in two or three centuries, as twelve nations of the middle age in a thousand.

God's most powerful means of creating and increasing distinctive originality, is to maintain the world harmoniously divided into those great and beautiful systems called nations, each of which, opening to man a different sphere of activity, is a living education. The more man advances, the more he enters into the genius of his native land, the better he concurs in the harmony of the globe. He learns to know this native land both in its proper and relative value, as a note in the grand concert, takes a part in it through her, and in her loves the world. One's native country forms the necessary initiation into the universal country. And so union progresses, without there being any danger of its ever attaining unity, since every nation, at every step it takes towards concord, is more original in itself. If, by an impossibility, diversities should cease and unity be established, as every nation would sing the same note, the concert would be over. Harmony would give place to a confused, unmeaning noise; and the world, relapsed into monotony and barbarism, might perish without leaving a single regret.

But nothing, I feel assured, will perish; neither soul of man, nor soul of people. We are in too good hands. No, on the contrary, we shall go on ever living more, — that is, strengthening our individuality, and acquiring more potent and fecundating influences. God keeps us from losing ourselves in him! . . . And if no soul perishes, how shall these great souls of nations, with their vivid genius, their history rich in martyrs and heroic sacrifices, a history replete with immortality, how shall they be extinguished? When but one of them is eclipsed for a moment, the whole world is sick in all its nations, and the world of the heart in its fibers, responsive to the nations. . . . Reader, the agonized fiber which I see in your heart, is Poland and Italy. Nationality and our country are the life of the world. Their death would be the death of all. Ask the people. They feel this, and will tell you so. Ask science, history, the experience of mankind. These two great voices are in unison. Two voices? No, two realities; that which is and that which was, opposed to vain abstraction. This was the belief on which I set my heart and my history, firm as upon a rock. I wanted no one to confirm me in my faith. But I have gone among the multitude; have questioned the people, young and old, little and great. All have borne witness to their country: 'Tis the living fiber which dies last in their heart. I have found it among the dead. I have been in the charnel-houses called prisons, *bagnes*, and there have dissected; and in these corpses, where the breast was a void, what think you I found? . . . France still; the last spark, perhaps, which offered a chance of recalling them to life.

Say not, I beseech you, that it is nothing to be born in the land surrounded by the Pyrenees, the Alps, the Rhine, the ocean. Take the poorest being, ragged, starved, one whom you would believe absorbed in material wants; he will tell you that to have a share in this immense glory, this unique legend which forms the theme of the world, is a rich inheritance. He knows that if he went to the world's extremest desert, alike under the equator or at the poles, he would find Napoleon, our armies, our grand history to shield and protect him; that the children would flock to him, and the aged be mute, and entreat him to speak; that to hear him only name those names, they would kiss the hem of his tattered vestments. For me, whatever my fate, poor or rich, happy or unhappy, I shall ever bless God for having given me this great country—France. And this, not alone on account of her many and glorious deeds, but, most of all, because I find her to be at once the representative of the liberties of the world, and the country which forms the bond of sympathy with all the rest, the initiation into universal love. This last characteristic is so strong in France, that she has often forgotten herself. And I must now recall her to herself, and beseech her to love all nations less than herself.

Undoubtedly, every great nation represents an idea important to universal man. But, great God, how much more true is this of France! Suppose her eclipsed, or that she perish; the bond of sympathy between the world is relaxed, dissolved, broken, probably destroyed. The love that constitutes the life of the globe would be affected in its most vital part. The earth would enter the frozen age where other globes, close at hand, have entered. . . .

A Chronology of European Romanticism (1789–1848)

1789 The French Revolution begins; the Bastille is stormed on July 14.

In August, the newly created National Assembly adopts the Declaration of the Rights of Man and of the Citizen.

William Blake publishes *Songs of Innocence*.

1790 The Civil Constitution of the Clergy subordinates the Catholic Church to the French state.

Edmund Burke publishes *Reflections on the Revolution in France*.

1792 Thomas Paine publishes *The Rights of Man* (1791–1792).

Provoked by antirevolutionary decrees from Austria and Prussia, France declares war and defeats an invading Austrian-Prussian army at Valmy.

1793 Louis XVI of France is executed in January; the Queen, Marie Antoinette, is guillotined in October.

Britain, Austria, Prussia, Spain, and Holland form the first of seven coalitions that will oppose France during the next twenty-three years.

The Jacobins, led by Maximilien Robespierre, come to power in France; the reign of terror begins in June.

Facing internal rebellion and military setbacks, the Jacobins establish mass conscription (Levée en Masse).

1794 The Jacobins fall in July, and Robespierre is guillotined.

William Blake publishes *Songs of Experience*.

Johann Gottlieb Fichte publishes the *Wissenschaftslehre* (Theory of Knowledge).

1795 Friedrich Schiller publishes *On Naive and Sentimental Poetry* and *On the Aesthetic Education of Mankind*.

In reaction against the Jacobin Terror, the French National Convention institutes a new government known as the Directory, with a bicameral legislature and a weak executive composed of five members.

1796 Johann Wolfgang Goethe publishes *Wilhelm Meister's Apprenticeship*, the archetype of the German *Bildungsroman*.

1797 W. H. Wackenroder publishes *Outpourings of an Art-Loving Friar*.

Friedrich Wilhelm Joseph Schelling publishes *Ideas for a Philosophy of Nature*.

1798 Friedrich and August Wilhelm Schlegel create the journal *Athenaeum* in Jena.

William Wordsworth and Samuel Taylor Coleridge publish *Lyrical Ballads*.

1799 Novalis presents "Christianity or Europe: A Fragment" to the Jena circle.

The German Protestant theologian Friedrich Daniel Ernst Schleiermacher publishes *Religion: Speeches to Its Cultured Despisers*, strengthening the German Romantic turn toward religion.

During November and December, Napoleon Bonaparte overthrows the Directory and establishes a dictatorship under the Consulate.

1800 Novalis publishes *Hymns to the Night*.

The second edition of Coleridge and Wordsworth's *Lyrical Ballads* is published with a preface by Wordsworth.

Friedrich Schlegel publishes "On Incomprehensibility."

Napoleon defeats Austria at Marengo, leaving France the dominant power on the Continent.

1802 Novalis publishes *Heinrich von Ofterdingen* and *The Apprentices of Saïs*.

François-René Chateaubriand publishes *The Genius of Christianity*.

1804 Napoleon Bonaparte is proclaimed Emperor Napoleon I in May.

Étienne Pivert de Senancour publishes his novel *Oberman* in France.

1805 Clemens Brentano and Achim von Arnim publish *The Youth's Cornucopia*, a collection of German folk songs.

William Wordsworth completes *The Prelude; or, Growth of a Poet's Mind*.

1806 Napoleon dissolves the Holy Roman Empire.

1807 Hegel publishes *Phenomenology of Spirit*.

Ludwig van Beethoven composes his Symphony No. 5.

After Prussia's defeat by France, Fichte delivers lectures on German nationalism in Berlin (published in 1808 as *Addresses to the German Nation*).

Madame de Staël gains European fame with her novel *Corinne, or Italy*.

1808 Goethe publishes a complete version of *Faust: A Tragedy*, Part I.

1809 Art students leave the Vienna Academy and create the Brotherhood of St. Luke, the first secessionist movement in art history; gathered in Rome, they become known as the Nazarenes.

Caspar David Friedrich completes his painting *Monk by the Sea*.

August Wilhelm Schlegel publishes *Lectures on Dramatic Art and Letters*.

Adam Heinrich Müller publishes *Elements of Statecraft*.

1810 Madame de Staël publishes *On Germany* in France, but Napoleon confiscates the entire print run.

1812 Napoleon wages a disastrous military campaign against Russia.

Wilhelm and Jacob Grimm publish the first volume of their fairy tale collection, known in English as *Grimm's Fairy Tales*, with further volumes following in 1815 and 1822.

Lord Byron's European fame is established with the publication of the narrative poem *Childe Harold's Pilgrimage* between 1812 and 1818.

1813 The War of Liberation begins, allying Prussia, Russia, Austria, Great Britain, and Sweden against France, accompanied by mass patriotic mobilization in Central Europe.

Ernst Theodor Amadeus Hoffmann publishes "Beethoven's Instrumental Music," one of the ground-laying works of modern music criticism.

Madame de Staël publishes French and English editions of *On Germany* in England.

1814 The Allied coalition conquers France in March; Napoleon abdicates in April and leaves for exile on the island of Elba. The Congress of Vienna convenes in October to redraw Europe's political map after the defeat of Napoleon.

Walter Scott publishes *Waverley*, his first novel; in ensuing years, his historical novels will make him the most successful novelist of the era and inspire a European-wide taste for historical fiction.

1815 Napoleon escapes from Elba and raises an army in France; the "One Hundred Days" comes to an end with defeat at the Battle of

Waterloo on June 18, and Napoleon is sent to the remote island of Saint Helena.

The Congress of Vienna concludes its work nine days before Napoleon's final defeat.

Louis XVIII is crowned King of France in July.

The Holy Alliance is formed between Russia, Austria, and Prussia to suppress liberal movements.

1816 Madame de Staël publishes "The Spirit of Translation" in a Milan journal, provoking widespread debate in Italy about the place of Romanticism in Italian culture.

1818 Mary Wollstonecraft Shelley publishes *Frankenstein, or the Modern Prometheus.*

Lord Byron begins *Don Juan,* his satirical, libertine, picaresque masterpiece. Work on the poem continues up to his death in 1824.

1819 The Carlsbad Decrees introduce repressive measures against liberal and nationalist tendencies in the German states.

A period of political unrest in Britain climaxes in the "Peterloo Massacre" in Manchester, becoming a symbol of the ruling class's continuing fear of democratic reform.

Painter Théodore Géricault completes his masterpiece, *The Raft of the Medusa.*

Victor Hugo and his brothers launch *Le Conservateur littéraire,* a short-lived conservative Romantic journal inspired by Chateaubriand.

1821 The Greek War of Independence against the Ottoman Empire begins.

Carl Maria Weber's *Der Freischütz* premieres in Berlin, considered the quintessential Romantic opera.

Percy Bysshe Shelley composes *A Defence of Poetry.*

1823 Stendhal publishes *Racine and Shakespeare,* spurred by the ill-treatment of a visiting English Shakespeare troupe in Paris.

Victor Hugo and friends create *La Muse française,* a literary journal supporting royalism and Catholicism.

1824 At the Paris Salon, critics remark on the large number of paintings done in "Romantic" style; Stendhal publishes a lengthy critique of "The Salon of 1824."

Lord Byron dies of fever in Missolonghi, Greece, in April.

1825 The Decembrist Revolt in Russia unsuccessfully attempts to create a constitutional monarchy by preventing Nicolas I's accession to the throne.

1827 Victor Hugo publishes the preface to his play *Cromwell*, expressing Hugo's move to the political left.

Eugène Delacroix exhibits his painting *Death of Sardanapalus* at the Paris Salon, causing much scandal.

Alessandro Manzoni publishes *The Betrothed*, a masterpiece of Romantic historical fiction.

1829 Frédéric Chopin begins to compose his *Études*.

1830 The premiere of Victor Hugo's play *Hernani* in Paris is disrupted by fights between supporters of Romanticism and defenders of Classicism.

The July Revolution in Paris brings down the Bourbon monarchy; Louis Philippe, Duke d'Orléans is crowned king.

Polish uprising against Russian occupation in November.

Hector Berlioz premieres his *Symphonie fantastique* in Paris, seen by many to be the beginning of Romantic music in France.

1831 Giuseppe Mazzini founds Young Italy to work toward a united, republican Italy.

Victor Hugo publishes *Notre-Dame de Paris* (*Hunchback of Notre-Dame*).

1832 The First British Reform Bill is passed, redistributing constituencies so as to give more power to the industrial towns and expanding the electorate modestly to include propertied middle-class men.

Goethe publishes Part II of *Faust: A Tragedy*.

Thomas Carlyle publishes *Sartor Resartus*, a work satirizing Romanticism, in serial form in *Frazer's Magazine*.

George Sand publishes *Indiana*, with *Lélia* following in 1833. Both novels explore the unequal status of women in French society.

The Treaty of Constantinople grants Greek independence from the Ottoman Empire.

1833 Alexander Pushkin publishes his verse epic *Eugene Onegin*.

1835 Bettina von Arnim publishes *Goethe's Correspondence with a Child*.

Alfred de Musset publishes *The Confession of a Child of the Century*.

1836 Heinrich Heine publishes *The Romantic School*, a scathing critique of the rightward shift of German Romanticism.

1837 Jules Michelet publishes the first volume of his monumental *History of France*.

Honoré de Balzac publishes the first installments of *Lost Illusions*, a critical novel of the Revolution of 1830.

1838   Chartism, a movement for democratic political reforms, begins in England.

Stendhal publishes his first novel, *The Red and the Black.*

1839   Stendhal publishes *The Charterhouse of Parma.*

1840   Mikhail Lermontov publishes *A Hero of Our Time* in Russia.

1843   William Wordsworth becomes England's poet laureate, succeeding Robert Southey.

1846   Jules Michelet publishes *The People.*

1848   Revolutions break out in Sicily, Italy, France, Germany, and the Austrian Empire.

Questions for Consideration

1. Romanticism is sometimes derided as escapist, dreamy, otherworldly, and passive. Does that strike you as an accurate description? Many consider the legacy of Romanticism to continue into our own time. Do you think that is the case? Do the concerns of the Romantic period strike you as still relevant?

2. From your reading of these selected texts, would you support the argument that Romanticism existed as a coherent phenomenon? What common themes do you perceive? What differences emerge? What is the proper balance between our need to respect diversity and our impulse to seek unity?

3. The Romantics judged their own age to be one of dualism and division. Why did they arrive at this conclusion? How does Romanticism itself reflect and respond to this concern with dualism?

4. Romanticism is frequently presented as anti-Enlightenment. How appropriate is this image? In what ways do the Romantics react against the Enlightenment? Do you see any continuities?

5. What is the relationship between Romanticism and the French Revolution? How does that relationship change over time? More generally, how should we conceptualize the relationship between cultural and intellectual phenomena like Romanticism and political and social events?

6. How important is national context in shaping the diverse expressions of Romanticism? How does national context help to explain the different time frames of Romanticism's appearance and development? What other kinds of contexts might help to explain Romanticism?

7. Novalis wrote that all philosophy is "homesickness." What does Novalis mean? Why would the Romantics be particularly aware of the metaphor of homesickness? Does homesickness look backward or forward?

8. Romantic aesthetics is often contrasted to Classicism (or Neoclassicism). What is Classicism? How do the Romantics themselves distinguish between the Romantic and the Classic? How rigid is this

distinction? What larger issues did the Romantics perceive in this debate over aesthetic form and style?

9. Romanticism has been called the "age of subjectivity." What does that mean? What concepts of the self emerge during this period? How do the Romantics imagine the relationship between self and world? How do these ideas differ from and relate to eighteenth-century concepts of the person?

10. Does gender play a role in the form and content of Romantic ideas? What does Romanticism suggest about the actual relationship between the sexes in the late eighteenth and early nineteenth centuries?

11. What is the variety of Romantic religious experience? Do you think Romanticism is best understood as an attempt to revive religion in the wake of Enlightenment skepticism or as a search for surrogate religions?

12. The nation and nationalism became important themes in Romantic political thought. What factors contributed to the development of Romantic nationalism? How does one reconcile nationalism's emphasis on collectivity with Romanticism's emphasis on individuality?

Selected Bibliography

The following includes only books that are broad in their coverage, and the list is far from exhaustive. Works devoted to individual figures are too numerous to begin listing here.

Abrams, Meyer Howard. *The Mirror and the Lamp: Romantic Theory and the Critical Tradition.* New York: Norton, 1958.
———. *Natural Supernaturalism: Tradition and Revolution in Romantic Literature.* New York: Norton, 1971.
Allen, James Smith. *Popular French Romanticism: Authors, Readers, and Books in the 19th Century.* Syracuse, N.Y.: Syracuse University Press, 1981.
Bann, Stephen. *Romanticism and the Rise of History.* New York: Twayne, 1995.
Behler, Ernst. *German Romantic Literary Theory.* Cambridge: Cambridge University Press, 1993.
Beiser, Frederick. *Enlightenment, Revolution, and Romanticism: The Genesis of Modern German Political Thought, 1790–1800.* Cambridge, Mass.: Harvard University Press, 1992.
———. *The Romantic Imperative: The Concept of Early German Romanticism.* Cambridge, Mass.: Harvard University Press, 2003.
Benichou, Paul. *The Consecration of the Writer, 1750–1830.* Trans. Mark K. Jensen. Lincoln: University of Nebraska Press, 1999.
Berlin, Isaiah. *The Roots of Romanticism.* Princeton, N.J.: Princeton University Press, 1999.
Bowman, Frank Paul. *French Romanticism: Intertextual and Interdisciplinary Readings.* Baltimore, Md.: Johns Hopkins University Press, 1990.
Brown, David Blayney. *Romanticism.* New York: Phaidon Press, 2001.
Brown, Marshall. *The Shape of German Romanticism.* Ithaca, N.Y.: Cornell University Press, 1979.
———, ed. *The Cambridge History of Literary Criticism. Volume V: Romanticism.* Cambridge: Cambridge University Press, 2000.
Butler, Marilyn. *Romantics, Rebels, and Reactionaries: English Literature and Its Background, 1760–1830.* New York: Oxford University Press, 1982.

Curran, Stuart, ed. *Cambridge Companion to British Romanticism*. Cambridge: Cambridge University Press, 1993.

Dahlhaus, Carl, *Nineteenth-Century Music*. Trans. J. Bradford Robinson. Berkeley: University of California Press, 1989.

Frank, Manfred. *The Philosophical Foundations of Early German Romanticism*. Trans. Elizabeth Millán-Zaubert. Albany: State University of New York Press, 2004.

Furst, Lilian. *The Contours of European Romanticism*. Lincoln: University of Nebraska Press, 1979.

Goodman, Katherine R., and Edith Waldstein, eds. *In the Shadow of Olympus: German Women Writers around 1800*. Albany: State University of New York Press, 1992.

Hoffmeister, Gerhart, ed. *European Romanticism: Literary Cross-Currents, Modes and Models*. Detroit: Wayne State University Press, 1990.

Honour, Hugh. *Romanticism*. New York: Harper & Row, 1979.

Izenberg, Gerald. *Impossible Individuality: Romanticism, Revolution, and the Origins of Modern Selfhood, 1787–1802*. Princeton, N.J.: Princeton University Press, 1992.

Kaiser, David Aram. *Romanticism, Aesthetics, and Nationalism*. Cambridge: Cambridge University Press, 1999.

McGann, Jerome. *The Romantic Ideology: A Critical Introduction*. Chicago: University of Chicago Press, 1983.

Mellor, Anne, ed. *Romanticism and Feminism*. Bloomington: Indiana University Press, 1988.

Nemoianu, Virgil. *The Taming of Romanticism: European Literature and the Age of Biedermeier*. Cambridge, Mass.: Harvard University Press, 1984.

Porter, Roy, and M. Teich, eds. *Romanticism in National Context*. Cambridge: Cambridge University Press, 1988.

Reardon, Bernard. *Religion in the Age of Romanticism: Studies in Early Nineteenth-Century Thought*. Cambridge: Cambridge University Press, 1985.

Redfield, Marc. *The Politics of Aesthetics: Nationalism, Gender, Romanticism*. Stanford, Calif.: Stanford University Press, 2003.

Richards, Robert J. *The Romantic Conception of Life: Science and Life in the Age of Goethe*. Chicago: University of Chicago Press, 2002.

Richardson, Alan. *Literature, Education, and Romanticism: Reading as a Social Practice, 1780–1832*. Cambridge: Cambridge University Press, 1994.

Schenk, H. G. *The Mind of the European Romantics*. New York: Frederick Ungar, 1966.

Vaughan, William. *German Romantic Painting*. 2nd ed. New Haven, Conn.: Yale University Press, 1994.

Walicki, Andrzej. *Philosophy and Romantic Nationalism: The Case of Poland*. Oxford: Oxford University Press, 1982.

Williamson, George. *The Longing for Myth in Germany: Religion and Aesthetic Culture from Romanticism to Nietzsche*. Chicago: University of Chicago Press, 2004.

Woodmansee, Martha. *The Author, Art, and the Market: Rereading the History of Aesthetics*. New York: Columbia University Press, 1994.

Ziolkowsik, Theodore. *Clio the Romantic Muse: Historicizing the Faculties in Germany*. Ithaca, N.Y.: Cornell University Press, 2004.

———. *German Romanticism and Its Institutions*. Princeton, N.J.: Princeton University Press, 1990.

Acknowledgments (continued from p. iv)

Document 1: By kind permission of Continuum International Publishing Group.

Document 2: From Frederick Beiser, ed. and trans. *The Early Political Writings of the German Romantics.* © Cambridge University Press, 1996. Reprinted with the permission of Cambridge University Press.

Documents 5 and 6: From *Lucinde and the Fragments,* translated and with an Introduction by Peter Firchow (University of Minnesota Press). © University of Minnesota Press, 1971. Reprinted by permission.

Document 13: From David Charlton (ed.) and Martyn Clarke (trans.). *E. T. A. Hoffmann's Musical Writings.* © Cambridge University Press, 1989. Reprinted with the permission of Cambridge University Press.

Document 14: From Joseph Luzzi (trans.), "The Spirit of Translation," in *Romanic Review* 97:1/2, May 1, 2006. Reprinted with the permission of the *Romanic Review* and the author.

Index

Académie Française, 28
Addresses to the German Nation (Fichte), 122
Aeneid (Virgil), 106
aesthetic theory. *See also* beauty
  French Revolution and, 14–15
  literature and, 76
  Neoclassical period, 10–11
  painting, 11–12
  religion, 85
  Romanticism and, 10–12, 38
  value of, 103–4
aisthetikos (sensuous perception), 104*n*.1
Alps, 139–40, 154–55*f*
analysis, principle of, 143
ancien régime, 29, 30, 120*n*
antirationalism, 8
anti-urbanism, 63
Apprentices of Saïs, The (Novalis), 195
Archimedes, 122–23, 124
architecture
  classical, 108–9
  forests and, 90
  Gothic, 89–90, 108–9
Ariosto, Ludovico, 106
Aristotle, 68, 175*n*.2
Arnim, Achim von, 35, 195, 198
Arnim, Bettine von, 94, 95
artistic freedom, 2. *See also* self-expression; individual freedom
artistic taste
  French art exhibitions and, 158, 162, 163
  genius and, 177
  personal, 162, 177
  in poetry, 176–77
arts
  academic formulas for, 159
  artists, 162–63
  beauty in, 172–73
  comedy in, 173, 174

creativity and, 38
criticism of, 158–67, 173–77
Denmark, 36
development of, 159
expression in, 158–59, 164–66, 170
Frankenstein and, 139
Germany, 11, 23–24, 79
God and, 46
grotesque, 173, 174
harmony in, 109
imitation in, 9, 161–62, 163, 176
language of, 45–47
mechanics of, 164–65
nationalism and, 34–35
Nazarene painters, 11, 23–24, 196
nudity in, 161–62, 167
painting and sculpture, 11–12, 108
passion in, 165
patronage system, 159
poetry and, 108*n*.4
powers of, 16, 44
revolution in, 14, 161–62
Romantic, 158–59, 166–67
rules of, 3, 9, 12, 170
rural motifs, 34–35
as self-expression, 12
standards, 38
Switzerland, 36
unity of, 99, 112
universal history of, 105
arts exhibitions
  artistic taste and, 158, 162, 163
  Salon of 1824, 158–67
association, nationalism and, 183–88
Athalie (Racine), 137
atheism, 113
Athenaeum, 76, 78, 80, 81, 82, 83, 195
Athenaeum Fragment No. 116 (Schlegel), 76–77
Augustus, 87*n*.1
Austria, 24

India, 57
Indiana (Sand), 198
individual freedom, 3–4, 18–19. *See also*
  freedom
  in German Romanticism, 8
  intellectual development and, 5–6
individuals and individualism. *See also* self-
    expression
  in art, 12
  concept of state and, 124–25
  liberty of, 178
  in literature, 9
  love of fatherland, 114
  nationalism and, 34
  noble-minded men, 115–17
  rights of, 179–82
  Romantic legacy of, 38–39
  self-expression, 144–45
  self-love, 117
  self-sacrifice for country, 117
  universal and, 18–19, 31, 33
Industrial Revolution, 17
Inferno, The (Dante), 2
infinity, 21, 78
instrumental music
  criticism of, 126–31
  vocal music *vs.*, 126
irony, 17, 77–84
  as form of paradox, 81
  incomprehensibility and, 82–84
  in literature, 126
  long-lasting effects of, 82
  misunderstanding of, 79–80
Isaac Newton (Blake), 6*f*
Italian language, translation and, 136,
    138–39
Italy, 29, 35
  literature, 138–39
  nationalism, 30–31, 34, 178–88, 192
  natural boundaries of, 184–85
  Romanticism, 30, 133
  unification of, 187–88
  working classes, 178–83

Jacobin Terror, 15, 16, 169, 194
Jena, University of, 113
Jena Romantics, 58*n*.17, 76, 78*n*.1, 102,
    113
  poetry, 47
  women and, 94
Jerusalem Delivered (Tasso), 165
Jesuits, 56, 56*n*.12
Journal des Débats, 159, 167
July Revolution, 198

Kant, Immanuel, 8, 10, 15, 52*n*.6, 79*n*.2,
    104*n*.1, 126
Keats, John, 11, 25, 26
Kierkegaard, Søren, 78
Klopstock, Friedrich Gottlieb, 9
Køpke, Christen, 36

Kosciusko, Thaddeus, 26
Kreisler, Johannes, 126. *See also* Hoffmann,
    Ernst Theodor Amadeus
Kunstreligion (religion of art), 3, 44

Lady of the Woods, 92
landscape, 20–21
landscape painting, 35–36
language
  of art and nature, 45–47
  Latin, 133
  nationalism and, 185
  national style and, 134
  of poetry, 64–65, 67–68, 144–45
  power of, 44–45
  translation, 131–39
Larra, Mariano José de, 29
Latin, 133
*Leben und Tod der Heiligen Genoveva (Life
    and Death of St. Genevieve)* (Tieck),
    83*n*.7
Lectures on Dramatic Art and Letters
    (Schlegel), 28–29, 102–12, 196
Leibniz, Gottfried Wilhelm, 79
Lélia (Sand), 198
Leopardi, Giacomo, 29, 30
Lermontov, Mikhail, 29, 30, 199
Lessing, Gotthold Ephraim, 81
letter-writing, 94
liberalism
  defined, 2*n*
  1848 and, 37
  German Romanticism and, 29
  Romanticism and, 29–30, 33–34
liberty of conscience, 52*n*.5
*Lines Composed a Few Miles above Tintern
    Abbey, On Revisiting the Banks of the
    Wye during a Tour* (Wordsworth),
    71–75
Liszt, Franz, 35
literature. *See also* classical literature;
    dramatic literature
  aesthetic theory and, 76
  genius in, 176–77
  German, 10, 25, 34, 98–100, 133
  Greek, 133–37, 149
  imitation in, 9, 133
  Italian, 138–39
  Neoclassical, 167
  Renaissance, 133
  Romantic appreciation of, 1–2
  sublimity in, 140–41
  translation of, 131–39
  women writers, 7
  world, 131
Locke, John, 8, 148
Lord of the Rings, The (Tolkien), 34
Lost Illusions (Balzac), 199
Louis Philippe, Duke d'Orléans, 198
Louis XIV, 170
Louis XVI, 132, 194